THE
Basic·Basics·

JAMS, PRESERVES AND CHUTNEYS HANDBOOK

MARGUERITE PATTEN

GRUB STREET · LONDON

This new edition published by Grub Street
4 Rainham Close, London SW11 6SS

Reprinted 2001
Reprinted 2002 (twice)
Reprinted 2003, 2004, 2005 (twice) 2006, 2007

British Library Cataloguing in Publication Data
Patten, Marguerite
    The basic basics jams, preserves and chutneys
    1. Cookery (Jam) 2. Canning and preserving 3. Chutncy
    I. Title II. Jams, preserves and chutneys
    641.8′52

ISBN 1 902304 72 1

Typeset by Pearl Graphics, Hemel Hempstead
Printed and bound in Great Britain by MPG Books Ltd. Bodmin, Cornwall

Grub Street only uses FSC (Forest Stewardship Council) paper for its books.

I would like to acknowledge the helpful information about certain fruits
in the following two books:
    The Complete Book of Fruit, Leslie John and Violet Stevenson, 1979,
Angus and Robertson.
    The Fresh Fruit Cookbook, Vo Bacon, the Department of Agriculture,
New South Wales, Australia.

CONTENTS

INTRODUCTION

━━━●━━━

Throughout history we can read of efforts made to preserve food for use in winter. In the case of meats and fish this was done by salting or drying. Fruits and herbs were dried too. People preserved certain fruits in brandy and pickled suitable vegetables in vinegar. These preserves are excellent and the recipes are on pages 138 to 159.

Cane sugar, although known as a scarce luxury in the Western world since the fourteenth century, did not become a major food in Britain until the nineteenth century. Beetroot was a well-known vegetable but it was not grown for its sugar content until the discovery made by A. S. Marggraf in 1747. He realised that the sugar content of beet is similar to that of sugar cane. When sugar became plentiful, cooks could use it for all forms of cooking, which led to the development of preserving as we know it today. Fruits and vegetables of all kinds could be turned into delicious jams, and other produce, which were made for storage.

It was in Victorian and Edwardian times that great pride was taken in having plentiful stores of preserves. Housewives depended upon their own resources and filled capacious larders and store cupboards with their home-made handiwork. Cookery books of that era abounded with recipes for jams, jellies and catsups (known nowadays as ketchups) together with chutneys and pickles of all kinds. Many of the recipes we use today are similar to the ones created in those faraway days. Thanks to the popularity of ethnic foods and various restaurants we have had the chance to sample preserves from all around the world, some of which are classics in their own countries. Fascinating recipes from abroad are included in this book.

Nowadays, with smaller houses and less storage space, together with the availability of commercially made preserves, huge stocks of the home-made variety may not be required, but there are few things that give one more pride and pleasure than carefully selected home-made jams, pickles or other foods. You can choose just those fruits or vegetables that please you most and base your preserves on them. With the wonderful range of exotic fruits and vegetables brought into our country nowadays it is possible to make chutneys, pickles and jellies, etc., which may not be on sale.

Home-made products, if made correctly, generally have a better flavour than those produced commercially in large quantities and, in consequence, have a great appeal. As many readers will know, jars of home-made preserves make wonderful presents and they are an excellent way of raising funds at charity bazaars – they can even become a source of income. If one compares the cost of making preserves at home with the cost of buying them, you realise that you can save an appreciable amount of money and, at the same time, produce preserves that have a finer flavour, made just as you would like them. This means that you can retain large, chunky pieces of fruit by preparing conserves, rather than jams, or sieve the fruits to make old-fashioned traditional fruit cheeses, free from pips or stones and skins.

There is great emphasis today on reducing the amount of sugar we eat. However, it must be appreciated that sugar is a very important ingredient when making jams or similar products: it is the preservative. If you reduce the sugar content in the preserves, they will not keep well if stored under normal conditions. There are, however, ways of making low sugar preserves that will keep, either by sterilizing the jars when filled or by placing them in the freezer. These methods are described on page 15.

Preserves have to be made with care. There must be a correct relationship between the amount of fruit and sugar used, or sugar and vinegar in the case of chutney, to give the best flavour and texture and to make sure the preserves set and keep well. This is why it is important to read through the advice given at the beginning of each section, which sets out the 'golden rules' for that particular kind of preserve.

Bottling of fruit and vegetables is less popular today due to the success in freezing these ingredients. There are, however, certain foods, such as peaches and pears, which have a better flavour when they are bottled. Details of this method of preservation are given on pages 124 to 126.

The following pages offer advice on making preserves that will please you and your family and give you a real sense of pride in your achievements.

Marguerite Patten

ESSENTIAL INFORMATION

In this section the most popular preserves – jams, conserves, jellies and marmalades – are given. Although the different groups of preserves vary in their requirements, they do have certain points in common.

Equipment: you should choose the equipment you use carefully; that does not mean you need to buy a lot of specialist equipment, for you may already own most of this. It is, however, sensible to read through the suggestions that follow and make sure you have everything in readiness *before* you begin making the preserve.

Speed of cooking: this is mentioned a great deal in the recipes in this section and it is important that the recommendations are followed. Simmering is essential when cooking the fruit in jams, jellies and marmalades. The speed of boiling when the sugar is added is equally important, see pages 18 to 19.

Testing: it is essential to test for setting point and details of how to test are on pages 8 to 9. These are followed by the method of testing the pectin content of the fruit.

Alternatives to sugar in preserves: sugar acts as the preservative; other forms of sweetening are not as effective but can be used to give a different flavour, see pages 11 and 12.

EQUIPMENT NEEDED WHEN MAKING PRESERVES

Although it is quite possible to make preserves with normal household utensils, it is worthwhile considering purchasing special equipment if you intend to prepare an appreciable amount of jams, jellies and chutneys. The first requirement is a large pan in which to cook the preserve.

Preserving pan: a large saucepan can be used but it is important that this is sufficiently large to allow rapid boiling, without fear of the contents boiling over. When making jam or jelly, the pan should never be more than half full of the fruit, or fruit juice, and sugar. This gives adequate space for rapid boiling.

Special preserving pans are wide in shape; this is ideal, for it aids evaporation and therefore allows the preserve to reach setting point more rapidly. Most preserving pans have a bucket-type handle so that the pan can be suspended when not in use, ensuring it is kept well aired. If possible, do *not* shut the pan away in a cupboard without good air circulation, for it may smell musty when used again. This could affect the flavour of the preserve unless the pan is well washed several times and then left in the air for as long as possible before use.

Pans made of aluminium or stainless steel can be used when making jams, conserves and other sweet preserves, and for chutneys and pickles. Enamel pans are excellent *unless* they are chipped, in which case they are unsuitable, for the acid in the fruit or vinegar (when making chutneys or pickles) would come into contact with the metal under the chipped enamel and this could affect the colour of the preserve. Iron or zinc pans are not suitable – they spoil both the colour and flavour of the fruit. Brass and copper preserving pans can be used when making jams and fruit preserves. If these are kept looking immaculate with metal polish, make absolutely certain the pans are well washed before use, so all traces of polish are removed. Even the slightest hint would adversely affect the taste of the preserve. Brass, copper or iron pans must *not* be used when making chutneys or pickles or sauces containing vinegar.

Pressure cooker or microwave: these can be used in making preserves, see the special instructions on pages 12 to 14.

Spoons and other utensils: a wooden spoon is ideal for stirring the preserve when dissolving the sugar. Buy one with a very long handle so your hands are kept as far away as possible from the extremely hot preserve. A perforated spoon (often called a slotted spoon) is ideal for removing scum from the preserve and also for removing stones from damsons, etc., when making the jam. A large metal spoon or ladle is needed if you are going to spoon the preserve into the containers. If you prefer to use a jug, then make sure this is heat-proof and has a handle so you can scoop up the preserve without burning your hands. A funnel, which can fit into the top of the jars or other containers, is another excellent way of filling them. Make sure the funnel is secure in the top of the container then spoon or pour the preserve through it. Its use avoids any possibility of the preserve dropping on to the surface of the jars or table.

Sugar thermometer: this is essential if you prefer to test for setting by temperature, as suggested on page 8.

Containers: most jams and conserves are put into jam jars. Standard jam jars are not sold, so keep any you have. Good stores sell a variety of glass containers which could be used. Put the waxed circles on to the jam, as described on page 19. Bottling jars could be used and are ideal for chutneys and pickles if they have glass lids – metal lids must not be placed on them (see page 139).

Covers: buy packs of special jam pot covers containing waxed rounds and transparent covers plus elastic bands. These are perfectly adequate for covering jams, conserves, jellies and fruit cheeses. Make sure you have the right size for the particular jars; the waxed circles should form a perfect fit over the hot preserve, so the air is excluded.

Muslin: this is needed to enclose pips and stones, as mentioned in various recipes. It can be used instead of the proper **jelly bag**, described on page 70. Buy muslin gauze from a chemist for this purpose.

Labels: these make the jars of preserves *look* more professional and are an ideal way of identifying the contents. Put the date on the label if you make a large amount of preserves, so they can be used in sequence.

Wooden board: most preserves are cooked to a very high temperature and the jars in which they are placed are very hot. It is essential to check that these are not put on cold or damp surfaces in the kitchen. It is wise to place them on a wooden board until the contents are cold.

Other useful utensils: use a sharp stainless steel knife when peeling, halving or chopping fruits, etc., so the colour of the food is not spoiled.

Use a special cherry stoner to remove the stones from the fruit. If this is not available, then substitute a firm, fine new hairpin. Insert the bent end into the cherry. Move it gently until you feel it has hooked around the stone then pull sharply, bringing the stone out. Whatever method you choose, stone the cherries over a basin, so no fruit juice is wasted. The juice is used in the preserve.

Use a hair or nylon sieve and *not* a metal one when sieving fruit or preserves containing acid ingredients, such as vinegar. Metal sieves spoil the colour slightly and tend to give a faint metallic taste to the preserve. Hair sieves were used in the past, well before nylon sieves were made. If you still own one of these excellent utensils, do not feel you must invest in a nylon sieve. The hair mesh is ideal for sieving acid fruits and for vegetables also.

Use a bowl of boiling water to remove the skins from peaches or tomatoes. Leave the fruit in this for about half a minute, remove and place in cold water, then pull away the skin.

SIMMERING THE FRUIT

Reference is made in most recipes to simmering the fruit, or fruit and liquid, before adding the sugar. The fruit should cook slowly until softened. The preserving pan is *not* covered during this period, so it is very important to check that the fruit does not stick to the pan and burn. Frequent stirring over a low heat will prevent this and will extract the maximum juice. If you are worried about the lack of juice, then add a little more water to the pan. The amount of water given in recipes is the minimum to use. If the fruit is rather firmer than usual, you will need a little more. Do not overcook the fruit during this first stage of cooking, for this will spoil both the colour and the taste of the preserve.

TESTING FOR SETTING POINT

There are various ways by which one can tell if a preserve has reached the correct setting point. With methods 1 and 2, below, remove the pan from the heat while testing the preserve. With method 3 move the thermometer around in the preserve, as described, then take the pan away from the heat as you check the reading.

It is stressed on page 18, point 9, that one should test for setting early so there is no possibility of the preserve becoming over-cooked.

There are fairly obvious signs when the preserve is reaching setting point: the fruit mixture does not rise as vigorously in the preserving pan, it makes more noise as it boils and fairly large bubbles begin to form on the surface of the preserve.

METHOD 1 – The Wrinkle Test

Spoon a little boiling preserve on to a *cold* plate or saucer. Allow this to become cool then push it with your finger. If the preserve has reached setting point the top will have set and the preserve will wrinkle when you push it with your forefinger. If the preserve shows signs of wrinkling only slightly, return the pan to the heat and give it another 1 or 2 minutes' boiling, then test again.

METHOD 2 – The Flake Test

Take a clean wooden spoon, not one that may already have been used to stir the sugar as it dissolves. Stir the spoon around in the preserve until it is well coated then allow it to cool slightly. Hold the spoon horizontally over the preserving pan. If the preserve has reached setting point it will hang on the edge of the spoon, forming a flake, and this will not drop off until given a very vigorous shake.

METHOD 3 – The Temperature Test

Use a proper sugar thermometer. This is made to be placed into mixtures that reach high temperatures. Turn the thermometer around in the preserve so you have an overall reading, then check this.

Jams and marmalades reach setting point at temperatures between 104° and 105.5°C/219°F to 222°F; **jellies** between 104° and 105°C/219° to 221°F. Use the lower setting if you require a less firm preserve – this is recommended in the case of conserves (see page 57). The higher setting is better for fruit cheeses (see page 103). After use, take great care to place the hot thermometer on a wooden board, and not on a cold or damp surface.

METHOD 4 – The Yield Test

This test is really a confirmation that the cooked preserve has the right proportion of sugar, but it also acts as another check that you have a satisfactory preserve that will keep well.

The pectin in fruit makes the jam set but it is the sugar that acts as the preservative. Too little sugar means the preserve is unlikely to keep well unless special precautions are followed, as described on page 15. Jams and similar preserves should consist of 60% sugar if they are to keep well. At the top of each recipe you will find the approximate amount of preserve that should result, e.g.

From each 450 g/1 lb (2 cups) of sugar used you should make 750 g/1⅔ lb of preserve.

If you find you have *more* than this, either reboil the jam for a short time or consider it has a lower than average sugar content and store it accordingly (see page 15). If you find you have *less* than this, sadly the jam will be somewhat oversweet and stiff. You probably boiled it for too long before testing for setting point.

Why do jams or similar preserves sometimes ferment?
There are a number of possibilities

- The fruit was over-ripe; while one should select ripe fruit for the best flavour, it must never be over-ripe.
- Too little sugar was used in the preserve. If the sugar content is reduced then the preserve must be used within a short time and stored in the refrigerator or frozen until required; or sterilised as pages 15 to 16.
- The preserve was poured into the jam jars before it was adequately set. See page 8 for methods of testing for setting point.
- The storage conditions were inadequate (see page 16). The storage cupboard or larder should be cool and dry.
- The preserve was not adequately covered. This means the preserve is not protected from adverse storage conditions, and is therefore more inclined to ferment or go mouldy (see page 19 – point 13 for details on covering jams and other preserves).

GOLDEN RULES FOR SUCCESS

The points that follow are important for they can make the difference between first-class preserves and those that are only average in taste and texture.

The jam section begins on page 17 and the various fruits are in alphabetical order, though with some variations under the main recipes.

Conserves – which can be termed a luxury preserve, with large pieces of fruit or whole fruit – begin on page 57.

Jellies are not only ideal as a sweet preserve to use as a filling in cakes, tarts and pastries; many form excellent accompaniments to main dishes. These begin on page 68, where you will find important information to ensure the jellies are full of flavour and beautifully clear in colour.

Marmalade is an essential preserve at breakfast time. There are many types of marmalade from which to choose and the recipes begin on page 87.

Fruit butters and cheeses are not as well known as they should be, for they are delicious. The recipes begin on page 103.

USING HONEY OR SYRUP IN PRESERVES

It is possible to substitute a certain amount of honey or golden syrup (corn syrup) for the sugar in jams, conserves, marmalade and fruit cheeses. An indication is given in recipes where these ingredients enhance the flavour of the fruit. It is still wise to use 75% sugar and only 25% honey or syrup. Even so, the preserve will be a little less stiff than when all sugar is used. Honey or syrup also give a pleasant taste to many sweet pickles and chutneys. These ingredients are included in some recipes in those sections, which begin on pages 138 and 160. A little black treacle, or molasses, gives an interesting taste to some marmalades and chutneys, see page 99.

TESTING FOR PECTIN CONTENT

The various recipes in this book are planned to give exactly the right amount of pectin for each type of preserve. It must be appreciated, however, that a fruit can vary a little in its pectin content. For example, strawberries are usually low in pectin *but* if you pick the fruit when it is absolutely perfect, i.e. *just* ripe but not over-ripe, and make jam within an hour of picking, the pectin content will be higher than average and you could manage with less lemon juice (see page 51). The test given on this page will enable you to make your own checks. You may decide to make preserves with a mixture of fruits and therefore not know just how good the pectin content will be. There is a simple way to check this.

1. Cook the fruit until soft then remove from the heat. Spoon a little fruit from the preserving pan, and strain this to give 2 teaspoons of juice.
2. Place the juice in a container and leave until cold.
3. To the 2 teaspoons of juice, add 6 teaspoons of methylated spirit, stir or shake gently and leave for a minute.
4. a)   If the fruit contains a **high** percentage of pectin the mixture will form a clear jelly type lump. In this case no extra lemon juice need be added when making the preserve and ordinary sugar could be used.
b)   If the fruit contains a **medium** amount of pectin the mixture will form several softer lumps. It would be advisable to add 1 tablespoon (1¼ tablespoons) lemon juice with each 450 g/1 lb (2 cups) sugar used to ensure a good setting preserve; or to use sugar containing extra pectin instead of ordinary sugar.
c)   If the fruit contains a **low** amount of pectin virtually no firm lumps will form. In this case add 2 tablespoons (2½ tablespoons) lemon juice with each 450 g/1 lb (2 cups) sugar. If preferred, use the special sugar plus just 1 tablespoon (1¼ tablespoons) lemon juice to each 450 g/1 lb (2 cups) sugar. N.B. American measures are given in brackets.

USING COMMERCIAL PECTIN

It is possible to buy bottles of commercial pectin, which is a natural product based on apples. It helps all jams to set well but it also allows one to use a smaller proportion of fruit to the sugar content. This is extremely useful when fruit is scarce or very expensive. There is a selection of recipes provided with the product (trade name Certo) but an example is given on pages 55 to 56.

USING APPLE JUICE

Advice from the Diabetes UK recommends using unsweetened apple juice in some preserves. This adds natural sweetness and also helps the jam, or other preserve, to set. An example of a jam recipe using apple juice is on pags 130 to 131. Pure apple juice can be obtained from health food stores.

MICROWAVE OVENS FOR PRESERVES

It is possible to make many preserves in a microwave oven, although for small amounts only.

1. Always use a suitable bowl for the purpose, for when making jams or other preserves from start to finish in a microwave oven, the bowl has to withstand the contents being heated to the high temperatures required for setting point. Do *not* use a metal bowl. The bowl should never be more than half filled with the food.
2. The maximum weight of contents that should be cooked must not exceed 1.12 kg/2½ lb. This is the weight of the fruit plus the weight of the sugar for jams, conserves, etc., or the total weight of all

ingredients when making chutneys. In jellies it is the weight of juice plus sugar.

3. Microwaving is less efficient than conventional cooking for softening citrus fruit peel for marmalade or dried fruit or fruits with tough skins, so it is better to choose conventional methods when making these preserves.

4. Use the proportions of fruit and sugar in the recipes in this book. When *no* water is used in the conventional method it is advisable to use 2 tablespoons (2½ tablespoons) to each 450 g/1 lb fruit in the microwave. In the recipes where more water than that is used, follow the recipe.

5. Cover the bowl in which the fruit is to be softened and use full power. Consult your manufacturer's instruction book for timing to soften fruits but, since the quality of fruit varies considerably, check very carefully during cooking that it is not over-cooked.

6. When making chutney, take care to chop all ingredients very evenly in size so the cooking will be uniform.

7. Add the same amount of sugar, or sugar and lemon juice, as given in the recipe. Stir well until dissolved. Caster sugar gives the best result in microwave cooking since it dissolves more rapidly than any other. Sugar that contains pectin could be used where recommended in the recipe. If the sugar does not completely dissolve in the hot fruit, return the bowl to the microwave for a few seconds only, using full power, remove and stir again.

8. After the sugar has dissolved, return the bowl to the microwave. Do *not* cover it at this stage. Allow the contents to boil on full power until setting point is reached. *Stir every minute* during this time to ensure an even distribution of heat. Do *not* stir more often or you will delay setting point. When making chutney, cook until the desired consistency is reached.

9. Allow the bowl to stand in the microwave with the power switched off for 1 minute, until the contents have ceased bubbling in the bowl. Even so, be careful how you handle it; use protective gloves and take care not to place the bowl on a damp cloth or very damp surface when it comes out of the microwave, for the contents are still extremely hot and the bowl could crack.

10. Cover the preserve as given in the instructions, on page 19.

PRESSURE COOKERS FOR PRESERVES

A pressure cooker can be used for making some preserves. It is suitable for small amounts only and is better for fruits that normally take quite a time to become tender – e.g. whole or sliced oranges or other citrus fruits, damsons, rather hard gooseberries, dried fruits, etc. In a pressure cooker these are tenderised within a very short time. Strangely enough, the rapid cooking of the fruit under pressure does not harm the pectin content. It is not, however, as good for fruits, like raspberries, that soften within minutes in an ordinary preserving pan as they could become over-cooked.

Here are the essential points to remember when using a pressure cooker for making preserves:

1. The pan should never be more than half-filled with fruit and liquid.

2. Even if the recipe gives a smaller amount of water, it is advisable to use 150 ml/¼ pint (⅔ cup) water with the fruit. In recipes, such as marmalade, where a large amount of water is used – generally a minimum of 1.2 litres/2 pints (5 cups) – you can reduce this by *half*, due to the shorter cooking time.
3. Do not use the trivet – the fruit and water are placed in the pan, the lid fixed and the cooker brought up to pressure.
4. Modern pressure cookers have three rings on top. By using these you can adjust the pressure.

>   1 ring – minimum pressure (5 lb)
>   2 rings – medium pressure (10 lb)
>   3 rings – maximum pressure (15 lb)

5. I like to use 10 lb pressure for cooking most fruits for all jams, jellies, conserves and fruit preserves and for chutneys, and the following examples of timings are based on that. Some people, however, prefer to use 15 lb pressure, in which case deduct 1 minute from the cooking time given. Fruits vary in their tenderness, so if in doubt allow the pressure to drop and check the softness of the fruit, or other ingredients if making a chutney. If inadequately cooked, bring up to pressure once again and cook for a short time.

    Here are some samples of cooking times:

>   Apple and Damson Jam (pages 21 to 22) 6 minutes at 10 lb pressure
>   Blackcurrant Jam (page 29) 3 minutes at 10 lb pressure if ripe; 4 minutes if very firm
>   Dried Apricot Jam (page 53) 10 minutes at 15 lb pressure
>   Lemon Marmalade (pages 93 to 94) 8 minutes at 10 lb pressure
>   Sweet Seville Orange Marmalade (page 98) 10 minutes at 10 lb pressure
>   Mango Chutney (pages 171 to 172) 6 minutes at 10 lb pressure

6. Always allow the pressure to drop at room temperature. Do not try to hurry this.
7. When the pressure has dropped, remove the lid, check the fruit and, if adequately softened, add the sugar, or sugar and lemon juice where recommended in the recipe.
8. *Do not put the lid back on.* Treat the pressure cooker as an ordinary preserving pan from this stage onwards. Stir over a low heat until the sugar has dissolved, then raise the heat and continue as the recipe.

USING FROZEN FRUIT

Often it is not possible to make the preserves when you pick or buy the fruit. This may happen with Seville oranges which have a very short season. It is therefore sensible to buy the fruit and freeze it. The Seville oranges, like any other fruits, will be perfectly satisfactory for making the preserves but during freezing a certain amount of the natural setting quality (pectin) is destroyed. To compensate for this either increase the amount of fruit by 10%, i.e. instead of 450 g/1 lb use nearly 500 g/1 lb 2 oz, or use double the amount of lemon juice in the recipe. If no lemon juice is given in the recipe when using fresh fruit, add 1 tablespoon (1¼ tablespoons) to each 450 g/ 1 lb (2 cups) of sugar.

USING CANNED FRUITS FOR PRESERVES

There may be occasions when a certain fresh fruit is not available and you must use canned fruit instead. If canned in syrup, you need to reduce the amount of sugar used with the fruit. If canned in natural juice, you should use the normal amount of sugar. In either case, increase the amount of lemon juice in the recipe. An example of this appears in Lychee Jam (see pages 40 to 41). Where no lemon juice is used in the recipe with fresh fruit add 1 tablespoon (1¼ tablespoons) to each 450 g/ 1 lb (2 cups) sugar.

LOWER SUGAR PRESERVES

Any of the recipes in this book for jam, conserves, jellies, marmalades or chutneys can be made with a lower amount of sugar. Although pectin and adequate boiling make the preserves set, the sugar is the preservative so it is a very important ingredient.

Preserves made with less sugar will not keep well unless special precautions are taken, but the flavour is excellent for you will have the true taste of the fruit, or other ingredients in the case of chutneys.

The sugar in any of the recipes can be reduced by half, i.e. where 450 g/1 lb (2 cups) sugar is given in the recipe use just 225 g/8 oz (1 cup).

If you make a very small batch of preserve, keep it in jars in the refrigerator and use within 3 to 4 weeks, especially after the jars are opened. If making larger batches, there are two ways to keep the preserves for a long period:

1. Freezing

Fill the jars to within 2.5 cm/1 inch of the top only. Cover, and when the preserve is absolutely cold place it in the freezer. The air space at the top of the jars is essential for the food expands during freezing. Instead of using jars, the preserve can be placed in suitable freezer containers for storage. Always make sure the container(s) used will not react with the vinegar in the chutney. Chutneys keep less well with freezing than jams, jellies and conserves, for their flavour needs to mature and that does not happen when frozen. Chutneys need to be stored at room temperature for the many flavours to mingle and mature.

2. Sterilizing

Use proper bottling jars. Make sure these are very well heated before filling them with the hot preserve. Put on the rubber bands and lids and then the screw bands. Loosen these bands by half a turn to allow for the expansion of the glass during sterilization.

Have ready a sterilizer or deep pan filled with boiling water. A proper sterilizer has a rack at the bottom of the pan on which to stand the jars. If using an ordinary saucepan, pad the base with a thick layer of cloth or paper to protect the glass jars.

Carefully lower the very hot jars into the water and allow this to come back to boiling. Boil briskly for 15 minutes. Remove the jars and tighten the bands. Next day check that the lids have sealed. If any have not, then the preserve in that jar must be eaten quickly or the sterilizing process repeated. The latter could spoil the flavour of the preserve for it would taste over-cooked. If you need to re-sterilize the preserve because the jars have not sealed, tip out of the containers into the preserving pan. Heat to boiling point, spoon the hot preserve into clean, heated bottling jars, cover with the lids and proceed as instructed above.

Why do jams and similar preserves form mould on top?
- The fruit was picked on a wet day and was damp.
- Too little sugar was used in making the preserve. As explained on page 9 if you reduce the sugar content you are losing some of the preservative and therefore mould could form unless the preserve is correctly stored.
- Too short a boiling time, so the completed preserve lacked the right proportion of sugar through too great a yield. Recipes detail the right yield.
- The preserve was stored in a damp place.
- The jars were inadequately covered (see page 19 – point 13).
- Too large an air space was left in the jars at the top of the preserve. The smaller the air space the less the possibility of mould forming (see page 19 – point 12 for details on filling jars).

JAMS OF ALL KINDS

The dictionary defines jam as a preserve of whole fruit, slightly crushed and boiled with sugar. Of course that is how good jam should be, except we simmer the fruit first to soften it before adding the sugar. A conserve is a preserve in which one should *always* find large pieces of fruit or even whole fruit.

Jams can be made with most fruit and the import of varied produce from other countries means we can choose from a very wide selection.

When the less common fruits are very expensive you can make them go further by carefully blending them with economical apples, rhubarb or marrow.

Some flowers or their leaves add an interesting flavour to jams, see Rose Petal Jam on pages 50 to 51, Gooseberry and Elderflower Jam on page 37 and Rhubarb and Geranium Jam on page 50.

PERFECT JAMS AND CONSERVES

These points are very important when making jams and conserves. They should be followed for fruit jellies and cheeses, together with the information on pages 6 to 10.

1. **Choosing the fruit.** Select this carefully: it should be ripe, so the full flavour has developed, but not be over-ripe, for that could cause the jam to ferment (see page 10). The fresher the fruit the better, for this will have the maximum flavour and setting quality.

2. **Proportions of fruit and sugar.** Follow the proportions given in the recipes. It is a mistake to think that one should allow 450 g/1 lb (2 cups) sugar to each 450 g/1 lb fruit for every jam. If a fruit has lower than average pectin, e.g. strawberries and dessert cherries, it is a good idea to use slightly more fruit than sugar, so you can increase the pectin content. Also, it may be advisable to add lemon juice or redcurrant juice (both rich in pectin) to build up the amount of natural setting quality in the recipe. A method of testing for pectin content is given on pages 11 to 12.

3. **Preparing the fruit.** Check the fruit carefully and discard any soft fruit that is bruised. With large plums, peaches and similar fruit, cut away any bruised parts. Unless the fruit has been freshly picked in dry weather it is important to rinse it in cold water. The best method is to put the fruit in a sieve or colander and run cold water over it; this prevents the fruit absorbing too much liquid. Drain on absorbent paper. Wash and prepare the fruit immediately before using, as it deteriorates if left standing for any length of time. Washing the fruit is mentioned in recipes using blackberries (brambles) because the wild fruit, growing beside roads, is likely to be dusty.

Hull strawberries, top and tail gooseberries, peel apples and pears, etc., unless sieving the fruit. Stones can be removed before or during cooking. The recipes suggest the best method.

4.   **Sugar to use.**
Special sugar: it is possible to obtain granulated sugar that includes a certain amount of pectin. Buy this when making preserves with fruits that are low in pectin. Where a fruit is rich in pectin, e.g. blackcurrants, you get a better textured jam if slightly *less* fruit is used in relation to the amount of sugar. Use ordinary sugar for this jam. If you are not using the special sugar that contains pectin, it is a good idea to buy preserving sugar. The small lumps take longer to dissolve than finer sugar and this helps to prevent scum. Loaf (lump) sugar can be used, as can granulated or caster sugar.
American measures: 2 American cups are given in recipes as the equivalent measure for 450 g/1 lb sugar. This is correct when using granulated sugar. If using preserving or loaf sugar buy them by weight. In a few recipes for jams and conserves you will find it recommended that a certain percentage of brown sugar is used to give a slightly different taste. Various kinds of brown sugar are used in chutneys and sweet pickles (see pages 151 and 161). Some honey or syrup can be used, see page 11. If you are anxious to lower the percentage of sugar in the jam, or other preserve, then follow the advice on pages 15 to 16 for low-percentage preserves.

5.   **Warming the sugar.** If the sugar is left in a warm place, such as an airing cupboard, for 1 or 2 hours before making the preserve it will dissolve more readily, see point 7.

6.   **Speed of cooking the fruit.** *Always* simmer the fruit slowly before adding the sugar. This is essential for it:
      a) extracts the pectin better;
      b) softens the skins of the fruit better.
Test the skins are absolutely soft before you add the sugar, for they do not soften once the sugar has been mixed into the fruit.
See the information about simmering on page 8.

7.   **Dissolving the sugar.** Make sure the sugar is *completely* dissolved before allowing the preserve to come to the boil. If the sugar remains partially undissolved you are more likely to have a preserve that will crystallize in due course. Stir all the time over a low heat until the sugar has dissolved.

8.   **Boiling the preserve.** Choose a pan sufficiently large to allow the preserve to boil rapidly after the sugar has been added without fear of it boiling over. Rapid boiling is essential to ensure setting point is reached in the shortest possible time.
      When making conserves you are advised to boil steadily, rather than rapidly. This is to keep the large pieces of fruit intact. *Do not stir* when the jam is boiling rapidly, or the conserve is boiling steadily. Stirring lowers the temperature and delays setting point – and the shorter the cooking time the better the flavour of the preserve.

9.   **The importance of early testing for setting.** Some jams reach setting point in 3 to 5 minutes, especially if only a small amount is being made. Others take 10 to 15 minutes, or even longer. Always remove the pan from the heat while testing for setting. For details of the

ways to test see pages 8 to 9. Some fruits pass setting point if overboiled, so early testing is essential.

10. **Dealing with scum on preserves.** Even when preserving sugar is used, a layer of scum may form on the top of the preserve. It is wasteful to try to remove this several times during cooking. It is better to wait until the preserve has reached setting point and then give a very brisk stir. This may disperse the scum. If any remains then remove with a metal spoon. A small knob of butter, about 25 g/1 oz (2 tablespoons), to each 900 g/2 lb fruit can be put into the preserving pan when the sugar is added; this helps to minimise the formation of scum. Scum on preserves is not harmful in any way, it just spoils the clarity of the finished product.

11. **Preparing the jam jars.** Make sure the jars into which the jam is to be put are well prepared.

    a) Wash them well in very hot water; if a detergent has been used, rinse thoroughly in very hot clear water afterwards.

    b) Dry the jars with an absolutely clean cloth, then warm them in the oven on a very low setting. It is a good idea to stand them on a baking tin padded with paper, so they will not get too hot and crack.

12. **Filling the jars.** The jam and conserve recipes read 'spoon the jam into the hot jars'. You will find it more convenient to use a jug to pour the preserve into the jars, although this can be difficult if it contains large pieces of fruit. If the preserve does have large chunks of fruit or slices of peel (as in marmalade), allow it to stand in the preserving pan for a short time until it begins to stiffen slightly. Stir briskly to distribute the pieces of fruit or peel and then put into the jars. Fill to within 3 to 6 mm/⅛ to ¼ inch from the top of each jar. This is very important for the less air space there is in the jars the better the preserve will keep. Any half-filled jars should be consumed within the shortest possible time.

13. **Covering the preserves.** Place the waxed circles from packs of jam pot covers on the hot preserve immediately it is spooned into the jars. These form a seal. If you are able to put the final transparent covers or lids over the preserve immediately after putting on the waxed circles then do so. This makes a good seal and the jars will be virtually airtight. If you have to delay this stage because you are filling a number of jars it is better to wait until the preserve has become absolutely cold before adding the transparent covers or the lids. It is wrong to cover half-warm preserves; these are likely to produce a certain amount of condensation within the jar.

14. **Storing preserves.** Choose a cool and dry place. A dark cupboard is ideal, for some preserves lose a little colour if continually exposed to bright sunlight. For details on storing preserves made with a low sugar content see page 15.

APPLE JAMS

The apple is a member of the rose family and is of the genus *Malus*. Apples have been known in Britain since the Stone Age and today there are thousands of different varieties, both for cooking and eating raw. The fruit has always been considered of great value to health. The old adage, known to most people, is 'An apple a day keeps the doctor away.'

A jam based on apples alone is not the most exciting of preserves but when mixed with a spice, as in the first recipe, or with other fruits you can achieve very interesting results. Apple Jellies (see pages 72 to 73) and Blackberry and Apple Butter (see page 106) have an excellent flavour. No specific varieties of apple are given in the recipes: choose a good cooking apple, unless stated to the contrary.

Apples are excellent partners to soft berry fruit, so if you have insufficient raspberries, strawberries or other fruits, use half apple purée and half soft fruit, as in the example on page 23.

APPLE GINGER JAM (1)

Cooking time: 30 minutes • Makes 750 g/1²/₃ lb jam

Metric/Imperial	Ingredients	American
450 g/1 lb	cooking apples, weight when peeled and cored (but retain peel and cores)	1 lb
450 g/1 lb	sugar	2 cups
4 tablespoons	diced preserved ginger	5 tablespoons
1 tablespoon	water	1¹/₄ tablespoons

Cut the apples into 1.5 cm/½ inch dice, put into the preserving pan with the sugar, ginger and water. Tie the peel and cores in a piece of muslin and add to the pan. Allow to stand for several hours. During this time some juice will flow from the apples. Simmer the fruit over a low heat, stirring regularly, until all the sugar has dissolved; raise the heat and boil steadily, rather than rapidly, until setting point is reached. Remove the bag of peel and cores. Spoon into the hot jars and seal down.

Variations

• Instead of using preserved ginger use 1 to 1½ teaspoons ground ginger.

Spiced Apple Jam: instead of ginger flavouring use ½ to 1 teaspoon ground cinnamon or cloves.

Apple and Date Preserve: omit the ginger in the recipe but add 175 g/6 oz (generous cup) chopped dates, 1 tablespoon (1¹/₄ tablespoons) lemon juice and 450 g/1 lb (2 cups) sugar. Prepare the apples as above, put into the preserving pan with the dates, lemon juice and sugar. Tie the peel and cores in a piece of muslin and add to the pan. Allow to stand for several hours then proceed as in the recipe above. Raisins, sultanas (golden raisins) and diced dried tenderised apricots, figs or prunes could be used instead of the dates. Instead of lemon juice use water in the recipe with a good pinch of ground cinnamon or mixed spice to flavour the jam.

APPLE GINGER JAM (2)

Cooking time: 30 minutes • Makes 750 g/1²/₃ lb jam

Use 550 g/1¼ lb cooking apples, 2 tablespoons (2½ tablespoons) water, 450 g/1 lb (2 cups) sugar and 4 tablespoons (5 tablespoons) chopped preserved ginger with 3 teaspoons syrup from the jar.

Wash the apples and cut into small pieces – do not peel or core the fruit. Put into a pan with the water and simmer gently until a purée.
 Rub through a nylon sieve and return to the pan. Heat gently then add the sugar and stir over the heat until the sugar has dissolved. Add the ginger and syrup, stir well to blend and boil rapidly until the setting point is reached. Spoon into hot jars and seal down.

APPLE AND CHERRY JAM

Cooking time: 30 minutes • Makes 1.5 kg/3¹/₃ lb jam

The main recipe is based on ripe dessert cherries. As these have little natural pectin you need a slightly more generous amount of the fruit than given in the variation, which uses more acid cooking cherries.

Metric/Imperial	Ingredients	American
450 g/1 lb	cooking apples, weight when peeled and cored	1 lb
550 g/1¼ lb	ripe dessert cherries	1¼ lb
4 tablespoons	cherry juice or water, see method	5 tablespoons
900 g/2 lb	sugar	4 cups

Cut the peeled and cored apples into 1.5 cm/½ inch dice; stone the cherries over a basin so no juice is wasted. Measure this juice and add water if necessary to give the right amount. Put the apples, cherries and juice or water into the preserving pan and simmer gently until the fruit is softened – try to prevent it breaking up too much. Add the sugar and stir over a low heat until this has dissolved, then raise the heat and boil steadily, not rapidly, until setting point is reached. Allow the jam to cool slightly in the pan, stir to distribute the pieces of fruit, then spoon into hot jars and seal down.

Variation

• If using Morello or other cooking cherries, you need only 450 g/1 lb. It is not easy to stone firm cherries, so cook them with their stones in, then remove the stones with a perforated spoon before adding the sugar. As there will not be any cherry juice, use water as in the recipe above.

APPLE AND DAMSON JAM

Cooking time: 30 to 35 minutes • Makes 1.75 kg/3³/₄ lb jam

Apples and damsons are a very good partnership. It is advisable to use slightly more damsons than apples because of the weight of the stones in the small fruit.

Metric/Imperial	Ingredients	American
450 g/1 lb	cooking apples, weight when peeled and cored	1 lb
675 g/1½ lb	damsons	1½ lb
150 to 225 ml/ 5 to 7½ fl oz	water	⅔ to scant 1 cup
1 kg/2¼ lb	sugar	4½ cups

Cut the apples into small pieces, put into the preserving pan with the washed damsons and the water. Use the larger quantity of water if the damsons are very firm. Simmer gently until a soft pulp; make certain the damson skins are soft. Remove the damson stones with a perforated spoon. Add the sugar and stir over a low heat until this has dissolved, then raise the heat and boil rapidly until setting point is reached. Spoon into hot jars and seal down.

APPLE AND LEMON JAM

Cooking time: 30 minutes • Makes 750 g/1⅔ lb jam

Use 550g /1¼ lb cooking apples, 2 tablespoons (2½ tablespoons) lemon juice, 2 teaspoons finely grated lemon rind, 450 g/1 lb (2 cups) sugar.

Wash the apples and cut into small pieces – do not peel or core the fruit. Put into a pan with the lemon juice and simmer gently until a purée. Rub through a nylon sieve and return to the pan with the grated lemon rind. Heat gently then add the sugar and stir over the heat until the sugar has dissolved. Bring to the boil then cook rapidly until setting point is reached. Spoon into hot jars and seal down.

Variations

Apple and Orange Jam: follow the recipe for Apple and Lemon Jam but use the same quantity of orange juice and 3 teaspoons grated orange rind instead of lemon rind. Other citrus fruits could be used instead: if using grapefruit follow the recipe for Apple and Lemon Jam above; if using clementines then follow the quantities for Apple and Orange Jam.

APPLE AND PINEAPPLE JAM

Cooking time: 35 minutes • Makes 1.5 kg/3⅓ lb jam

Use 450g/1 lb apples, weight when peeled and cored, 450 g/1 lb pineapple, weight when peeled and centre hard core removed, 3 tablespoons (3¾ tablespoons) water, 2 tablespoons (2½ tablespoons) lemon juice and 900 g/2 lb (4 cups) sugar.

Cut the apples and pineapple into 1.5 cm/½ inch dice, put into the pan with the water and lemon juice. Simmer gently until the fruit is soft then stir in the sugar and proceed as the Apple and Cherry Jam, page 21.

Variation

- Use canned pineapple in natural juice instead of fresh pineapple. Drain the fruit and cut it into dice, as above. Use the liquid from the can instead of water.

APPLE AND PLUM JAM

Cooking time: 30 minutes • Makes 2.25 kg/5 lb jam

As apples have a somewhat stronger flavour than many plums it is better to use a smaller amount of the apples, as in the recipe below.

Metric/Imperial	Ingredients	American
450 g/1 lb	cooking apples, weight when peeled and cored	1 lb
900 g/2 lb	cooking plums, weight when stoned	2 lb
4 to 8 tablespoons	water	5 to 10 tablespoons
1.35 kg/3 lb	sugar	6 cups

Chop the peeled and cored apples; halve the plums and remove the stones. Put the fruit into the preserving pan with the required amount of water – use the smaller quantity if the fruit is very ripe but the larger amount if it is very firm. Simmer gently until a soft purée, then add the sugar and stir over a low heat until this has dissolved. Raise the heat and boil rapidly until setting point is reached. If there are large pieces of fruit in the jam, cool slightly then stir briskly to distribute the fruit and spoon into hot jars. Seal down.

Variations

Apple and Raspberry Jam: use the same proportions of apples as in the recipe above and 900 g/2 lb raspberries instead of plums. Use only 2 tablespoons (2½ tablespoons) water. Simmer the apples with the water until a soft purée, add the raspberries and heat for 4 to 5 minutes only. Add the sugar and stir over a low heat until the sugar has dissolved. Boil rapidly until setting point is reached, then spoon into hot jars and seal down.

Apple and Strawberry Jam: use strawberries instead of raspberries. Follow exactly the same cooking method but use 2 tablespoons (2½ tablespoons) lemon juice or half lemon juice and half water to add extra pectin to the fruit.

APPLE AND RHUBARB JAM

Cooking time: 30 minutes • Makes 1.5 kg/3⅓ lb jam

Rhubarb is not a fruit, although it is generally classed as one.
The edible parts are stalks of a large plant of the Polygonaceae *family.*
A jam made from equal amounts of apples and rhubarb has an excellent

flavour. The more robust garden rhubarb is better for this particular preserve. The delicate forced variety is delicious in the conserve on page 67.

Metric/Imperial	Ingredients	American
450 g/1 lb	**cooking apples, weight when peeled and cored**	1 lb
450 g/1 lb	**rhubarb**	1 lb
3 tablespoons	**water**	3³/₄ tablespoons
900 g/2 lb	**sugar**	4 cups

Chop the apples finely; wipe and cut the rhubarb into 1.5 cm/¹/₂ inch lengths. Put the apples and rhubarb with the water into the pan and simmer gently until a purée. Add the sugar and stir over a low heat until dissolved, then raise the heat and cook rapidly until setting point is reached. Spoon into hot jars and seal down.

Variations

Apple and Tomato Jam: this makes a very unusual and pleasant jam. It is an ideal alternative to marmalade at breakfast time. Substitute 450 g/1 lb red or green tomatoes for the rhubarb in the recipe above.

If using red tomatoes: skin and halve the tomatoes, the seeds could be removed but this is not essential. Chop the fruit into small pieces. Simmer with the prepared apples and continue as the recipe above.

If using green tomatoes: it is difficult to skin these, so simply chop the fruit finely. Simmer the tomatoes in 6 tablespoons (7¹/₂ tablespoons) water until they begin to soften, then add the apples and cook until both fruits form a soft purée. Continue as the recipe above. You could add 1 to 2 teaspoons ground ginger to the fruits, as this is particularly good with green tomatoes.

APRICOT JAM

Cooking time: 25 to 30 minutes • Makes 750 g/1²/₃ lb jam

Apricots were introduced into Arab countries from China and the Far East, where they had grown for centuries. The Romans brought the fruit to Europe and by the sixteenth century the trees could be found in some sheltered British gardens. Apricots are now grown extensively in America, Australia, South Africa and New Zealand. They are one of the most popular canned fruits. As the apricot has a low level of pectin, it is advisable to add lemon juice and also to use the sugar that contains pectin, where this is available.

Metric/Imperial	Ingredients	American
450 g/1 lb	**apricots**	1 lb
2 to 4 tablespoons	**water**	2¹/₂ to 5 tablespoons
450 g/1 lb	**sugar**	2 cups
1 tablespoon	**lemon juice**	1¹/₄ tablespoons

Halve the fruit and remove the stones. Some of these can be cracked and the kernels added to the jam just before it reaches setting point – do not add them too early since this will make them over-soft. Put the fruit into the preserving pan. Add the water to the fruit – use the smaller amount if the fruit is ripe and the larger quantity if less than ripe. Simmer gently until soft, add the sugar and lemon juice, stir over a low heat until this has dissolved, then boil rapidly until setting point is reached. If there are fairly large pieces of apricot in the jam, leave until slightly thickened, stir to distribute the fruit, then spoon into hot jars and seal down.

Variations

Apricot and Almond Jam: use the recipe above but to each 450 g/1 lb apricots allow 50 g/2 oz (½ cup) blanched almonds, chopped and flaked. Add these to the jam when it has reached setting point and stir to distribute.

Apricot and Maraschino Jam: use the syrup from a jar of Maraschino cherries instead of the water in the recipe. Allow 2 tablespoons (2½ tablespoons) well-drained Maraschino cherries to each 450 g/1 lb apricots. Make the jam as the recipe then add the cherries just before the jam reaches setting point. See Apricot and Maraschino Cherry Conserve, page 59.

BANANA JAM

Cooking time: 30 minutes • Makes 2.25 kg/5 lb jam

Bananas are probably the favourite fruit in Britain today. It is believed that they were first brought from China early in the nineteenth century. They grow prolifically in most tropical regions. The banana is a fruit rarely used in jam-making, but this recipe is extremely good. The apples give body to the jam and, with the lemons, add flavour; both fruits ensure that the jam sets well and help to prevent the bananas discolouring. The Banana and Apple Cheese (see page 106) makes an equally good preserve. An Orange and Banana Marmalade (see page 90) is an excellent breakfast preserve.

Metric/Imperial	Ingredients	American
450 g/1 lb	cooking apples, weight when peeled and cored	1 lb
2 large	lemons	2 large
3 tablespoons	water	3¾ tablespoons
900 g/2 lb	bananas, weight when peeled	2 lb
1.35 kg/3 lb	sugar	6 cups

Cut the apples into 1.5 cm/½ inch dice. Grate the rind from the lemons, halve the fruit and squeeze out the juice. Put the apples with the lemon rind and water into a preserving pan. Simmer for approximately 15 minutes. Mash the peeled bananas, blend with the lemon juice, add to the pan and simmer for a few minutes. Put in the sugar, stir over a low heat until dissolved, then boil rapidly until setting point is reached. Spoon into hot jars and seal down.

Variations

Banana and Grape Jam: follow the recipe above but substitute 450 g/ 1 lb black grapes for the cooking apples. Split the grapes before cooking and remove any pips. Cook the grapes for 10 minutes with the lemon rind and water then add the bananas, mashed with the lemon juice, and proceed as the recipe.

Banana and Rhubarb Jam: follow the recipe but substitute 450g/1 lb diced rhubarb for the cooking apples. The rhubarb gives a very pleasing colour to the bananas. As rhubarb contains a high percentage of water, use only 1 tablespoon (1¼ tablespoons) water in the pan. Cook the diced rhubarb for 10 minutes with the lemon rind then add the bananas, mashed with the lemon juice, and proceed as the recipe.

BLACKBERRY JAM

Cooking time: 20 to 25 minutes • Makes 1.5 kg/3⅓ lb jam

Blackberries have a low amount of natural pectin, which is why a blend of cooking apples and blackberries ensures a jam that will set well. Lemon juice is added in the jam recipe below to ensure setting quality and the special sugar that contains pectin could be used. Blackberry pips are rather hard, so a jam based on a smooth blackberry purée is generally more popular than one in which the pips are left in (see Variations). Bramble Jelly is one of the best ways of using this fruit (see pages 74 to 75).

Metric/Imperial	Ingredients	American
900 g/2 lb	**blackberries**	2 lb
900 g/2 lb	sugar	4 cups
2 tablespoons	**lemon juice**	2½ tablespoons

Wash the fruit in cold water and allow to drain well. Put into the preserving pan and cook over a low heat until a soft pulp. As it cools it is advisable to press the fruit from time to time to extract the maximum juice – this makes sure it does not stick to the pan. Add the sugar and lemon juice, stir over a low heat until the sugar has dissolved then raise the heat and boil rapidly until setting point is reached. Spoon into hot jars and seal down.

Variations

Seedless Blackberry Jam: simmer the fruit as in the recipe above, rub through a nylon sieve, then measure the pulp. To each 600 ml/1 pint (2½ cups) purée allow 450 g/1 lb (2 cups) sugar and 1 tablespoon (1¼ tablespoons) lemon juice. Heat the purée and proceed as the recipe above.

Spiced Blackberry Jam: follow the recipes for Blackberry and Apple Jam (see below) or Blackberry Jam (page 26). To each 450 g/1 lb fruit allow 1 teaspoon ground cinnamon or mixed spice. This should be added with the sugar and blended with the hot fruit.

Boysenberry Jam: Cooking time: 20 to 25 minutes • Makes 1.5 kg/3½ lb jam.

These berries were obtained by crossing blackberries with loganberries and raspberries. They are a large berry fruit with a very fine flavour, and were named after their creator Rudolf Boysen. Follow the recipes for Blackberry Jams above but substitute boysenberries for blackberries. There is an excellent Boysenberry and Citrus Fruit jam on page 30.

Cloudberry Jam: Cooking time: 20 to 25 minutes • Makes 1.5 kg/3⅓ lb jam.

These fruits look like large golden blackberries; they grow on low bushes and are highly esteemed in Norway. The flavour is very subtle and not to everyone's taste but devotees of the fruit seek it out eagerly. Cloudberry Jam is made like Blackberry Jam on page 26, but it has a sharper taste. It is better to use cloudberries without adding other fruits.

BLACKBERRY AND APPLE JAM

Cooking time: 25 to 30 minutes • Makes 1.5 kg/3⅓ lb jam

Blackberries, like apples, belong to the rose family. They grow prolifically in the wild and, while the cultivated variety may look rather more impressive, the wild blackberries, often known as brambles, tend to have more flavour.

Metric/Imperial	Ingredients	American
450 g/1 lb	blackberries	1 lb
450 g/1 lb	cooking apples, weight when peeled and cored	1 lb
2 tablespoons	water	2½ tablespoons
900 g/2 lb	sugar	4 cups

Wash the berries in cold water and allow to drain well. Chop the apples into small pieces and put into the preserving pan with the water. Simmer for 10 minutes then add the blackberries and continue cooking slowly until a soft purée. Add the sugar and stir over a low heat until dissolved then raise the heat and boil rapidly until setting point is reached. Spoon into hot jars and seal down.

Variation

- An interesting jam can be made by simmering the apples until a smooth purée then adding the blackberries. Cook gently for 5 to 6 minutes before putting in the sugar. Proceed as above. This gives a good distribution of whole fruit in the apple purée.

BLACKBERRY AND ELDERBERRY JAM

Cooking time: 20 to 25 minutes • Makes 1.5 kg/3⅓ lb jam

The combination of these two fruits makes an excellent jam.

Use 450 g/1 lb blackberries with 450 g/1 lb elderberries, 900 g/2 lb (4 cups) sugar and 4 tablespoons (5 tablespoons) lemon juice.

Wash the berries in cold water, drain well then put into the preserving pan. Simmer until just soft. Add the sugar and lemon juice, stir over a low heat until the sugar has dissolved, then boil rapidly until setting point is reached. Spoon into hot jars and seal down.

BLACKBERRY AND PINEAPPLE PRESERVE

Cooking time: 35 to 40 minutes • Makes 2.25 kg/5 lb jam

This is an interesting and unusual combination of fruits. The apples seem to emphasise the flavour of the other two fruits and give a good texture to the preserve.

Metric/Imperial	Ingredients	American
450 g/1 lb	pineapple, weight when peeled and cored	1 lb
450 g/1 lb	cooking apples, weight when peeled and cored	1 lb
4 tablespoons	water	5 tablespoons
450 g/1 lb	blackberries	1 lb
1.35 kg/3 lb	sugar	6 cups
3 tablespoons	lemon juice	3¾ tablespoons

Cut the pineapple and apple into 1.5 cm/½ inch dice. Put into the preserving pan with the water and simmer for 15 minutes. Meanwhile wash the blackberries, drain well then add to the pan and continue simmering until all the fruit has softened. Add the sugar and lemon juice. Stir over a low heat until the sugar has dissolved then boil rapidly until setting point is reached. Cool for a short time in the pan, stir to distribute the fruit then spoon into hot jars and seal down.

Variation

• Use canned pineapple in natural juice instead of fresh pineapple. Strain and chop the fruit, and use the juice from the can instead of water.

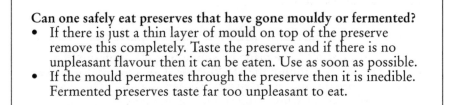

Can one safely eat preserves that have gone mouldy or fermented?
• If there is just a thin layer of mould on top of the preserve remove this completely. Taste the preserve and if there is no unpleasant flavour then it can be eaten. Use as soon as possible.
• If the mould permeates through the preserve then it is inedible. Fermented preserves taste far too unpleasant to eat.

BLACKCURRANT JAM

Cooking time: 35 to 40 minutes • Makes 900 g/2 lb jam

These small berries can be found growing in most of the northern hemisphere and even in northern Asia, as far as the Himalayas. They were originally found wild in Britain and other European countries. Some people like to cut away the remains of the flower on the berries but this is not really essential. It is, however, important to make sure the very firm skins are soft before adding the sugar, for they do not soften when this is added. The fruit is very rich in pectin and therefore it is possible to use slightly more sugar than fruit, as in the recipe that follows.

Metric/Imperial	Ingredients	American
450 g/1 lb	**blackcurrants**	1 lb
300 to 450 ml/¹/₂ to ³/₄ pint	**water**	1¹/₄ cups to scant 2 cups
550 g/1¹/₄ lb	**sugar**	2¹/₂ cups

Put the washed fruit and water into the preserving pan; use the smaller amount of water if the blackcurrants are very ripe. Simmer slowly until the blackcurrants are very soft – test one or two, you should be able to rub the skin with your fingers. Add the sugar, stir over a low heat until this has dissolved then boil rapidly until setting point is reached. Spoon into hot jars and seal down.

Variation

• The above makes a soft, delicately textured jam. For a firmer texture reduce the amount of water to 225 ml/7¹/₂ fl oz (scant cup) for ripe fruit and 300 ml/¹/₂ pint (1¹/₄ cups) for less ripe fruit. The amount of sugar is as above.

BLACKCURRANT AND APPLE JAM

Cooking time: 35 to 40 minutes • Makes 1.8 kg/4 lb jam

Use 450 g/1 lb blackcurrants, 300 ml/¹/₂ pint (1¹/₄ cups) water, 450 g/1 lb cooking apples (weight when peeled and cored) and 1 kg/2¹/₄ lb (4¹/₂ cups) sugar.

Put the washed blackcurrants into the preserving pan with the water. Simmer gently for 10 to 15 minutes. Slice the apples thinly, add to the blackcurrants and continue cooking gently until the fruit is soft. Add the sugar, stir until dissolved, then boil rapidly until setting point is reached. Spoon into hot jars and seal down.

BLUEBERRY JAM

Cooking time: 20 minutes • Makes 750 g/1²/₃ lb jam

Blueberries belong to the heather family (Ericaceae), and the most commonly used variety is Vaccinium myrtillus. *The fruit grows on small trees or low bushes, and has a variety of different names, the best known being blaeberries, bilberries, huckleberries and whortleberries. The berries soften very quickly and, because the fruit has a good amount of pectin, the jam will set in a short time.*

Metric/Imperial	Ingredients	American
450 g/1 lb	**blueberries**	1 lb
450 g/1 lb	**sugar**	2 cups

Put the fruit into the preserving pan, simmer over a low heat, stirring well at first, so the juice flows. As soon as the berries begin to soften add the sugar. Stir over a low heat until the sugar has dissolved then boil rapidly until setting point is reached. Spoon into hot jars and seal down.

Variations

• If the berries are not quite ripe, simmer in 4 tablespoons (5 tablespoons) water. Although it is better to make most jam with ripe – but not over-ripe – fruit, a jam made from blueberries that are slightly red in colour has an excellent flavour.

Spiced Blueberry Jam: add just ½ teaspoon ground cinnamon with each 450 g/1 lb (2 cups) sugar.

BOYSENBERRY AND CITRUS FRUIT JAM

Cooking time: 20 to 25 minutes • Makes 1.5 kg/3¹/₃ lb jam

The secret of this jam is to remove half the berries when tender, boil the rest of the fruit with the sugar until the setting point is nearly reached, then return the berries to the purée.

Metric/Imperial	Ingredients	American
900 g/2 lb	**boysenberries**	2 lb
6 tablespoons	**orange juice**	7¹/₂ tablespoons
2 tablespoons	**lemon juice**	2¹/₂ tablespoons
3 teaspoons	**finely grated orange rind**	3 teaspoons
2 teaspoons	**finely grated lemon rind**	2 teaspoons
900 g/2 lb	**sugar**	4 cups

Put the boysenberries with the orange and lemon juice and rinds into the preserving pan. Simmer gently until the fruit is *just* softened. Carefully remove half the berries and put on one side. Stir the sugar into the remaining fruit and continue to stir over a low heat until dissolved. Boil rapidly until setting point is almost reached then return the whole fruit to the pan and complete the cooking process. Allow the jam to cool slightly, stir to distribute the whole fruit, then spoon into hot jars and seal down.

Variations

- Sieve the puréed fruit to give a smooth mixture, free from pips. Return to the pan, heat gently, then add the sugar and continue as the recipe above.

Loganberry and Citrus Fruit Jam: use loganberries instead of boysenberries. As loganberries are not quite as firm as boysenberries you may prefer to purée all the fruit before adding the sugar.

Tayberry and Citrus Fruit Jam: use tayberries (a cross between a raspberry and a blackberry) instead of boysenberries in the recipe.

CAPE GOOSEBERRY JAM (1)

Cooking time: 30 minutes • Makes 1.5 kg/3⅓ lb jam

Cape gooseberries are members of the tomato family; they form part of a very spectacular plant called peruviana Physalis. *The fruit is often known as Chinese Lanterns. The fruit is not as plentiful as one would wish for it has a very pleasant flavour. It makes an excellent jam if combined with a certain amount of apples to provide bulk.*

Metric/Imperial	Ingredients	American
450 g/1 lb	cape gooseberries, weight when seed pods removed, see method	1 lb
450 g/1 lb	cooking apples, weight when peeled and cored	1 lb
3 tablespoons	water	3¾ tablespoons
900 g/2 lb	sugar	4 cups

Remove the outer cases and weigh the fruit. Cut the apples into thin slices. Put both fruits into the preserving pan with the water and simmer gently until a soft purée. Add the sugar and stir over a low heat until this has dissolved then raise the heat and boil rapidly until setting point is reached. Spoon into hot jars and seal down.

Variations

Cape Gooseberry Jam (2): omit the apples in the recipe above and use 900 g/2 lb cape gooseberries (weight after seed pods removed). Put the fruit and the water, plus the pulp and finely grated rind from 2 medium lemons, into a saucepan. Simmer until soft, add the sugar and continue as the recipe above.

Tamarillo Jam: tamarillos are also known as tree tomatoes. Skin the fruit, then weigh the pulp and use this instead of the cape gooseberries in either of the recipes above.

CHERRY JAM

Cooking time: 20 to 25 minutes • Makes 675 g/1½ lb jam

Cherry trees are members of the rose family. There are hundreds of cherry varieties (Prunus spp.) grown in many parts of the world. It is believed that the Romans brought cherry trees to Britain as long ago as AD 100. Cherry Jam is one of the most delicious preserves, the most famous being Swiss Black Cherry Jam, which you will find under Conserves on page 59. Both sweet dessert and the sourer cooking cherries make excellent jam. In order to achieve the best results the amounts of lemon juice and sugar need to be adjusted to suit each type. With ripe dessert cherries it is better to use more fruit than sugar; the special sugar that contains pectin could be used.

Metric/Imperial	Ingredients	American
450 g/1 lb	**ripe but firm dessert cherries**	1 lb
	weight when stoned, but see method	
400 g/14 oz	**sugar**	1¾cups
1 tablespoon	**lemon juice**	1¼ tablespoons

It is quite easy to stone ripe cherries: use a proper stoner or insert the bent end of a new firm hairpin into the cherry and pull out the stone. Do this over a basin so no juice is wasted. If you prefer to leave the stones in the fruit and remove them during cooking, allow 675 g/1½ lb cherries. Put the prepared fruit and its juice into the preserving pan. If you are leaving the stones in then add just 1 tablespoon (1¼ tablespoons) water if the fruit is very ripe or 3 tablespoons (3¾ tablespoons) if firm. Simmer gently until the fruit softens – do not over-cook. Add the sugar and lemon juice. Stir over a low heat until the sugar has dissolved then boil rapidly until setting point is reached. Cool for a short time, stir to distribute the fruit then spoon into hot jars and seal down.

Variations

• The cherry stones do add flavour to the jam, so if you have removed these before cooking they can be tied in muslin and left in the preserve until just before setting point is reached.

Morello Cherry Jam: allow the same amount of fruit but 450 g/1 lb (2 cups) sugar with only 2 teaspoons lemon juice. If using the special sugar that contains pectin, the lemon juice can be omitted. This will yield 750 g/1⅔ lb jam.

CRANBERRY JAM

Cooking time: 25 to 30 minutes • Makes 900 g/2 lb jam

Cranberries are related to blueberries, for they are another member of the heather family. The botanical name for the fruit grown extensively in America and Canada is Vaccinium macrocarpum. The berries are found on low evergreen shrubs and are chiefly famous in sauces to serve with turkey and in drinks. They also make an excellent jam. Cranberries are rich in Vitamin C and pectin, so a higher amount of sugar than fruit is used.

Metric/Imperial	Ingredients	American
450 g/1 lb	cranberries	1 lb
150 ml/¼ pint	water	⅔ cup
550 g/1¼ lb	sugar	2½ cups

Put the cranberries and water into a preserving pan or large saucepan with a tightly fitting lid. This is essential, for the berries are very inclined to jump up as they are heated. Simmer gently for 10 minutes or until the 'popping' noise ends and the berries have softened. Add the sugar, stir over a low heat until dissolved, then boil rapidly until setting point is reached. Spoon into heated jars and seal down.

Variations

Cranberry and Orange Jam: add the finely grated rind of 2 oranges to the fruit and use orange juice instead of water.

Cranberry and Port Wine Jam: add 4 tablespoons (5 tablespoons) water and 4 tablespoons (5 tablespoons) port wine to the fruit instead of all water.

CRANBERRY AND APPLE JAM

Cooking time: 25 to 30 minutes • Makes 1.5 kg/3⅓ lb jam

The inclusion of apples in this recipe is an excellent way of making cranberries go further. When fresh cranberries are not available, use the frozen variety in this or the previous recipes.

Metric/Imperial	Ingredients	American
450 g/1 lb	cooking apples, weight when peeled and cored	1 lb
150 ml/¼ pint	water	⅔ cup
450 g/1 lb	cranberries	1 lb
900 g/2 lb	sugar	4 cups

Cut the apples into thin slices. Put into the preserving pan with the water and cranberries. Cover the pan tightly and cook slowly for 10 minutes, or until the 'popping' noise ends. Add the sugar, stir over a low heat until dissolved, then boil rapidly until setting point is reached. Spoon into heated jars and seal down.

Variation

- This is a recipe in which a little honey could be used. Choose clear honey. Instead of 900 g/2 lb (4 cups) sugar use 675 g/1½ lb (3 cups) plus 225 g/8 oz (⅔ cup) honey. Add the honey with the sugar and stir well until these ingredients have dissolved.

DAMSON JAM

Cooking time: 25 to 30 minutes • For yield see end of recipe

Like plums and greengages, the damson comes from a Prunus tree, which is a member of the rose family. The true damson – Prunus damascena – is oval in shape with a blue-black colour. The fruit makes wonderfully rich preserves. In addition to this jam there are recipes for Apple and Damson Jam, Damson Jelly and Damson Cheese (see pages 21 to 22, 78 and 106). The amount of water and sugar required for the jam varies according to the ripeness of the fruit. Because damsons have such a definite flavour it is not essential to use more than 450 g/1 lb fruit, even when considering the weight of the stones, but see under Variations.

Metric/Imperial	Ingredients	American
450 g/1 lb	damsons	1 lb
4 tablespoons to 300 ml/½ pint	water	5 tablespoons to 1¼ cups
450 to 550 g/ 1 to 1¼ lb	sugar	2 to 2½ cups

Put the fruit and water into a preserving pan; use the smaller amount of water with very ripe fruit but the larger amount if the fruit is very firm and slightly under-ripe. Simmer until soft, then remove as many stones as possible with a perforated spoon. Add the sugar; use the smaller amount with ripe fruit and the greater quantity if the fruit is very under-ripe. Stir over a low heat until the sugar has dissolved, then boil rapidly until the setting point is reached. Spoon into hot jars and seal down.

Variations

• The amount of fruit can be raised to 550 g/1¼ lb if you like a strongly flavoured jam. The measurements of water and sugar should remain as in the recipe.

Damson and Marrow Jam: use 450 g/1 lb damsons, 450 g/1 lb marrow (weight when peeled and diced), 4 tablespoons (5 tablespoons) water and 900 g/2 lb (4 cups) sugar. Follow the recipe for Damson Jam, above.

Damson Plum Jam: follow the recipe for Damson jam, adjusting the amounts of water and sugar according to the ripeness of the fruit.

Yield

450 g/1 lb (2 cups) sugar gives 750 g/1²/₃ lb jam; 550 g/1¼ lb (2½ cups) sugar gives 900 g/2 lb jam; 900 g/2 lb (4 cups) sugar gives 1.5 kg/3⅓ lb jam.

ELDERBERRY JAM

Cooking time: 20 to 25 minutes • Makes 750 g/1²/₃ lb jam

Elderberries belong to the honeysuckle family and the fruit is highly esteemed in wine-making. It has a fairly strong taste, so many people prefer it mixed with blackberries, as in the recipe on page 28, or with apples, pears and quinces, as in the recipes that follow. The flowers of elderberries are excellent for adding a subtle flavour to fruit cheeses (see page 73). European elderberries are generally black in colour when fully ripe, whereas in America there are golden elderberries too.

Metric/Imperial	Ingredients	American
450 g/1 lb	elderberries	1 lb
450 g/1 lb	sugar	2 cups
2 tablespoons	lemon juice	2¹/₂ tablespoons

Put the fruit into the preserving pan, press it firmly to extract the juice, then simmer until soft. Add the sugar and lemon juice, stir over a low heat until the sugar has dissolved then boil rapidly until setting point is reached. Spoon into hot jars and seal down.

ELDERBERRY AND APPLE JAM

Cooking time: 30 minutes • Makes 1.5 kg/3¹/₃ lb jam

Use 450 g/1 lb cooking apples (weight when peeled and cored), 3 tablespoons (3³/₄ tablespoons) water, 450 g/1 lb elderberries, 900 g/2 lb (4 cups) sugar, 2 tablespoons (2¹/₂ tablespoons) lemon juice.

Cut the apples into very small pieces, put into the pan with the water and simmer for 10 minutes. Add the elderberries and continue cooking until soft. Add the sugar and lemon juice, stir over a low heat until the sugar has dissolved then boil rapidly until setting point is reached. Spoon into hot jars and seal down.

Variations

Elderberry and Pear Jam: use firm dessert pears instead of cooking apples (weigh these when peeled and cored). Follow the method for the Elderberry and Apple Jam but increase the amount of lemon juice to 3 tablespoons (3³/₄ tablespoons).

Elderberry and Quince Jam: use quinces instead of apples in the recipe.

FRESH FIG JAM

Cooking time: 40 to 45 minutes • Makes 750 g/1²/₃ lb jam

Figs – Ficus carica – belong to the mulberry family. The fruit makes an excellent jam, although it is better as a conserve (see page 61). Use the purple or green figs when they are ripe – they lack flavour when under-ripe. Dried figs too can be used for making jam (see page 54).

Metric/Imperial	Ingredients	American
450 g/1 lb	**figs**	1 lb
2 tablespoons	**water**	2½ tablespoons
450 g/1 lb	**sugar**	2 cups
2 tablespoons	**lemon juice**	2½ tablespoons

Cut the figs into small pieces and put into the preserving pan with the water. Simmer until soft then add the sugar and lemon juice. Stir over a low heat until the sugar has dissolved then boil rapidly until setting point is reached. If there are fairly firm pieces of fruit, allow to cool slightly then stir to distribute. Spoon into hot jars and seal down.

Why does a jam, or similar preserve form sugary crystals after storage?
- The sugar was not completely stirred and dissolved before rapid boiling began (see page 18 – stage 7).
- Too much sugar was used in relation to the amount of fruit.
- The preserve was over-cooked. This can be ascertained by the yield. If this is considerably less than given in the recipe there is a possibility of crystals forming in the preserve.

Can anything be done to correct a crystallised preserve?
- Not really, for re-boiling would only mean that when the preserve cooled and set again the crystals would re-form. A second boiling would tend to emphasise the problem. The best plan is to heat the preserve when required and use it as a hot sauce.

GOOSEBERRY JAM

Cooking time: 25 to 35 minutes • For yield see below

The gooseberry plant belongs to the Saxifrage family, as do blackcurrants, redcurrants and raspberries. There are many different gooseberries, each variety giving its own particular flavour to preserves. If you want to make a green gooseberry jam, the fruit must be very firm and hard and somewhat under-ripe. Although ripe gooseberries usually look green when cooked in jam, they generally produce a pinkish coloured preserve.

Metric/Imperial	Ingredients	American
450 g/1 lb	**gooseberries**	1 lb
3 tablespoons to 300 ml/½ pint	**water**	3¾ tablespoons to 1¼ cups
450 to 550 g/ 1 to 1¼ lb	**sugar**	2 to 2½ cups

Top and tail the gooseberries and put into the saucepan with the water – use the smaller amount for really ripe fruit but up to the maximum amount if the fruit is very hard. Simmer gently until the skins are soft – these will not soften after adding the sugar. Use the larger amount of sugar with under-ripe fruit. Stir over a low heat until the sugar has dissolved. Boil rapidly until setting point is reached. Spoon into hot jars and seal down.

Variations

Gooseberry and Elderflower Jam: use 1 small head of elderflowers to each 450 g/1 lb fruit. Remove the flowers from the stalks, wash in cold water, and add to the gooseberries at the beginning of the cooking period.

Gooseberry and Orange Jam: add 1 to 2 teaspoons finely grated orange rind to each 450 g/1 lb gooseberries and simmer the fruit in orange juice instead of water. The rind and juice of clementines could be used instead of oranges.

Yield

450 g/1 lb (2 cups) sugar will produce 750 g/1²/₃ lb jam; 550 g/1¼ lb (2½ cups) sugar will produce 900 g/2 lb jam.

GOOSEBERRY AND STRAWBERRY JAM

Cooking time: 25 minutes • Makes 1.5 kg/3⅓ lb jam

Gooseberries blend well with many other fruits and, as they are generally inexpensive, are an excellent way of making more expensive fruit go further. They also help fruits low in pectin, such as cherries and strawberries, to set. Ripe but firm gooseberries are best in the following recipes.

Metric/Imperial	Ingredients	American
450 g/1 lb	small ripe gooseberries	1 lb
3 tablespoons	water	3³/₄ tablespoons
450 g/1 lb	small ripe strawberries	1 lb
900 g/2 lb	sugar	4 cups

Top and tail the gooseberries and put into the preserving pan with the water. Simmer until nearly soft then add the strawberries and cook for a further few minutes. Add the sugar and stir over a low heat until dissolved. Boil rapidly until setting point is reached. Cool slightly, stir to distribute the fruit and then spoon into hot jars and seal down.

Variations

Gooseberry and Apple Jam: use 450 g/1 lb cooking apples (weight when peeled and cored) instead of strawberries. Simmer the apples with the gooseberries then add the sugar and follow the recipe above. You could put 1 or 2 small bunches of elderberry flowers in with the two fruits as these give a very delicate and interesting taste.

Gooseberry and Cherry Jam: use 550 g/1¼ lb stoned ripe dessert cherries in place of strawberries. Cook as the recipe above. You could use 450 g/ 1 lb Morello (cooking) cherries instead of the dessert cherries. Remove the stones before adding the sugar.

Gooseberry and Loganberry Jam: substitute loganberries for strawberries.

Gooseberry and Raspberry Jam: substitute raspberries for strawberries.

Gooseberry and Rhubarb Jam: use 450 g/1 lb diced rhubarb in place of the strawberries in the recipe. Simmer the two fruits together in just 2 tablespoons (2½ tablespoons) water. Add 2 tablespoons (2½ tablespoons) lemon juice and 900 g/2 lb (4 cups) sugar and proceed as the recipe.

Gooseberry and Tayberry Jam: these two fruits blend well together. Use tayberries in place of strawberries in the recipe.

GREENGAGE JAM

Cooking time: 20 to 25 minutes • Makes 750 g/1²/₃ lb jam

Greengages, like plums and damsons, are members of the Prunus *family. There is often confusion between real greengages and greengage-plums: the former are not completely round in shape but the greengage-plum is quite round. Try to use greengages when they are just ripe for then you need virtually no water when making the preserve. True greengages make a perfect conserve (see page 62).*

Metric/Imperial	Ingredients	American
450 g/1 lb	**greengages, weight when stoned, see method**	1 lb
1 to 4 tablespoons	water	1¼ to 5 tablespoons
450 g/1 lb	sugar	2 cups

Halve the fruit and carefully remove the stones. These can be cracked and the kernels added to the jam just before setting point is reached. If the fruit is too firm to halve before cooking then allow 550 g/1¼ lb fruit and remove the stones when the fruit has softened. Put the fruit into the preserving pan. If very ripe use just 1 tablespoon (1¼ tablespoons) water; increase this up to the 4 tablespoons (5 tablespoons) according to the ripeness of the fruit. Simmer gently until a soft pulp. Add the sugar and stir over a low heat until this has dissolved, then raise the heat and boil rapidly until setting point is reached. Spoon into hot jars and seal down.

Variation

- Use greengage-plums with the full amount of water instead of greengages.

KIWI FRUIT JAM

Cooking time: 20 minutes • Makes 750 g/1²/₃ lb jam

This fruit, which has become so popular in recent times, is also known as Chinese gooseberry; its botanical name is Actinidia chinensis. *It is not related in any way to the gooseberry and it grows on climbing shrubs. The fruit originated in China and is now grown extensively in New Zealand, Russia, Israel, America and many European countries. Choose*

*firm and just-ripe fruit when making jam. The Kiwifruit Marmalade on
pages 92 to 93 is another excellent way of using the green pulp in a preserve.*

Metric/Imperial	Ingredients	American
450 g/1 lb	kiwi fruit pulp, see method	1 lb
1 tablespoon	water	1¼ tablespoons
450 g/1 lb	sugar, see note	2 cups

Halve the kiwi fruits, then scoop out the pulp with a teaspoon and weigh
it. Chop the pulp finely and tip into the preserving pan. Make certain you
add any juice from the board on which it was chopped. Add the water
and stir briskly to extract the juice from the fruit. Simmer gently for
about 5 minutes only, then add the sugar. Stir over a low heat until the
sugar has dissolved then boil briskly until setting point is reached.
Spoon into hot jars and seal down.

NOTE: kiwi fruit has a strongly sharp taste when just ripe and additional
lemon juice might make the preserve too tart for some tastes. It is a good
idea to use the sugar that contains pectin for this recipe. If the fruit is
rather ripe, add 1 tablespoon (1¼ tablespoons) lemon juice with the sugar.

LOGANBERRY JAM

Cooking time: 20 to 25 minutes • Makes 750 g/1²/₃ lb jam

*This fruit makes one of the richest and most delicious jams. It is excellent
in a jelly or fruit cheese too (see pages 75 and 108). Loganberries are
members of the rose family. They can be used in any of the preserves made
with either raspberries or blackberries. The large red berries are not as
sweet as raspberries and, as they are firmer in texture, they do need
slightly longer cooking.*

Metric/Imperial	Ingredients	American
450 g/1 lb	loganberries	1 lb
450 g/1 lb	sugar	2 cups

Put the fruit into the preserving pan and stir over a low heat until the
juice flows and the fruit is tender. Add the sugar, continue stirring until
this has dissolved then raise the heat and boil rapidly until setting point is
reached. Spoon into hot jars and seal down.

Variations

Loganberry and Cherry Jam: these two fruits form a very good
partnership, especially if the jam is made with ripe dessert red or white
cherries. Black cherries are less suitable, for they spoil the bright colour
of the jam. If stoning the cherries before cooking, use 450 g/1 lb; if
stoning them after cooking, and before adding the sugar, then allow
550 g/1¼ lb. Put 450 g/1 lb loganberries into the preserving pan with
1 tablespoon (1¼ tablespoons) water, simmer for a few minutes, or until
the juice begins to flow. Add the cherries and cook until both fruits are
tender. Add 1 tablespoon (1¼ tablespoons) lemon juice with 900 g/2 lb

(4 cups) sugar. Stir over a low heat until the sugar has dissolved then raise the heat and boil until setting point is reached. Allow the jam to cool for a short time in the pan, stir to distribute any whole fruit then spoon into hot jars and seal down.

Loganberry and Redcurrant Jam: put 450 g/1 lb redcurrants and 450 g/ 1 lb loganberries into the preserving pan with 150 ml/¼ pint (⅔ cup) water. Simmer until the fruit is tender then add 900 g/2 lb (4 cups) sugar. Stir over a low heat until the sugar has dissolved then raise the temperature and boil rapidly until setting point is reached. Spoon into hot jars and seal down.

Loganberry and Raspberry Jam: put 450 g/1 lb loganberries into the preserving pan. Simmer for 5 to 10 minutes, or until the fruit is almost tender. Add 450 g/1 lb raspberries and cook for 3 to 5 minutes only. Stir in 900 g/2 lb (4 cups) sugar and continue as Loganberry Jam above.

Yield

In these variations 900 g/2 lb (4 cups) sugar makes 1.5 kg/3⅓ lb jam.

LYCHEE JAM

Cooking time: 15 minutes • Makes 750 g/1⅔ lb jam

Lychees, known botanically as Litchi chinensis, *are among the many fruits that originated in China. While fresh lychees are fairly easy to obtain, the canned variety are more plentiful, so recipes using both kinds are given. Lychees have poor setting quality so either use the amount of lemon juice in the recipes below or use just half the lemon juice with the special sugar that contains pectin.*

Metric/Imperial	Ingredients	American
450 g/1 lb	lychees, weight when peeled and stoned	1 lb
2 tablespoons	lemon juice	2½ tablespoons
450 g/1 lb	sugar	2 cups

Remove the hard shells, halve the fruit and take out the stones. Put the fruit into the preserving pan and simmer very slowly, pressing down to extract the juice, until well heated. Add the lemon juice and sugar. Stir over a low heat until the sugar has dissolved then boil rapidly until setting point is reached. Allow the jam to cool in the pan until slightly thickened, stir to distribute the fruit then spoon into hot jars and seal down.

Variations

Lychee and Redcurrant Jam: use only 350 g/12 oz (¾ lb lychees) (weight when stoned), together with 225 g/8 oz (½ lb) redcurrants. Rub the uncooked redcurrants through a nylon sieve. Simmer the lychees with the redcurrant purée, then add the sugar, stir until dissolved then follow the recipe above. This combination of fruits makes a very attractive coloured jam.

Canned Lychee Jam: if the fruit is canned in light syrup drain this and weigh out 450 g/1 lb fruit – without stones. Heat for a few minutes only, as the fruit has been softened in canning. Add 3 tablespoons (3¾ tablespoons) lemon juice but only 350 g/12 oz (1½ cups) sugar. Follow the main recipe above. If the fruit is canned in heavy syrup use only 225 g/8 oz (1 cup) sugar with the 3 tablespoons (3¾ tablespoons) lemon juice. If the fruit is canned in natural juice use the same amount of sugar as in the first recipe for 450 g/1 lb stoned fruit but 3 tablespoons (3¾ tablespoons) lemon juice.

Rambutan Jam: this fruit, while being of a different botanical family from the lychee, has much the same flavour and can be used in the jam recipes above. It is sometimes called a 'hairy lychee'.

MARROW AND GINGER JAM

Cooking time: 30 minutes • Makes 750 g/1²⁄₃ lb jam

Vegetable marrow is used quite often in preserves, both sweet and savoury. It makes an excellent ginger flavoured jam and is also good when blended with lemons or oranges. Some of the recipes for various kinds of pickle, which begin on page 138, include marrow. Use the autumn-grown vegetables – they have a much better flavour than those produced in the early summer. Larger and more mature marrows are best.

Metric/Imperial	Ingredients	American
450 g/1 lb	marrow, weight when peeled and seeds removed	1 lb
3 tablespoons	chopped crystallized or preserved ginger	3¾ tablespoons
450 g/1 lb	sugar	2 cups
2 tablespoons	lemon juice	2½ tablespoons

Cut the marrow into 1.5 cm/½ inch dice. Put into the preserving pan with the ginger and sugar and leave overnight. Stir well before cooking – this encourages the juice to flow from the marrow. Stir over a low heat until the sugar has dissolved. Add the lemon juice then boil steadily until setting point is reached. The marrow tends to remain in dice, so allow the preserve to cool slightly in the pan, stir to distribute the pieces then spoon into hot jars and seal down.

Variations

Marrow and Orange Jam: omit the ginger in the recipe above, add the finely grated rind of 2 oranges to the diced marrow and sugar together with the pulp from 2 oranges. Continue as the recipe above.

Pumpkin Jam: use diced pumpkin instead of marrow in either of the recipes above.

MELON JAM

Cooking time: 25 minutes • Makes 750 g/1²/₃ lb jam

Melons are members of a large family of plants, known botanically as
Cucurbitaceae, *which includes cucumbers, marrows, pumpkins and gourds*
of all kinds. Melons can be used to make jam, but they are rather nicer as
a conserve (see pages 62 to 63). The various kinds of melon produce
different flavoured jams, the most interesting made by mixing honeydew
and Gallia melons together. Choose fruit that is just ripe but not over-soft.
Melon contains very little pectin so it is advisable to use lemon juice when
making the jam; this also enhances the flavour of the melon. If using the
special sugar that contains pectin reduce the lemon juice by 1 tablespoon
(1¼ tablespoons).

Metric/Imperial	Ingredients	American
450 g/1 lb	melon, weight when peeled and seeds removed	1 lb
4 tablespoons	lemon juice	5 tablespoons
450 g/1 lb	sugar	2 cups

Halve the melon(s) and cut away the skin, then scoop out the seeds.
Cut the melon flesh into 1.5 cm/½ inch dice. Put into the preserving pan
with half the lemon juice and simmer gently until just soft. Mash the pulp
with a wooden spoon or potato masher to make it quite smooth. Add the
rest of the lemon juice and the sugar, then stir over a low heat until this
has dissolved. Raise the heat and boil rapidly until setting point is
reached. Spoon into hot jars and seal down.

Variations

Melon and Rum Jam: allow 1 tablespoon (1¼ tablespoons) rum for each
450 g/1 lb (2 cups) sugar. Stir this into the preserve just before it reaches
setting point.

Melon and Ginger Jam: allow 1 to 2 teaspoons ground ginger for each
450 g/1 lb melon. Stir this into the melon when it has been made into a
smooth purée.

Papaya Jam: this fruit, also known as pawpaw, can be used in exactly the
same recipes as melon. It should be ripe for jam, but when under-ripe it
makes an excellent chutney (see page 163).

Cucumber Jam: this is an unusual jam but very good to serve as a sauce
with cold meats or pâtés or as a breakfast preserve. Peel and dice the
cucumber; there is no need to remove the small seeds. Cook as melon
jam. The colour is fairly pale and rather uninteresting, so a few drops of
culinary pale green colouring could be used to tint the jam when it has
reached setting point.

MULBERRY JAM

Cooking time: 25 to 30 minutes • Makes 750 g/1²/₃ lb jam

It is believed that mulberries have been grown in Asia and parts of Europe since ancient times. They were valued both for their fruit and their leaves, on which silkworms feed. Trees were planted in Britain in the sixteenth century and by King James I in the seventeenth century in an attempt to improve the economy of the country by producing silk. It is thought that 100,000 trees were planted and some may still be flourishing in gardens today. The fruit has a wonderful richness of flavour and colour – take care when handling the fruit that your hands and tables do not become stained. Mulberries make an excellent jelly and cheese as well as a jam (see pages 80 and 107). The fruit blends well with apples, so add these if you have only a small amount of mulberries.

Metric/Imperial	Ingredients	American
450 g/1 lb	*mulberries*	1 lb
2 to 4 tablespoons	*water*	2¹/₂ to 5 tablespoons
450 g/1 lb	*sugar*	2 cups

Put the mulberries into the preserving pan. If really ripe, use the lower amount of water but if fairly firm add the larger amount. Simmer gently until soft then add the sugar. Stir over a low heat until this has dissolved then boil rapidly until setting point is reached. Spoon into hot jars and seal down.

Variation

Mulberry and Apple Jam: use the recipe above with 225 g/8 oz (¹/₂ lb) cooking apples (weight when peeled, cored and sliced). Simmer the two fruits together then add 675 g/1¹/₂ lb (3 cups) sugar and proceed as the recipe. This variation makes 1.125 kg/2¹/₂ lb jam.

PASSION FRUIT JAM

Cooking time: 15 to 20 minutes • Makes 750 g/1²/₃ lb jam

Passion fruit, or granadilla as it is often called, originated in South America and Mexico but is now grown in most hot climates. It is a favourite fruit in Australia and New Zealand. There are quite a number of types of passion fruit, all belonging to the Passiflora family. The pulp has a most delicious flavour, but because it is rather soft and liquid it is better to measure rather than weigh it.

Metric/Imperial	Ingredients	American
600 ml/1 pint	*passion fruit pulp*	2¹/₂ cups
450 g/1 lb	*sugar*	2 cups
2 tablespoons	*lemon juice*	2¹/₂ tablespoons

Halve the fruit and scoop out the pulp. Measure this and pour into the preserving pan. Heat for a few minutes only, then add the sugar and lemon juice. Stir over a low heat until the sugar has dissolved then boil rapidly until setting point is reached. Spoon into hot jars and seal down.

Variation

Guava Jam: halve ripe guavas, scoop out the pulp and sieve this to remove the seeds. Measure the pulp and use as the passion fruit in the recipe above. See also Guava Jelly on pages 78 to 79.

PEACH JAM

Cooking time: 30 minutes • Makes 750 g/1²/₃ lb jam

Peach trees belong to the rose family and they are mentioned in Chinese literature as far back as 551 BC. While peaches have a wonderful flavour when eaten raw, or even when canned, they seem to lack a definite taste when turned into jam. The addition of lemon which helps the jam set gives some flavour, as well as keeping the peaches a good colour; but a mixture of lemon and orange with the peaches is even better. The yellow-fleshed peaches give a better jam than the white-fleshed variety.

Metric/Imperial	Ingredients	American
550 g/1¹/₄ lb	peaches	1¹/₄ lb
2 tablespoons	water	2¹/₂ tablespoons
2 tablespoons	lemon juice	2¹/₂ tablespoons
450 g/1 lb	sugar	2 cups

Lower the peaches carefully into boiling water, leave for 30 seconds then remove and put into cold water. Remove the skins and halve the fruit. Take out the stones – these can be cracked and the kernels added to the jam just before setting point is reached. Cut the peaches into small dice and put into the preserving pan with the water and lemon juice. Simmer gently until the fruit is soft, then add the sugar and stir over a low heat until dissolved. Raise the heat and boil rapidly until setting point is reached. Spoon into hot jars and seal down.

Variations

Peach and Orange Jam: finely grate the rind of 2 oranges, halve the fruit and scoop out the orange pulp; avoid any pips, pith or skin. Put the peaches with the orange rind and pulp into a preserving pan. Add the lemon juice, as in the recipe above, but do not add water. Simmer until the fruit is soft then continue as the recipe above.

Mango Jam: cut away the peel and scoop out the pulp from around the mango stones. Use 450 g/1 lb pulp from ripe mangoes instead of peaches in either of the Peach Jam recipes above.

Nectarine Jam: this fruit is treated in exactly the same way as peaches. It has rather more flavour, so makes an excellent jam.

PEAR JAM

Cooking time: 30 to 35 minutes • Makes 750 g/1²/₃ lb jam

Pears are rather better when in a conserve, so you can enjoy fairly firm pieces of fruit (see page 64). If, however, you have an abundance of pears then some can also be made into jam. As pears do not have a great deal of flavour the addition of spices improves the preserve. The first recipe is based on dessert pears. If using unripe cooking pears see the Variations below.

Metric/Imperial	Ingredients	American
450 g/1 lb	**pears, weight when peeled and cored**	1 lb
3 tablespoons	**white wine or rosé wine or orange juice**	3³/₄ tablespoons
¹/₄ teaspoon or to taste	**ground cloves or cinnamon**	¹/₄ teaspoon, or to taste
450 g/1 lb	**sugar**	˙2 cups
2 tablespoons	**lemon juice**	2¹/₂ tablespoons

Cut the pears into 1.5 cm/¹/₂ inch dice. Put into the preserving pan with the liquid and spice. Simmer gently until tender. Add the sugar and lemon juice, stir over a low heat until the sugar is dissolved then boil rapidly until setting point is reached. Cool for a short time in the preserving pan, stir to distribute any pieces of fruit, then spoon into hot jars and seal down.

Variations

- If using cooking pears allow 225 ml/7¹/₂ fl oz (scant cup) liquid and cover the pan so the pears cook gently for about 30 minutes without the liquid evaporating, then proceed as the recipe above.
- Pears can be used in recipes based upon cooking apples, see pages 20 and 21, but in each case allow a little more liquid if the pears are firm and use 2 tablespoons (2¹/₂ tablespoons) lemon juice with each 450 g/ 1 lb (2 cups) sugar. In the Apple and Lemon Jam on page 22 use ripe dessert pears that can be sieved easily after cooking. Peel these first and weigh after peeling. Increase the amount of lemon juice in the recipe by 1 tablespoon (1¹/₄ tablespoons). In the Apple and Orange Jam on page 22 add 2 tablespoons (2¹/₂ tablespoons) lemon juice.

PLUM JAM

Cooking time: 20 to 30 minutes • Makes 750 g/1²/₃ lb jam

Each kind of plum gives its own individual flavour to jam. The superb Victoria plums are best made into a conserve, because this contains the large juicy pieces of fruit (see page 58). Some plums have a slightly wax-like substance around the stones – this is a feature of certain types and quite harmless. There is great variation in the pectin levels and in the ripeness of plums. If using really ripe dessert plums, add the amount of lemon juice indicated in the recipe below or use jam-making sugar that contains pectin. If the plums are firm and of the cooking variety, they will have sufficient natural pectin. The kernels from plum stones have a very good flavour and can be added just before setting point is reached.

Metric/Imperial	Ingredients	American
450 g/1 lb	plums, weight when stoned see method and Variations	1 lb
up to 4 tablespoons	water	up to 5 tablespoons
450 g/1 lb	sugar	2 cups

Halve the fruit and carefully remove the stones. These can be cracked and the kernels added to the jam just before setting point is reached. If the fruit is too firm to halve before cooking then allow 550 g/1¼ lb fruit and remove the stones when the fruit has softened. You can still crack the stones at this point and remove the kernels. Put the fruit into the preserving pan. If the plums have been halved and they are very ripe do not add any water at all, but if very firm and under-ripe use up to the 4 tablespoons (5 tablespoons). Simmer the fruit gently until a soft pulp. Add the sugar and stir over a low heat until this has dissolved then raise the heat and boil rapidly until the setting point is reached. Spoon into hot jars and seal down.

Variations

Cherry-Plum Jam: this fruit has a very interesting flavour. Use the recipe above with 550 g/1¼ lb fruit as the stones have to be removed when the fruit has softened. Use the minimum amount of water as the small fruits soften quickly during cooking. Add 1 tablespoon (1¼ tablespoons) lemon juice with the sugar.

Plum and Greengage Jam: use 450 g/1 lb of each fruit and double the amount of sugar in the Plum Jam recipe above. Keep the amount of water used to the minimum, so you retain the maximum flavour of the two fruits. If one of the fruits is much riper than the other, simmer the under-ripe fruit first for 5 to 10 minutes, then add the second kind of fruit.

Plum and Prune Jam: add 4 tablespoons (5 tablespoons) finely chopped tenderised (ready-to-eat) prunes to the fruit purée before adding the sugar. The dried fruit gives a richness to the jam. This is a recipe in which you can use three-quarters white sugar and a quarter Demerara sugar or clear honey to give a more interesting taste.

POMEGRANATE JAM

Cooking time: 25 minutes • Makes 750 g/1²/₃ lb jam

The word pomegranate means 'grain apple' and the profusion of seeds inside the outer skin are not unlike juicy grains. The fruit comes from a plant called Punica granatum, *which grows in India and throughout the whole of the Mediterranean area, especially in Spain. It was mentioned in the Bible when Moses promised the Israelites pomegranates as well as wheat and barley and vines and fig trees. Children generally love to eat the fruit and it does make an interesting jam.*

Metric/Imperial	Ingredients	American
450 g/1 lb	pomegranate seeds, weight when skin is removed	1 lb
3 tablespoons	orange juice	3³/₄ tablespoons
450 g/1 lb	sugar	2 cups
3 tablespoons	lemon juice	3³/₄ tablespoons

Cut the pomegranates into halves and scoop out all the seeds then weigh them. Discard the pith that surrounds the seeds for this has a very bitter taste. Put the seeds into a preserving pan with the orange juice and simmer slowly until softened. Stir in the sugar and lemon juice and continue stirring until the sugar has dissolved, then raise the heat and boil rapidly until setting point is reached. Spoon into hot jars and seal down.

Variation

- For a smooth-textured jam rub the seeds through a fine sieve to get a purée-like pulp. Use this in the recipe above. Allow 600 ml/1 pint (2½ cups) to the other ingredients in the recipe.

QUINCE JAM

Cooking time: 35 to 40 minutes • Makes 750 g/1²/₃ lb jam

The origin of the quince tree is doubtful; it is a member of the rose family and it is believed to have come from a region around Iran, for a wild edible fruit very similar to the cultivated quince can still be found there. It was a fruit very much esteemed by both the Greeks and Romans and was dedicated to Venus and Aphrodite as a symbol of love, fertility and happiness. Quinces make good partners to apples in all forms of cooking. There are recipes for Quince Conserves and Quince Cheese on pages 65 to 66 and 111.

Metric/Imperial	Ingredients	American
450 g/1 lb	quinces, weight when peeled and cored	1 lb
150 to 300 ml/¹/₄ to ¹/₂ pint	water	²/₃ to 1¹/₄ cups
450 g/1 lb	sugar	2 cups
1 tablespoon	lemon juice	1¹/₄ tablespoons

Peel, core and weigh the fruit then cut it into small pieces. The flesh is hard and quite difficult to cut if the fruit is not perfectly ripe – in this case it is a good idea to shred or grate it. Put the fruit into the preserving pan with the water. Use the smaller amount if the fruit is ripe. Simmer gently until soft then add the sugar and lemon juice. Stir over a low heat until the sugar has dissolved then raise the heat and boil rapidly until the setting point is reached. Spoon into hot jars and seal down.

Variations

- For a stronger flavour, the peel and cores of the quinces can be tied in muslin and simmered with the fruit. Remove before adding the sugar and lemon juice.

Quince and Apple Jam: use 450 g/1 lb quinces and 450 g/1 lb cooking apples (weight when peeled and cored), with 300 to 450 ml/½ to ¾ pint (1¼ to scant 2 cups) water, according to the ripeness of the fruit. Add 900 g/2 lb (4 cups) sugar. The lemon juice can be omitted, as the apples help to set the jam, but 2 tablespoons (2½ tablespoons) lemon juice does enhance the flavour. Follow the recipe, using the peel and cores of the fruit, as described above, if a stronger taste is desired. In this variation 900 g/2 lb sugar makes 1.5 kg/3⅓ lb jam.

Japonica Jam: one form of Japanese quince is known as japonica. The fruits vary in size, according to the particular type of plant, but they are smaller than the usual quince. It is better to cook the fruit in a little water then sieve and measure this. To each 600 ml/1 pint (2½ cups) japonica pulp allow 450 g/1 lb (2 cups) sugar and 1 tablespoon (1¼ tablespoons) lemon juice. Heat the pulp, add the sugar and lemon juice, stir over a low heat until the sugar has dissolved then boil rapidly until setting point is reached. In this variation each 450 g/1 lb (2 cups) sugar makes 750 g/1⅔ lb jam.

RASPBERRY JAM

Cooking time: 10 to 12 minutes • Makes 750 g/1⅔ lb jam

Raspberries are Rubus *species within the rose family. Wild raspberries grew well throughout Europe and Northern Asia and the plant was brought into gardens and gradually cultivated. It was grown in Britain in the mid-sixteenth century. There can be no doubt that this is one of the favourite jams for most people. It has such a good flavour that it is ideal for fillings in sponges, for adding to trifles and in many other dishes. The only drawback is the number of pips in it, so a recipe for Seedless Raspberry Jam is given too. Raspberries contain an average amount of pectin and the jam should set quite easily. In addition to the classic recipe below there is a recipe for uncooked raspberry jam on page 49.*

Metric/Imperial	Ingredients	American
450 g/1 lb	raspberries	1 lb
450 g/1 lb	sugar	2 cups

Put the fruit into the preserving pan and mash it with a wooden spoon. Heat gently to boiling point. Add the sugar and stir over a low heat until this has dissolved then allow the jam to boil rapidly until setting point is reached. Spoon into hot jars and seal down.

Variations

Seedless Raspberry Jam: simmer the fruit then rub through a nylon sieve. Measure the purée and add 450 g/1 lb (2 cups) sugar to each 600 ml/ 1 pint (2 cups) raspberry pulp. Continue as the recipe above.

Raspberry and Redcurrant Jam: simmer 450 g/1 lb redcurrants in 4 tablespoons (5 tablespoons) water until a soft purée. Add 450 g/1 lb raspberries and continue cooking until the fruit is very hot. Add 900 g/ 2 lb (4 cups) sugar, stir over a low heat until dissolved then continue as the recipe. If preferred, the fruit can be rubbed through a nylon sieve when tender and measured. Add 450 g/1 lb (2 cups) sugar to each 600 ml/1 pint (2½ cups) purée then continue as the recipe.

Raspberry and Blackcurrant Jam: use blackcurrants instead of redcurrants in the recipe above.

Raspberry and Strawberry Jam: put 450 g/1 lb raspberries and 450 g/1 lb strawberries into the preserving pan. Simmer until tender. Add 900 g/2 lb (4 cups) sugar and 2 tablespoons (2½ tablespoons) lemon juice. Stir over a low heat until the sugar is dissolved then continue as for Raspberry Jam. In this variation 900 g/2 lb (4 cups) sugar makes 1.5 kg/3⅓ lb jam.

RASPBERRY JAM – UNCOOKED

Makes 900 g/2 lb jam

This is one of the most delicious jams, but in order to make it successfully the fruit must be ripe and perfect.

Metric/Imperial	Ingredients	American
450 g/1 lb	caster sugar	2 cups
450 g/1 lb	raspberries	1 lb

Put the sugar into an ovenproof dish and place it in the oven at the lowest heat for about 15 minutes until it is just warm. Put the raspberries into a bowl, add the sugar and mash together until the sugar has melted. Spoon into hot jars and seal down. This jam should be kept in the refrigerator. It can be frozen, in which case allow about 2.5 cm/1 inch space at the top of the jars for the expansion during freezing.

RHUBARB JAM

Cooking time: 25 minutes • Makes 750 g/1⅔ lb jam

As explained on page 23, rhubarb is an edible plant stalk, not a fruit. It blends well with a number of different fruits and is a good way of extending rather rarer fruits. Never be tempted to cook the leaves of rhubarb, they are poisonous. Because rhubarb has such a high water content it is better to let it stand with the sugar to draw out the liquid – in this way you avoid having to add water. The delicate forced rhubarb could be used but the autumn crop has a better flavour. If using sugar that contains pectin omit the lemon juice.

Metric/Imperial	Ingredients	American
450 g/1 lb	rhubarb	1 lb
450g/1 lb	sugar	2 cups
1 tablespoon	lemon juice	1¼ tablespoons

Wipe the rhubarb and cut it into 1.5 cm/½ inch lengths. Allow to stand with the sugar for several hours then cook gently, stirring well, Over a low heat until the sugar has dissolved. Add the lemon juice, raise the heat and boil rapidly until setting point is reached. Spoon into hot jars and seal down.

Variations

Rhubarb Ginger Jam: the rhubarb and sugar can be mixed with 1 teaspoon ground ginger or 2 to 3 tablespoons (2½ to 3¾ tablespoons) finely diced preserved or crystallized ginger.

Rhubarb and Geranium Jam: add 4 medium-sized lemon-scented or rose-scented geranium leaves to the rhubarb. Remove these just before potting the jam. Omit any other flavouring.

Rhubarb and Red or Whitecurrant Jam: allow the rhubarb to stand as in the recipe. Meanwhile cook and sieve or liquidize 450 g/1 lb redcurrants or whitecurrants. Add these to the rhubarb with another 450 g/1 lb (2 cups) sugar. Stir over a low heat until the sugar has dissolved then raise the heat and boil rapidly until setting point is reached. Spoon into hot jars and seal down.

Rhubarb and Strawberry Jam: use 450 g/1 lb rhubarb and allow this to stand with the sugar. Put into the preserving pan, add 450 g/1 lb strawberries together with 400 g/14 oz (1¾ cups) sugar. Stir over a low heat until all the sugar has dissolved, add 2 tablespoons (2½ tablespoons) lemon juice then boil rapidly until setting point is reached. Spoon into hot jars and seal down.

Rhubarb and Tomato Jam: use ripe tomatoes instead of strawberries in the recipe above. Skin and deseed the tomatoes and chop the pulp, then use 450 g/1 lb of this with 400 g/14 oz (1¾ cups) sugar and the juice of 2 lemons.

Yield

In these variations 900 g/2 lb (4 cups) sugar makes 1.5 kg/3⅓ lb jam; 850 g/1 lb 14 oz (3¾ cups) sugar makes 1.35 kg/3¼ lb jam.

ROSE PETAL JAM

Cooking time: 25 minutes • Makes 750 g/1⅔ lb jam

Keen gardeners may not enjoy making this jam for their cherished roses must be picked when they are just perfect. Scarlet roses give the best colour and flavour. Choose a dry day to pick the flowers so they are not moist. The jam has a pleasant, delicate flavour. It is made by boiling the sugar, water and lemon juice together first, so really the rose petals are crystallized within this syrup.

Metric/Imperial	Ingredients	American
450 g/1 lb	sugar	2 cups
300 ml/½ pint	water	1¼ cups
3 tablespoons	lemon juice	3¾ tablespoons
600 ml/1 pint	rose petals	2½ cups

Put the sugar and water into the preserving pan, stir over a low heat until the sugar has dissolved then add the lemon juice and allow the mixture to boil steadily until it makes a syrup-like consistency. Meanwhile, separate the rose petals, discarding any that are not perfect, and measure. Do not bruise them. Add the rose petals to the syrup, lower the heat. Turn the petals around in the syrup as this simmers. Continue cooking slowly until all the petals are tender and coated with syrup. Cool slightly and stir to distribute the petals then spoon into hot jars and seal down.

What is the reason for pieces of fruit or peel rising in the jars, and can this be rectified once the preserve has set in the jars?
You did not wait for the preserve to stiffen slightly in the preserving pan before stirring and spooning it into the jars. The preserve should not be reheated, for you will waste quite an amount and run the risk of over-boiling. Try stirring the contents of the jar with a small knife.

STRAWBERRY JAM

Cooking time: 15 minutes • Makes 700 g/good 1½ lb jam

Strawberries belong to the rose family. For many centuries wild strawberries were found in Europe, and in the fourteenth century Charles V of France planted a large number at the Louvre in Paris. In 1714 a French naval officer found strawberry plants with large fruit growing in Chile and brought some back to France. Later many varieties were produced in England, which now boasts the finest strawberries in the world. The tiny wild strawberries have become a sought-after delicacy – the recipes for Strawberry Conserves include these (see page 66).

Metric/Imperial	Ingredients	American
450 g/1 lb	strawberries	1 lb
400 g/14 oz	sugar	1¾ cups
2 tablespoons	lemon juice	2½ tablespoons
or		or
4 tablespoons	redcurrant juice, see note	5 tablespoons

If the strawberries are very large cut them into smaller pieces; this hastens the heating and retains more of the colour and flavour. Simmer gently until hot and add the sugar and lemon or redcurrant juice. Stir over a low heat until the sugar has dissolved then raise the heat and boil rapidly until setting point is reached. Spoon into hot jars and seal down.

NOTE: to obtain the redcurrant juice rub the fruit through a fine nylon sieve.

SUMMER FRUIT JAM

Cooking time: 25 minutes • Makes 1.5 kg/3⅓ lb jam

This is an ideal jam when only small amounts of the various fruits are available. Adjust the amount of water to the ripeness of the blackcurrants.

Metric/Imperial	Ingredients	American
225 g/8 oz	blackcurrants	½ lb
1 to 3 tablespoons	water	1¼ to 3¾ tablespoons
225 g/8 oz	redcurrants	½ lb
225 g/8 oz	small strawberries	½ lb
225 g/8 oz	raspberries	½ lb
900 g/2 lb	sugar	4 cups

Put the blackcurrants and water into the preserving pan, cook very slowly, pressing the fruit to extract the juice, and simmer until the skins are almost soft. Add the redcurrants and cook for a few minutes then put in the strawberries and finally the raspberries. Stir over a low heat until dissolved then boil rapidly until setting point is reached. Cool slightly in the pan, stir to distribute the fruit then spoon into hot jars and seal down.

Variation

• To make the soft fruits go further add 450 g/1 lb cooking apples (weight when peeled and cored). Chop the apples finely and cook, with the blackcurrants. Increase the amount of sugar to 1.35 kg/3 lb. This will produce 2.25 kg/5 lb jam.

THREE FRUIT JAM

Cooking time: 20 to 25 minutes • Makes 2.25 kg/5 lb jam

When mixing fruits together in a jam, cook the one that is firmest for a few minutes before adding the others – in this way all the fruits remain lightly cooked.

Metric/Imperial	Ingredients	American
450 g/1 lb	loganberries	1 lb
450 g/1 lb	raspberries	1 lb
450 g/1 lb	very small strawberries	1 lb
1.35 kg/3 lb	sugar	6 cups
2 tablespoons	lemon juice	2½ tablespoons

Put the loganberries into the preserving pan and simmer over a very low heat until the juice starts to flow and the fruit begins to soften. Add the raspberries and strawberries and continue cooking for a short time. Add the sugar and lemon juice and stir over a low heat until the sugar has dissolved, then raise the heat and boil rapidly until setting point is reached. Spoon into hot jars and seal down.

JAMS MADE WITH DRIED FRUIT

Dried fruits give an entirely different taste to jam. In the case of dried apricots and peaches, in particular, the jams have a very rich flavour.
In the past dried fruit had to be soaked for 48 or even 72 hours to soften it adequately before simmering. Today the modern tenderised fruits need only 3 to 4 hours' soaking before being cooked in jam. Check carefully which type you have bought for both are still sold. Another name for the tenderised fruit is 'ready-to-eat' and you can check on this point quite easily. If you want to make jam with a fairly smooth texture, as opposed to having larger pieces of fruit, then cut the fruit into small pieces *after* soaking. If the fruit is cut before, it absorbs too much water.

DRIED APRICOT JAM

Cooking time: 1 to 1¼ hours • Makes 2.25 kg/5 lb jam

Dried apricots have an excellent flavour, and they make a very good jam. The modern tenderised type, often known as ready-to-eat fruit, does not need soaking for a long period (see above). In fact, it can be cooked without soaking if more convenient, but that does slightly prolong the cooking time.

Metric/Imperial	Ingredients	American
450 g/1 lb	dried apricots	1 lb
1.7 litres/3 pints or 1.4 litres/2½ pints	water	7½ cups or 6¼ cups
1.35 kg/3 lb	sugar	6 cups
4 tablespoons	lemon juice	5 tablespoons

If using the older type of apricots put them into a bowl with the larger amount of water and leave to soak for 48 to 72 hours, then tip the fruit and water into the preserving pan. For tenderised fruit use the smaller amount of water and either soak for 3 to 4 hours or use at once. The cooking time is less with this tenderised fruit so you do not need quite as much water. Cover the pan tightly and simmer gently until the fruit is soft. Add the sugar and lemon juice; stir over a low heat until the sugar has dissolved then boil rapidly, without a lid on the pan, until setting point is reached. There will be fairly large firm pieces of apricot in the jam, so allow it to cool until slightly thickened. Stir to distribute the fruit then spoon into hot jars and seal down.

Variations

Dried Apricot and Almond Jam: add about 150 g/5 oz (1¼ cups) blanched and slivered almonds to the jam just before it reaches setting point. Stir well to distribute.

Dried Apricot and Lemon Jam: add 4 teaspoons finely grated lemon rind to the water in which the apricots are soaked and cooked. When adding the sugar include an extra 2 tablespoons (2½ tablespoons) lemon juice.

Dried Fig Jam: use dried figs instead of apricots and follow the recipe on page 53.

Dried Fig and Orange Jam: figs taste very pleasant if a delicate flavour of orange is introduced. Add 2 tablespoons (2½ tablespoons) finely grated orange rind to the water in which the figs are soaked and cooked. Instead of using all water, use half water and half fresh orange juice for soaking and cooking the fruit.

Dried Peach Jam: use dried peaches instead of apricots. Soak these as recommended for dried apricots. These soften more rapidly than apricots so use only 1.4 litres/2½ pints (6¼ cups) water with old-style dried fruit and 1.2 litres/2 pints (5 cups) water with the tenderised type. The peaches are large so cut into halves or quarters after soaking.

What should one do if the cold preserve has not set adequately?

- If you find that you have produced an appreciable amount *more* preserve than you should – each 450g/1 lb (2 cups) of sugar used should yield 750g/1⅔ lb of preserve – then tip it back into a preserving pan and boil briskly. After a few minutes test for setting point (see pages 8 and 9) and re-pot into heated jars and seal down.
- If you find you have made the *correct* amount of preserve but it has not set well, then re-boiling is not the answer. It means that the fruit was lacking in pectin (the setting quality). There is every chance that the rather liquid preserve will keep well.

  It could be used for sauces or you could make it set by using a little gelatin. Do this only when you require each pot of runny preserve as gelatin does not keep well.

  To 450g/1 lb of preserve allow 2 level teaspoons of gelatin. Soften this in 2 tablespoons (2½ tablespoons) of cold water. Heat the preserve, add the softened gelatin and stir over the heat until dissolved. Allow the preserve to cool and use within a

---

PRUNE JAM

Cooking time: 35 minutes to 1 hour • For yield see end of recipe

Dried prunes make a wonderfully rich-flavoured jam. Choose plump and very good quality fruit. The modern tenderised prunes are ideal.
If possible buy these stoned, but if the stones are included they are removed in sieving but must be taken out before liquidising the mixture.
The preserve has a richer flavour if the prunes are soaked and then cooked in very well-strained weak tea. China tea is perfect for this purpose.

Metric/Imperial	Ingredients	American
450 g/1 lb	prunes	1 lb
900 ml/1½ pints or 600 ml/1 pint	water or tea	3¾ cups or 2½ cups
	sugar, see method	
	lemon juice, see method	

Soak the prunes in the water or tea overnight. If using the tenderised type use the smaller amount of water and soak for only 2 to 3 hours. Put into the preserving pan, cover tightly and simmer until tender. Either rub the fruit through a nylon sieve or remove the stones and liquidize. Measure the pulp and allow 450 g/1 lb (2 cups) sugar and 2 tablespoons (2½ tablespoons) lemon juice to each 600 ml/1 pint (2½ cups). Return the pulp to the pan, heat well then add the sugar and lemon juice. Stir over a low heat until the sugar has dissolved then boil rapidly until setting point is reached. Spoon into hot jars and seal down.

Yield

Each 450 g/1 lb (2 cups) of sugar makes 750 g/1²⁄₃ lb jam.

Variations

Prune Conserve: in this recipe the whole prunes are really poached in the syrup. Choose 450 g/1 lb very good quality small prunes. If possible remove the stones after soaking or better still buy prunes without stones. Soak the 450 g/1 lb prunes in 600 ml/1 pint (2½ cups) liquid for the time given in the recipe above. Strain the liquid and return to the pan with 450 g/1 lb (2 cups) sugar and 4 tablespoons (5 tablespoons) lemon juice. Stir over a low heat until the sugar has dissolved then add the prunes and simmer gently for about 25 minutes or until the prunes are just tender. Spoon into hot jars and seal down.

   As this variation is more like a preserve, there will be about 900 g/2 lb conserve. When the prunes are nearly tender 1 to 2 tablespoons brandy can be added to the mixture.

Prune and Walnut Jam: add 1 tablespoon (1¼ tablespoons) finely grated lemon rind and the same amount of grated orange rind to the liquid in which the prunes are soaked. In this case water is better than tea. Add 175 g/6 oz (1½ cups) coarsely chopped walnuts to the jam just before it reaches setting point.

COMMERCIAL PECTIN (CERTO) JAMS

STRAWBERRY JAM WITH CERTO

Cooking time: 15 minutes • Makes 2.25 kg/5 lb jam

The following recipe shows how the amount of fruit can be reduced when commercial apple pectin (Certo) is used. This also helps to ensure that the jam sets perfectly. Examples of a conserve, a jelly and a marmalade using this pectin are on pages 60, 81 and 94. The bottles contain 250 ml/9 fl oz (1⅛ cups) of liquid. It is important to follow the special recipes for the product.

Metric/Imperial	Ingredients	American
1 kg/2¼ lb	strawberries	2¼ lb
1.35 kg/3 lb	sugar	6 cups
3 tablespoons	lemon juice	3¾ tablespoons
125 ml/4½ fl oz	Certo	just over ½ cup

Prepare the fruit, put into the preserving pan and crush slightly. Add the sugar and lemon juice, stir over a low heat until the sugar has dissolved. Raise the heat and bring to the boil. Boil rapidly for 2 minutes. For this recipe it is advised that the jam is stirred occasionally. Take from the heat and add the Certo; remove any scum if this has formed. A knob of butter can help to prevent this, as can using preserving sugar. Cool the jam slightly then spoon into hot jars and seal down.

RASPBERRY JAM WITH CERTO

Cooking time: 10 minutes • Makes 1.8 kg/4 lb jam

Raspberries are an expensive fruit to buy and this jam has a very good flavour even when using less fruit.

Metric/Imperial	Ingredients	American
900 g/2 lb	raspberries	2 lb
1.35 kg/3 lb	sugar	6 cups
125 ml/4½ fl oz	Certo	just over ½ cup

Put the fruit into the preserving pan, crush the berries then add the sugar. Stir over a low heat until the sugar has dissolved then bring to a rolling boil and boil rapidly for 2 minutes. Remove the pan from the heat and add the Certo. Stir briskly then spoon into hot jars and seal down.

CONSERVES OF ALL KINDS

The term 'conserve' is given to preserves that are somewhat similar to jam but retain whole large pieces of fruit, even when cooked. This makes them ideal to use as a filling for flan cases or as a topping for cold desserts, as well as being an alternative to jam. As conserves are considered more luxurious than jam, they offer an ideal opportunity to incorporate extra flavouring, such as alcohol, in some of the recipes and to use rather more exotic fruits.

The most interesting conserves are given on the pages following but most jam recipes can be converted into conserves if the methods of preparation and cooking, as given below, are followed. Choose firm soft fruit, and in the case of strawberries it is better to have small or medium rather than large berries.

As hard skins do not soften when sugar is added, you cannot make conserves with fruit like damsons or gooseberries, which have tough skins. These must be made into jam where the fruit is first simmered until tender before the sugar is added.

To keep the fruit whole, or in large slices or portions, allow it to stand for a time with the sugar and only little, if any, liquid. The sugar helps to keep the uncooked fruit firmer in texture and at the same time it extracts fruit juice before heating, so minimising the cooking time. Use a large bowl or the preserving pan for this purpose.

The process after that is to heat the preserve slowly, stirring all the time, until the sugar has dissolved. Do this gently for care must be taken not to break up the fruit. When the sugar has dissolved allow the preserve to boil steadily, *not* rapidly as for jam. Do *not* stir during this period. After that test for setting point as detailed on page 8. If using the saucer or flake on a wooden spoon methods, use the syrup part and not the whole fruit to ascertain setting point.

The conserve will need to cool in the pan for quite some time because of the large pieces of fruit; it can then be stirred and put into hot jars.

It is advisable to read through the points under Perfect Jams and Conserves on page 17 before beginning to prepare the conserve.

APRICOT CONSERVE

Cooking time: 30 to 35 minutes • Makes 750 g/1²/₃ lb conserve

Fresh apricots make a wonderful conserve. Choose fruit that is just ripe, for the halved fruit should remain fairly firm when cooked.

Metric/Imperial	Ingredients	American
450 g/1 lb	**ripe apricots, weight when stoned**	1 lb
450 g/1 lb	sugar	2 cups
2 tablespoons	**lemon juice**	2¹/₂ tablespoons

Halve the fruit, remove the stones then add the sugar and lemon juice. Allow to stand for only 15 minutes, for cut apricots tend to darken in colour. Stir once or twice, so the fruit becomes well coated with sugar and lemon juice. Heat gently, stirring all the time, until the sugar dissolves then raise the heat a little and cook steadily until the setting point is reached. Allow to cool slightly, stir to distribute the whole pieces of fruit then spoon into hot jars and seal down.

Variations

- The stones can be cracked and the kernels added to the conserve as described under Apricot Jam (see pages 24 to 25).

Luxury Apricot Conserve: add 2 tablespoons (2¹/₂ tablespoons) apricot brandy or Amaretto (almond liqueur) to the fruit, sugar and lemon juice.

Apricot and Cherry Conserve: use 450 g/1 lb apricots (weight when stoned) and 450 g/1 lb ripe dessert cherries (weight when stoned) with 900 g/2 lb (4 cups) sugar and 4 tablespoons (5 tablespoons) lemon juice. Halve or quarter the apricots and follow the method for Apricot Conserve. You could add 2 to 3 tablespoons apricot or cherry brandy to the fruit and sugar before cooking.

Apricot and Pineapple Conserve: use 450 g/1 lb apricots (weight when stoned) and 450 g/1 lb pineapple (weight when skinned and the hard centre core removed). Halve the apricots or quarter large ones; cut the pineapple into neat dice. Add 900 g/2 lb (4 cups) sugar and 4 tablespoons (5 tablespoons) lemon juice. Follow the method for Apricot Conserve. In this variation 900 g/2 lb (4 cups) sugar makes 1.5 kg/3¹/₃ lb conserve.

Peach Conserve: skin the peaches, then halve or quarter them; add the lemon juice with the sugar to prevent the fruit discolouring then follow the recipe for Apricot Conserve.

Victoria Plum Conserve: these particular plums make a wonderful conserve. Halve or quarter the fruit. The cut plums do discolour easily so add the lemon juice with the sugar and follow the recipe for Apricot Conserve.

APRICOT AND MARASCHINO CHERRY CONSERVE

Cooking time: 30 to 35 minutes • Makes 850 g/1 lb 14 oz conserve

Maraschino cherries are good partners to apricots. They are also used in the jam on page 25.

Metric/Imperial	Ingredients	American
450 g/1 lb	ripe apricots, weight when stoned	1 lb
2 tablespoons	Maraschino syrup from the jar of cherries	2½ tablespoons
2 tablespoons	lemon juice	2½ tablespoons
500 g/1 lb 2 oz	sugar	2¼ cups
100 g/4 oz	Maraschino cherries	1 cup

Halve the apricots, remove the stones, add the syrup, lemon juice and sugar. Stir well so the apricots absorb the syrup and lemon juice, as well as the sugar. Allow to stand for 15 to 30 minutes then heat gently, stirring all the time, until the sugar dissolves. Raise the heat and cook steadily until the conserve is almost at setting point. Add the cherries, stir to blend these with the apricots, then continue cooking for a very short time until setting point is reached. Allow to cool slightly, stir to distribute the fruits, then spoon into hot jars and seal down.

BLACK CHERRY CONSERVE

Cooking time: 30 to 35 minutes • Makes 750 g/1²/₃ lb conserve

This is often known as Swiss Cherry Jam for it is one of the most famous preserves in that country. Choose black cherries that are really ripe and stone them before cooking as described on page 32.

Metric/Imperial	Ingredients	American
550 g/1¼ lb	black cherries, weight when stoned	1¼ lb
450 g/1 lb	sugar	2 cups
2 tablespoons	lemon juice	2½ tablespoons

Stone and weigh the cherries, blend with the sugar and any juice that may have flowed from the fruit during stoning. Leave for several hours then stir over a low heat until the sugar has dissolved. Add the lemon juice and boil steadily until setting point is just reached. This particular preserve is never very stiff. Allow to cool until the syrup has stiffened slightly, stir to distribute the cherries then spoon into hot jars and seal down.

Variations

- The cherry stones can be tied in muslin and added to the conserve as in Cherry Jam (see page 32).
- Black cherries have so much natural flavour that a liqueur is not essential but 1 to 2 tablespoons cherry brandy could be added to the cherries while they are standing.

BLACK CHERRY CONSERVE WITH CERTO

Cooking time: 15 minutes • Makes 2.25 kg/5 lb conserve

Metric/Imperial	Ingredients	American
1.125 kg/2½ lb	black cherries, weight when stoned	2½ lb
1.35 kg/3 lb	sugar	6 cups
3 tablespoons	lemon juice	3¾ tablespoons
250 ml/9 fl oz	Certo	1⅛ cups

Put the fruit, with any juice that may have flowed during stoning, into the pan with the sugar. Stir well to blend. Stand for 1 hour to allow the juice to flow from the cherries. Stir over a low heat until the sugar has dissolved. Add the lemon juice then raise the heat. Boil rapidly for 3 minutes then remove from the heat. Add the Certo and stir well. Allow the conserve to cool in the pan until it is beginning to stiffen then stir to distribute the cherries. Spoon into hot jars and seal down.

CARROT AND ALMOND CONSERVE

Cooking time: 30 minutes • Makes 750 g/1⅔ lb conserve

I was given this recipe by a friend who had tasted it in New Zealand. While carrot conserve may sound a little like the preserves made in wartime when fruit was not always available, this is a luxury conserve.

Metric/Imperial	Ingredients	American
450 g/1 lb	young carrots, weight when peeled	1 lb
225 ml/7½ fl oz	water	scant 1 cup
2 teaspoons	grated lemon rind	2 teaspoons
450 g/1 lb	sugar	2 cups
4 tablespoons	lemon juice	5 tablespoons
2 tablespoons	sweet sherry or brandy	2½ tablespoons
75 g/3 oz	blanched and shredded almonds	¾ cup

Peel then weigh the carrots and cut them into wafer-thin slices. Put into the pan with the water and lemon rind. Cook steadily until just tender. Add the sugar, stir over a low heat until this has dissolved then add the lemon juice and sherry or brandy. Cook steadily until setting point is almost reached, add the almonds, combine thoroughly then continue cooking to setting point. Allow to cool for a short time in the pan, stir to distribute the whole pieces of carrot then spoon into hot jars and seal down.

Variation

Carrot and Almond Jam: cook the carrots with the water and lemon rind until tender. Sieve, mash or liquidize to give a smooth purée and return to the pan. Add the sugar, lemon juice and sherry or brandy. Stir over a low heat until the sugar has dissolved then raise the heat and boil rapidly until setting point is almost reached. Add the almonds to the jam and then continue boiling to setting point. (When making jam it is a good idea to chop the almonds fairly finely.) Spoon into hot jars and seal down.

FIG CONSERVE

Cooking time: 30 to 35 minutes • Makes 750 g/1²/₃ lb conserve

Choose absolutely ripe figs. Small fruits are better than large ones for these can be made into a conserve without cutting.

Metric/Imperial	Ingredients	American
450 g/1 lb	**green or purple figs**	1 lb
450 g/1 lb	sugar	2 cups
2 tablespoons	**lemon juice**	2¹/₂ tablespoons

For a conserve it is important to trim the ends of the figs neatly. If the fruit is large, halve or quarter it lengthways. Blend the figs with the sugar and allow to stand for 1 to 2 hours. Stir over a low heat until the sugar has dissolved then add the lemon juice and boil steadily until setting point is reached. Allow to cool slightly, stir to distribute the fruit then spoon into hot jars and seal down.

Variation

Fig and Honey Conserve: use 350 g/12 oz (1¹/₂ cups) sugar and 100 g/4 oz ¹/₃ cup) clear honey. Add the honey to the fruit with the sugar and allow to stand for 1 to 2 hours. Continue as above.

GRAPE CONSERVE

Cooking time: 20 to 25 minutes • Makes 750 g/1²/₃ lb jam

Grapes are acknowledged to be one of the oldest cultivated fruits. Vitis vinifera is the Latin name for grapes, of which there are a great many varieties. Choose medium-sized juicy fruit, preferably free from pips, or split the fruit and remove the pips as in the method below. If the skins are tough it is better to make jam (see Variation) or Grape Cheese or Jelly (see pages 78 and 108).

Metric/Imperial	Ingredients	American
450 g/1 lb	grapes	1 lb
450 g/1 lb	sugar	2 cups
2 tablespoons	**lemon juice, if required**	2¹/₂ tablespoons

If necessary, carefully slit the grapes, insert the tip of a small sharp knife and remove the pips. Add the sugar to the fruit and allow to stand for 1 to 2 hours until the juice flows. Stir over a low heat until the sugar has dissolved. If the grapes are green and sharp in flavour omit the lemon juice, but if very ripe then you will need the lemon juice. This is particularly important if using sweet black grapes. Raise the heat a little and boil steadily until setting point is reached. Allow to cool slightly then stir to distribute the fruit, spoon into hot jars and seal down.

Variation

Grape Jam: use the proportions given in the conserve. All sizes of grapes are suitable for making jam. Simmer the fruit with 2 tablespoons (2½ tablespoons) water or white or red wine, until tender. Add the sugar and lemon juice, if required. Stir over a low heat until the sugar has dissolved then raise the heat and boil rapidly until setting point is reached. Spoon into hot jars and seal down.

GREENGAGE CONSERVE

Cooking time: 25 minutes • Makes 750 g/1⅔ lb conserve

It is essential to use real greengages (see page 38) for a conserve as the skins of greengage-plums are fairly tough and it would be quite difficult to tenderise them by the following method of cooking. Make sure the fruit is sufficiently ripe but firm enough to extract the stones without damaging the pulp. As one needs really ripe fruit for a conserve it is wise to add a little lemon juice, or use sugar that contains pectin.

Metric/Imperial	Ingredients	American
450 g/1 lb	**greengages, weight when stoned**	1 lb
450 g/1 lb	**sugar**	2 cups
1 tablespoon	**lemon juice, optional**	1¼ tablespoons

Carefully slit the greengages and take out the stones. Try to keep the fruit whole if possible. The stones can be cracked if desired and the kernels added to the conserve just before setting point is reached. Mix the greengages and sugar and leave to soak for 2 to 3 hours. Simmer gently until the sugar has dissolved, stirring all the time, then add the lemon juice (if using) and cook steadily until setting point is reached. Cool slightly, stir to distribute the fruit then spoon into hot jars and seal down.

MELON CONSERVE

Cooking time: 25 to 30 minutes • Makes 750 g/1⅔ lb conserve

The flavour of melon is not a strong one, so other ingredients can be added, as in the suggestions which follow. More details about melon are given on page 42. Melon has little natural setting quality so a generous amount of lemon juice must be used. If you buy the sugar with added pectin, reduce the lemon juice by half. Some lemon juice is added early to flavour the melon and prevent some other fruits, such as apples, apricots, peaches and nectarines, darkening the colour.

Metric/Imperial	Ingredients	American
450 g/1 lb	melon, weight when peeled and seeds removed	1 lb
4 tablespoons	lemon juice	5 tablespoons
2 tablespoons	kirsch	2½ tablespoons
450 g/1 lb	sugar	2 cups

Halve the melon(s) and cut away the skin then remove the seeds.
Cut the flesh into 2 to 2.5 cm/³/₄ to 1 inch dice or into balls with a
vegetable scoop. Add half the lemon juice with all the kirsch and sugar
and allow to stand for about 2 hours. Stir over a low heat until the sugar
has dissolved then add the rest of the lemon juice and raise the heat a
little. Cook steadily until setting point is reached. Allow to cool slightly,
stir to distribute the melon then spoon into hot jars and seal down.

Variations

Melon and Ginger Conserve: omit the kirsch and add to the melon 2
tablespoons (2½ tablespoons) diced preserved ginger plus 1 tablespoon
(1¼ tablespoons) syrup from the jar of ginger, half the lemon juice and all
the sugar. Allow to stand as above and continue as the recipe. Add the
rest of the lemon juice when the sugar has dissolved.

Melon and Port Wine Conserve: follow the recipe but use port wine
instead of kirsch.

Melon and Mango Conserve: these two fruits blend well together.
Use 450 g/1 lb melon and prepare this as described above. Add 450 g/1 lb
neatly diced ripe mango pulp with 2 tablespoons (2½ tablespoons) lemon
juice and 900 g/2 lb (4 cups) sugar. Allow to stand for 30 minutes.
Stir over a low heat until the sugar has dissolved then add a further 2
tablespoons (2½ tablespoons) lemon juice and continue as the recipe.

Melon and Passion Fruit Conserve: use 450 g/1 lb melon and prepare this
as in the recipe. Add 600 ml/1 pint (2½ cups) passion fruit pulp, 2
tablespoons (2½ tablespoons) lemon juice and 900 g/2 lb (4 cups) sugar.
Allow to stand for 2 hours, then continue as the Melon Conserve, adding
another 2 tablespoons (2½ tablespoons) lemon juice when the sugar has
dissolved.

Melon and Peach Conserve: follow the recipe for Melon and Mango
Conserve, using skinned and diced peaches instead of mangoes.

Melon and Pineapple Conserve: use 450 g/1 lb melon and prepare this as
in the recipe. Add 450 g/1 lb neatly diced fresh pineapple and 900 g/2 lb
(4 cups) sugar. Allow to stand for 2 hours, then stir over a low heat until
the sugar has dissolved. Add 3 tablespoons (3³/₄ tablespoons) lemon juice
and continue as the Melon Conserve.

Yield

Variations using 900 g/2 lb (4 cups) sugar make 1.5 kg/3⅓ lb conserve.

PEAR CONSERVE

Cooking time: 35 to 40 minutes • Makes 750 g/1²/₃ lb conserve

The choice of pear is very important for a conserve. A dessert pear should be used and it must be almost, but not 100%, ripe so it does not become too soft when cooked. A Comice pear has the perfect flavour for a conserve; if unavailable choose a Conference pear. The best way of making the conserve is to poach the fruit in a lemon-and-wine-flavoured syrup.

Metric/Imperial	Ingredients	American
2 tablespoons	**lemon juice**	2¹/₂ tablespoons
3 tablespoons	**white wine**	3³/₄ tablespoons
450 g/1 lb	**sugar**	2 cups
450 g/1 lb	**pears, weight when peeled and cored**	1 lb

Put the lemon juice, wine and sugar into the preserving pan. Stir over a low heat until the sugar has dissolved. Prepare the pears and cut into neat dice about 2 to 2.5 cm/³/₄ to 1 inch in size. Put into the hot syrup and cook steadily until setting point is reached. Cool and stir to distribute the fruit then spoon into hot jars and seal down.

Variations

- You could add 2 tablespoons (2¹/₂ tablespoons) finely chopped preserved ginger to the conserve just before setting point is reached.
- Use orange juice and 2 to 3 teaspoons finely grated orange rind instead of white wine.

PLUM AND CITRUS CONSERVE

Cooking time: 35 minutes • Makes 1.5 kg/3¹/₃ lb conserve

Although Victoria plums are excellent in this conserve, the additional flavours of orange and lemon make the recipe suitable for any well-flavoured ripe dessert plums. Make sure the orange and lemon pulp are free from skin and pips.

Metric/Imperial	Ingredients	American
675 g/1¹/₂ lb	**plums, weight when stoned**	1¹/₂ lb
2 to 3	**large oranges**	2 to 3
1 to 2	**lemons**	1 to 2
900 g/2 lb	**sugar**	4 cups
2 tablespoons	**orange juice**	2¹/₂ tablespoons
1 tablespoon	**lemon juice**	1¹/₄ tablespoons
150 g/5 oz	**seedless raisins**	1 cup

Halve the plums, remove the stones and crack these to obtain the kernels. If you do not want to do this, see under Variations below. Grate the peel of the oranges and lemons to give 2 teaspoons of each. Halve the fruit and carefully scoop out the pulp. You need sufficient to weigh 175 g/6 oz (a generous cup) when mixed together. Blend the halved plums with the grated fruit rinds, the citrus pulp and the sugar. Leave to soak for 2 to 3 hours. Stir over a low heat until the sugar has dissolved. Add the orange and lemon juice and the raisins and cook steadily until nearly at setting point. Add the kernels from the plums then continue cooking until setting point is reached. Cool slightly, stir to distribute the ingredients then spoon into hot jars and seal down.

Variations

- Add 100 g/4 oz (scant cup) whole or flaked blanched almonds or chopped pecan nuts or walnuts instead of the plum kernels.

Apricot and Citrus Conserve: use apricots instead of plums.

QUINCE CONSERVE (1)

Cooking time: 1 hour • Makes approximately 1.5 kg/3⅓ lb conserve

This method of making a conserve is ideal when the quinces are firm. It may sound a little more bother than the Variation (2) below but it does produce a delicious conserve, for the sliced quinces are poached in the lemon-flavoured liquid.

Metric/Imperial	Ingredients	American
4	*lemons*	4
1.35 kg/3 lb	*quinces, weight before being peeled and cored*	*3 lb*
900 ml/1½ pints	*water*	*3¾ cups*
900 g/2 lb	*sugar*	*4 cups*

Before preparing the quinces have ready a bowl of cold water. Halve 2 of the lemons, squeeze out the juice and add this to the water together with the lemon skins. This will help to keep the quinces a good colour. Wash the quinces, remove the peel, halve the fruit and take out the cores. Cut the quince pulp into neat slices about 6 mm/¼ inch thick. You should have 900 g/2 lb of fruit. Put the slices into the lemon-flavoured water and cover with a plate so the fruit is kept under the liquid. Put the 900 ml/1½ pints (3¾ cups) water into a saucepan with the quince peel and cores. Bring to the boil, cover the pan and simmer for 30 minutes, then strain the liquid. Measure this: it should be reduced to 450 ml/¾ pint (scant 2 cups). Halve the remaining lemons, squeeze out the juice and add to the liquid. Bring this just to simmering. Drain the quinces well, place in the liquid in the pan and simmer gently until just tender; do not over-cook for the slices should remain a good shape. Add the sugar, stir over a low heat until this has dissolved then boil steadily until the syrup is thick. It does not reach setting point in quite the same way as most preserves. Cook until fairly thick then spoon into hot jars and seal down.

- To give a less pronounced lemon taste omit the lemon juice in the liquid in which the quinces are cooked but not in the liquid in which they stand.

Quince Conserve (2): follow the recipe for Pear Conserve (see page 64) but use ripe quinces instead of pears. Apple juice could be substituted for the white wine, for this blends well with quinces.

Quince and Lime Conserve: use lemons in the water in which the quince slices stand but substitute the juice of 2 limes in the cooking liquid.

STRAWBERRY CONSERVE

Cooking time: 10 to 12 minutes • Makes 750 g/1²/₃ lb conserve

The method of making a syrup before cooking the fruit is ideal for strawberries and other soft berry fruit for it helps to prevent the fruit breaking up too much. Choose small to medium-sized strawberries, which should be absolutely ripe but firm.

Metric/Imperial	Ingredients	American
450 g/1 lb	sugar	2 cups
2 tablespoons	lemon juice	2¹/₂ tablespoons
or		or
4 tablespoons	redcurrant juice, see note	5 tablespoons
450 g/1 lb	strawberries	1 lb

Put the sugar and lemon juice or redcurrant juice into the pan, then stir over a very low heat until the sugar has completely dissolved. Remove from the heat. Add the strawberries to the hot syrup, stir around gently so they are all covered and allow to stand for 15 to 30 minutes. Return the pan to the heat and cook steadily for 5 to 7 minutes or until setting point is reached. Allow to cool for a time, stir to distribute the fruit then spoon into hot jars and seal down.

NOTE: to obtain the redcurrant juice, press fresh redcurrants through a nylon sieve then strain to make sure the juice is clear.

- The above method is suitable for most berry fruits. Raspberries are really better made into a jam as the ripe fruit breaks easily.

Boysenberry Conserve: as boysenberries are firmer than strawberries, put them into the hot syrup and heat for 1 to 2 minutes, or until just softened on the outside. Remove the pan from the heat and allow to stand as in the recipe for Strawberry Conserve. Continue as this recipe.

Loganberry Conserve: follow the method for boysenberries.

Tayberry Conserve: tayberries are softer than boysenberries. If ripe, treat like strawberries in the recipe. If rather firm, treat like boysenberries.

Wild Strawberry Conserve: these delicious tiny berries make a wonderful conserve. Follow the recipe for Strawberry Conserve but take care not to over-cook the fruit.

STRAWBERRY AND RHUBARB CONSERVE

Cooking time: 15 to 20 minutes • Makes 1.5 kg/3⅓ lb conserve

It is advisable to use young and fairly narrow stalks of rhubarb for this particular conserve, so the size and flavour do not overwhelm that of the strawberries. Summer rhubarb is ideal. Choose small to medium-sized strawberries. The method of preparing redcurrant juice is given in the note on page 66.

Metric/Imperial	Ingredients	American
450 g/1 lb	rhubarb	1 lb
550 g/1¼ lb	strawberries	1¼ lb
3 tablespoons	lemon juice	3¾ tablespoons
or		or
6 tablespoons	redcurrant juice	7½ tablespoons
900 g/2 lb	sugar	4 cups

Wipe the rhubarb and cut into dice – make these as near to the size of the strawberries as possible. Mix the rhubarb and whole strawberries with the lemon juice or redcurrant juice and sugar. Allow to stand for 1 to 2 hours. Heat very slowly, stirring all the time, until the sugar has dissolved, then allow the conserve to cook steadily until setting point is reached. Cool slightly, stir to give an even distribution of rhubarb and strawberries then spoon into hot jars and seal down.

Variations

Rhubarb Conserve: use 450 g/1 lb autumn rhubarb if possible, for this has more flavour. Dice and allow to stand with 1 tablespoon (1¼ tablespoons) lemon juice or 2 tablespoons (2½ tablespoons) redcurrant juice and 450 g/1 lb (2 cups) sugar for 1 to 2 hours, or even longer, so plenty of juice can flow. Continue as the recipe above.

Rhubarb and Ginger Conserve: add 3 to 4 tablespoons (3¾ to 5 tablespoons) finely diced preserved or crystallized ginger or 1 to 2 teaspoons ground ginger to the rhubarb as it stands with the sugar. This makes certain it becomes well impregnated with the flavour. Continue as Rhubarb Conserve.

Yield

In these variations 450 g/1 lb (2 cups) sugar makes 750 g/1⅔ lb conserve.

JELLIES OF ALL KINDS

Fruit jellies are some of the most useful preserves. Most people consider that roast game birds or venison served without redcurrant, crab apple or rowan jelly would lack a very important accompaniment. Often a little jelly can be added to a gravy or savoury sauce to balance the flavour and to give it a pleasant gloss. Fruit flans, tarts and many gateaux need a glaze, generally made from a jelly, to enhance the look of the fruit or cake. Many fruit jellies can be given extra flavour by adding chopped herbs to the preserve, see pages 85 to 86; these are ideal to serve with meat and poultry. The golden rules of making jelly are given on page 69.

LOWER SUGAR JELLIES

The amount of sugar required for jellies is calculated on the amount of fruit juice after straining the purée. In most cases it is 450 g/1 lb (2 cups) to each 600 ml/1 pint (2½ cups) juice. The sugar can be reduced to 350 g/12 oz (1½ cups) or even to 225 g/8 oz (1 cup) to the same amount of juice but the jelly will be less firm, especially with the smaller quantity of sugar. You will need to freeze or sterilize the preserve, as explained on pages 15 to 16, unless you plan to use the jelly within a very short time. In this case keep the preserve in the refrigerator.

YIELD OF JELLY

It is not easy to say just how much jelly will result from the different recipes. An exact amount of water is given with each type of fruit but that does not mean the same amount of juice will flow from the purée, even if the same kind of fruit is used every time. It all depends upon the juiciness of that particular batch of fruit. This is why it is better to measure the juice *after* straining the purée, and allow 450 g/1 lb (2 cups) sugar to each 600 ml/1 pint (2½ cups) juice, unless you are reducing the proportion of sugar, as mentioned earlier. The completed jelly should have a 60% sugar content if it is to keep well in an ordinary store cupboard, so the yield is exactly as given for jam or similar preserves, i.e. as follows:

450 g/1 lb (2 cups) sugar should make 750 g/1⅔ lb jelly
900 g/2 lb (4 cups) sugar should make 1.5 kg/3⅓ lb jelly
1.35 kg/3 lb (6 cups) sugar should make 2.25 kg/5 lb jelly

PERFECT JELLIES

The comments at the beginning of this book about preserves are just as important for making jellies as they are for making jams and conserves. There are, however, additional steps to follow to make sure a jelly is perfect in flavour and colour.

1. While there is no need to peel or stone fruit before cooking, it is important to make sure the fruit is not bruised in any way or over-ripe; you can cut away any damaged or bruised portions of hard fruit, like apples.
2. Simmer the fruit in the recommended amount of water very slowly to extract the pectin and to make sure the liquid does not evaporate too much. It is advisable to cover the pan to prevent undue evaporation when cooking hard fruits, which take some time to become a complete pulp. Preserving pans rarely have a lid, so place a thick sheet of foil over the top while softening the fruit. Do *not* over-cook the fruit, for it would lose both colour and flavour.
3. Strain the fruit pulp with the greatest of care – this is the secret of a perfectly clear jelly. Do not press the jelly bag while the juice is dripping through it – it may be tempting to hasten the process with pressure but this results in a cloudy liquid.
    If straining the pulp through several layers of muslin the same rule applies: allow the juice to drip through at its own pace.
4. Heat the juice in the uncovered preserving pan before adding the sugar.
5. Add the sugar and stir over a low heat until this has completely dissolved, then raise the heat and allow the liquid to boil rapidly until setting point is reached. Details of testing for setting point are on pages 8 to 9.
6. Before potting remove any scum from the top of the jelly with a spoon. If you do not want to do this try stirring slowly; this often disperses the scum, which is quite harmless. If you do stir the scum into the jelly it may not look quite as clear as you would wish, but the taste will not be affected.
    It is not advisable to add a knob of butter to the pan when making a jelly, as one can for a jam or conserve, for this spoils the clarity of the product.
7. Prepare the jars and pour the very hot liquid jelly into them in exactly the same way as described on page 19, but tap the jar as you pour in the mixture so any air bubbles come out. This is only vital if you are making jellies for contests or for sale.
8. Jellies tend to set very quickly, so it is important to make sure the jam jars are very well heated and to pour the liquid jelly into the jars while it is very hot. If you are making a large batch of jelly and the last amount left in the pan begins to set, warm it for a very short time so that it liquifies once again.
9. Cover the jars as described on page 19.

USING A JELLY BAG

Jelly bags are obtainable from shops selling kitchen equipment. They are large in size and made of heavy-duty calico or flannel. They have a very close weave which allows only the juice from the fruit to flow through and none of the pulp or pips or skin. The bag has either four loops of tape or four lengths of tape to attach the bag to the legs of an upturned chair or stool.

Making a Jelly Bag

If you have suitable material in the house you can make a jelly bag yourself. You need a piece of fabric about 45 to 60 cm/18 to 24 inches square.

Fold this into a triangle as shown in the second sketch. Machine the seam BC to D very well. Be particularly careful about sewing the tip of the triangle, for that will be holding the weight of fruit. Sew four loops (sufficiently large to go over the legs of the chair or stool you intend using) or sew long pieces of tape at regular intervals to the top of the bag.

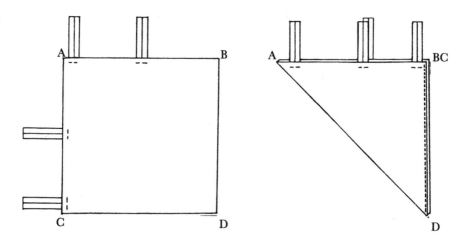

To Strain the Fruit Pulp

Tie the tapes firmly around the legs of the chair or stool or lift the loops over the legs; make sure these are secure, for the fruit and juice will be heavy. Place a very large bowl on the base of the chair or stool. Spoon or pour some of the hot fruit pulp into the bag and leave it for a while, then add more fruit. Continue like this until all the fruit has been put into the bag then allow to hang for several hours. During this time the juice will gradually drip into the bowl, as shown in the diagram. Leave until the fruit pulp in the jelly bag is completely dry. You can then remove the bag, which has the residue of the fruit, and the bowl of fruit juice, which is the basis for the jelly.

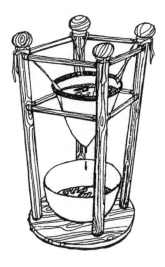

A Second Boiling

When using fruits that have a very high amount of pectin, such as crab or cooking apples, redcurrants, damsons, etc., you can reboil the fruit a second time. Allow only *half* the amount of water used the first time for this second boiling, strain the pulp, add the second batch of juice to the first batch and continue as the recipe. Do *not* try a second boiling with fruits that are low in pectin, such as strawberries, for the juice would be of poor quality.

Cleaning the Jelly Bag

Wash the jelly bag very thoroughly. If a detergent is used then rinse the bag several times in clear water to make sure there is no trace of detergent left. Dry thoroughly before storing. A jelly bag should last for many years.

Preparing the Jelly Bag Before Use

Whether you buy or make a jelly bag, it must be put into boiling water before use in order to sterilize it. Leave in the water until cold then remove and drain well. This same rule applies to the muslin you will use over a sieve, see below.

STRAINING JUICE THROUGH MUSLIN

About four thicknesses of fine muslin (sold as gauze by chemists) could be formed into a jelly bag but generally it is better to place the layers over a hair or nylon sieve (see page 103). Stand the sieve over a large bowl, then place the muslin on top of this. Add a little of the fruit and allow it to drip through. Continue like this, adding more fruit to the muslin and leave for several hours until the fruit pulp is absolutely dry.

PRESERVES FROM THE HEDGEROW

Throughout this book wild, as well as cultivated, ingredients are included to give interest and a new flavour to many preserves. Few late summer fruits have such a good taste as wild blackberries and these are used in several kinds of jam as well as an interesting fruit cheese and one of the most popular of all jellies – Bramble (see pages 26 to 28 and 74 to 75).

During the Second World War, when citrus fruit was virtually unobtainable, people hunted out rose hips to make a syrup that is rich in Vitamin C. The recipe for this is on page 117 and an unusual jelly, based on the same fruit, is on page 80.

Maybe you have not tried cooking with elderflowers or elderberries. The delicate sprays of white flowers add a subtle taste to gooseberries in both a jam or jelly and the dark berries have a richness of taste that is unique. Recipes using the flowers and the berries are on page 73.

If you are lucky enough to find a rowan tree, use the berries when they are really ripe and brilliant red to make a jelly. This jelly is excellent by itself or as a base for the Thyme Jelly on page 86.

Sloes have earned fame by being allied to gin but in a jelly they are also excellent as a partner to apples (see page 84).

Hunting wild mushrooms has become a popular pastime. Wild or cultivated mushrooms can be used for the Mushroom Ketchup on pages 181 to 182 and they are included in many pickles and chutneys in the sections that begin on pages 138 and 160.

QUANTITIES FOR JELLIES

A rather more generous amount of fruit is needed for jellies, and for butters and cheeses too, compared with that given in the recipes for jams and conserves. This is because there is a considerable amount of wastage of fruit skins and pips when straining the fruit pulp to make a jelly, or rubbing it through a sieve for a butter or cheese. In most cases it is not worth embarking on these preserves unless you are using at least of 900 g/2 lb of fruit.

APPLE JELLY

Cooking time: 30 to 35 minutes • For yield see page 68

A sharp cooking apple or crab apple makes the best jelly. You may like to experiment by mixing several different kinds of cooking apples to find the flavour you like best. The apples can be flavoured in various ways, as mentioned on page 73. Crab apples make an even better jelly than ordinary apples but their taste is so pronounced that it is advisable not to add extra ingredients.

Metric/Imperial	Ingredients	American
900 g/2 lb	*cooking apples*	2 lb
600 ml/1 pint	*water*	2½ cups
	sugar, see method	

Wipe or wash the apples – do *not* peel or core them, but remove any part that is bruised. Put into a pan with the water. Simmer gently until very soft, stirring or crushing the fruit from time to time to help extract the juice. Put the fruit through a jelly bag or through muslin, measure the juice and add 450 g/1 lb (2 cups) sugar to each 600 ml/1 pint (2½ cups) juice. You can boil the apple pulp a second time to give more juice (see page 71) but add only 300 ml/½ pint (1¼ cups) water. Cook the fruit again then strain and add the second batch of juice to the first one.
In any of the variations of Apple Jelly, a second boiling can be done. Heat the juice, add the sugar, stir over a low heat until the sugar has dissolved then boil rapidly until setting point is reached. Pour into hot jars and seal down.

Variations

- You can add 4 to 6 individual lemon balm leaves or mint leaves or rosemary leaves or sage leaves to the apples. These are excellent if you intend using the jelly with savoury dishes. See also Mint Jelly, Rosemary Jelly, Sage Jelly and Thyme Jelly on pages 85 to 86.

Apple and Cranberry Jelly: use 900 g/2 lb cooking apples and 450 g/1 lb cranberries with 825 ml/1 pint 7½ fl oz (scant 3½ cups) water. Cover the pan very tightly and do not raise the lid until the cranberries cease 'popping'.

Apple and Elderberry Jelly: use 900 g/2 lb cooking apples and 450 g/1 lb elderberries with 900 ml/1½ pints (3¾ cups) water. The fruit can be flavoured with the pared rind of 2 medium oranges. Use 150 ml/¼ pint (⅔ cup) orange juice instead of this amount of water. A little cinnamon can be used to flavour this jelly or the plain Apple Jelly above. Tie a 5 to 7.5 cm/2 to 3 inch cinnamon stick in muslin and simmer with the fruit. Remove before putting the fruit through the jelly bag or muslin.

Apple and Elderflower Jelly: add 2 small heads of elderflowers to the apples at the beginning of cooking time in the Apple Jelly recipe.

Apple and Geranium Jelly: add 3 or 4 lemon-scented or rose-scented geranium leaves to the apples in the Apple Jelly. Remove the leaves before straining the fruit through the jelly bag or muslin.

Apple and Lemon Jelly: as above, but pare the top rind from 2 large lemons – do not include any pith – add to the apples and water together with the juice from the 2 lemons. If giving a second boiling to the fruit use the rind and juice from just 1 lemon.

Apple and Orange Jelly: pare the rind from 3 oranges and add to the apples – do not include any pith or pips. Use 300 ml/½ pint (1¼ cups) orange juice and 300 ml/½ pint (1¼ cups) water instead of all water. If giving a second boiling to the fruit use the rind of 1 orange and 150 ml/¼ pint (⅔ cup) orange juice and 150 ml/¼ pint (⅔ cup) water.

APPLE STRUPER

Cooking time: 45 minutes • For yield see page 68

This particular jelly has a very unusual flavour due to the honey and spices that are added. It is a recipe I have known since childhood days.

Metric/Imperial	Ingredients	American
900 g/2 lb	*cooking apples or crab apples*	2 lb
600 ml/1 pint	*water*	2½ cups
	sugar, see method	
	clear honey, see method	
	grated or ground nutmeg, see method	
	mixed spice or ground cinnamon, see method	

If using cooking apples cut these into small pieces; leave crab apples whole unless they are large, in which case they can be halved. Put the fruit into the water and simmer gently until a thick purée. Strain through a jelly bag or through muslin. To each 600 ml/1 pint (2½ cups) juice allow 350 g/12 oz (1½ cups) sugar; 100 g/4 oz (⅓ cup) clear honey; ½ to 1 teaspoon grated or ground nutmeg and ½ to 1 teaspoon mixed spice or ground cinnamon. (It is advisable to use the smaller amounts of the spices first and add more later if desired.) Pour the juice into the pan, add the sugar, honey and spices and stir over a low heat until the sugar has dissolved. Raise the heat and boil rapidly until setting point is reached. Check the flavour just before this stage and add more spices if desired. Pour into hot jars and seal down.

Variations

Apple Struper Butter: instead of straining the juice, rub the cooked apple purée through a fine nylon sieve to give a smooth texture, free from peel and cores. Measure this and add the sugar, honey and spices as above. You could add 1 or 2 tablespoons Calvados (apple brandy) to this purée or to the jelly above. In this case be sparing with the spices, so they do not overwhelm the flavour of the Calvados.

BLACKBERRY (BRAMBLE) JELLY

Cooking time: 25 to 30 minutes • For yield see page 68

Blackberries have little natural pectin, so it is advisable to use lemon juice, as given in the method, or combine the blackberries with a small amount of cooking apples, see Blackberry with Apple Jelly (page 75). Soft fruits that need very little water could be cooked in a bowl in a microwave oven (see pages 12 to 13) or in the top of a double saucepan over boiling water so there is no possibility of the fruit sticking to the pan or burning. When the sugar has been added, the preserve must boil rapidly in an open pan. If using sugar that contains pectin, add only half the amount of lemon juice given in the recipes.

Metric/Imperial	Ingredients	American
900 g/2 lb	*blackberries*	2 lb
150 ml/¼ pint	*water*	⅔ cup
	sugar, see method	
	lemon juice, see method	

Wash the blackberries, put into the pan with the water and simmer gently until very soft. Press the fruit from time to time. Strain through a jelly bag or muslin, measure the juice and allow 450 g/1 lb (2 cups) sugar and 2 tablespoons (2½ tablespoons) lemon juice to each 600 ml/1 pint (2½ cups) juice. Heat the juice, add the sugar and lemon juice. Stir over a low heat until the sugar has dissolved then boil rapidly until setting point is reached. Pour into hot jars and seal down. Do not give a second boiling to this fruit or any of the other fruits below.

Variations

Blackberry with Apple Jelly: this is rather different from the Blackberry and Apple Jelly below in that to each 900 g/2 lb blackberries you need just 1 large cooking apple. Cut this in pieces and simmer with the blackberries. Omit the lemon juice. In this jelly the blackberry flavour is predominant.

Blackberry and Apple Jelly: use 900 g/2 lb blackberries and 900 g/2 lb cooking apples with 750 ml/1¼ pint (generous 3 cups) water. Cut up the apples and simmer in all the water for 10 minutes before adding the blackberries. In this jelly you have a pleasant blend of apple and blackberry flavours.

Boysenberry Jelly: use boysenberries instead of blackberries in the main recipe or the alternative recipes with apples.

Loganberry Jelly: use loganberries instead of blackberries. Since these are slightly firmer than blackberries allow 225 ml/7½ fl oz (scant cup) water to each 900 g/2 lb fruit. Measure the juice and allow 450 g/1 lb (2 cups) sugar and 1 tablespoon (1¼ tablespoons) lemon juice to each 600 ml/ 1 pint (2½ cups) juice.

Raspberry Jelly: follow the recipe for Blackberry Jelly. Use the same amount of sugar but only 1 tablespoon (1¼ tablespoons) lemon juice to each 600 ml/1 pint (2½ cups) juice.

Spiced Blackberry Jelly: a fairly generous amount of spice blends well with blackberries. Tie 4 cloves and a 2.5 cm/1 inch length of cinnamon stick in muslin and cook with the blackberries or blackberries and apples.

Strawberry Jelly: this fruit, used by itself, does not have a very strong flavour in a jelly and is therefore rather disappointing. The recipe following is better, or the mixture of fruits in Rhubarb and Strawberry Jelly on page 83. If you decide to make the jelly without adding any extra fruit, simmer the strawberries without any liquid. Measure the juice and to each 600 ml/1 pint (2½ cups) add only 400 g/14 oz (1¾ cups) sugar and 3 tablespoons (3¾ tablespoons) lemon juice. Continue as for Blackberry Jelly.

Strawberry and Redcurrant Jelly: use 450 g/1 lb strawberries and 450 g/ 1 lb redcurrants with no water. Simmer the fruit until soft, strain the juice and add the usual 450 g/1 lb (2 cups) sugar to each 600 ml/1 pint (2½ cups) juice.

Tayberry Jelly: use the recipe for Blackberry Jelly on pages 74 to 75.

Why was my apple jelly slightly cloudy? I did use a proper jelly bag. If you used a thick jelly bag then I am afraid you must have pressed this once or twice, possibly to speed up the process of the juice dripping through. Even a slight pressure through the bag or muslin (if using this) is sufficient to spoil the clarity of the liquid (see pages 69 to 71).

If using muslin, make sure you have sufficient layers, so only the juice can run through.

BLACKCURRANT JELLY

Cooking time: 30 to 35 minutes • For yield see page 68

Blackcurrants make an excellent jelly, full of rich flavour. The fiddliness of the fruit is worth the effort.

Metric/Imperial	Ingredients	American
900 g/2 lb	blackcurrants	2 lb
600 ml/1 pint	water	2½ cups
	sugar, see method	

Simmer the fruit in the water until very tender. Put through a jelly bag or muslin and strain the juice. While you can allow the usual 450 g/1 lb (2 cups) sugar to each 600 ml/1 pint (2½ cups) juice, you could make a slightly sweeter jelly with 500 g/1 lb 2 oz (2¼ cups) sugar to each 600 ml/1 pint (2½ cups) juice. Blackcurrants could be given a second boiling using only 300 ml/½ pint (1¼ cups) water.

Variations

Blackcurrant and Whitecurrant Jelly: if you have whitecurrants in the garden use these with the blackcurrants; the colour of the jelly will be excellent. Allow 450 g/1 lb blackcurrants and 450 g/1 lb whitecurrants with 450 ml/¾ pint (scant 2 cups) water if the whitecurrants are very firm. If ripe then allow just 300 ml/½ pint (1¼ cups) water. Do not give this mixture of fruits a second boiling.

Blackcurrant and Redcurrant Jelly: use the recipe above with red, instead of whitecurrants.

Cranberry Jelly: to each 900 g/2 lb cranberries allow 450 ml/¾ pint (scant 2 cups) water. Simmer the cranberries in a very tightly covered pan. Do not raise the lid until the cranberries cease 'popping' – they tend to jump out of the pan until tenderised. Use 450 g/1 lb (2 cups) sugar to each 600 ml/1 pint (2½ cups) juice. The cranberries could be given a second boiling with only 225 ml/7½ fl oz (scant cup) water.

Cranberry and Orange Jelly: to each 900 g/2 lb cranberries add the rind from 2 oranges, removing any pips and pith. Use 300 ml/½ pint (1¼ cups) water and 150 ml/¼ pint (⅔ cup) orange juice. To emphasise the orange flavour use 225 ml/7½ fl oz; (scant cup) orange juice and no water for the second boiling.

Redcurrant Jelly: it is surprising that redcurrants, which add pectin and extra flavour to many other fruits, must be cooked with very little, if any, water to produce a strongly flavoured jelly. Do not give a second boiling. To 900 g/2 lb redcurrants allow 300 ml/½ pint (1¼ cups) water if the fruit is very firm and slightly under-ripe. If moderately ripe then allow 150 ml/¼ pint (⅔ cup) water. If very ripe simmer without any water.

Redcurrant and Raspberry Jelly: use 450 g/1 lb redcurrants and 900 g/ 2 lb raspberries with 150 ml/¼ pint (⅔ cup) water only. Do not give a second boiling.

GOOSEBERRY JELLY

Cooking time: 25 to 30 minutes • For yield see page 68

Gooseberries make an excellent jelly and this is a good way of using very small fruit, although all kinds of gooseberries are suitable. The term 'levellers' may not be well known. This is the name given to large ripe dessert gooseberries in the south of England. They are wonderful in a jelly, although they do need some lemon juice to set well.

Metric/Imperial	Ingredients	American
900 g/2 lb	*gooseberries*	2 lb
300 to 600 ml/½ to 1 pint	*water*	1¼ to 2½ cups
	sugar, see method	
	lemon juice, see method	

The gooseberries need not be 'topped and tailed' when making jelly. Simply put them into the preserving pan with the water. Use the smaller amount with ripe fruit, including levellers, but the full amount with firm gooseberries. Simmer slowly until the fruit is soft then strain through the jelly bag or muslin. Allow 450 g/1 lb (2 cups) sugar to each 600 ml/1 pint (2½ cups) juice. There is no need to add lemon juice with cooking gooseberries but allow 1 tablespoon (1¼ tablespoons) to each 600 ml/ 1 pint (2½ cups) juice when cooking levellers. Heat the juice, add the sugar and stir over a low heat until the sugar has dissolved. Add the lemon juice if necessary. Raise the heat and boil rapidly until setting point is reached. Pour into hot jars and seal down. Do not give a second boiling to the fruit pulp unless the gooseberries were very green and firm. In this case use just 300 ml/½ pint (1¼ cups) water.

Variations

Gooseberry and Redcurrant Jelly: use 450 g/1 lb gooseberries and 450 g/1 lb redcurrants with the same amount of water.

Leveller Jelly: the fruit has a rather less sweet and more interesting flavour if only 400 g/14 oz (1¾ cups) sugar is used to each 600 ml/1 pint (2½ cups) juice. Use the lemon juice as given in the method above. If the levellers are very ripe reduce the amount of water to 150 ml/¼ pint (⅔ cup) to each 900 g/2 lb fruit.

Damson Jelly: do not try to stone the fruit before cooking. Use the same proportion of water as given under Gooseberry Jelly above. When the pulp is strained use the same amount of sugar. Lemon juice is not necessary for damsons.

GRAPE JELLY

Cooking time: 25 to 30 minutes • For yield see page 68

White or red grapes can be used but red grapes, which are really ripe and juicy, give the best flavour and colour to the jelly.

Metric/Imperial	Ingredients	American
1.35 kg/3 lb	grapes	3 lb
	sugar, see method	
	lemon juice, see method	

Halve a few of the grapes to encourage the juice to flow; there is no need to remove any pips. Simmer the fruit slowly, pressing it firmly from time to time, until a smooth purée. Strain through a jelly bag or muslin and measure the juice. To each 600 ml/1 pint (2½ cups) allow 450 g/1 lb (2 cups) sugar. If the grapes were white and very acid in flavour omit the lemon juice; if moderately sweet allow 1 tablespoon (1¼ tablespoons) lemon juice to each 600 ml/1 pint (2½ cups) of juice; but if red and ripe use 2 tablespoons (2½ tablespoons) lemon juice. Warm the juice, add the sugar and lemon juice and stir over a low heat until the sugar has dissolved. Raise the heat and boil briskly until setting point is reached. Pour into hot jars and seal down. Do not give a second boiling.

GUAVA JELLY

Cooking time: 25 minutes • For yield see page 68

The guava tree is related to the myrtle. Originally it was a native of Mexico and South America, but it is now grown extensively in many countries where the weather is sufficiently hot. The pulp is delicious as a dessert fruit or made into a jelly or butter, as in the following recipes. It is claimed that guavas contain more Vitamin C than oranges, so they are a very healthy as well as pleasant fruit.

Metric/Imperial	Ingredients	American
900 g/2 lb	*guava pulp*	2 lb
300 ml/½ pint	*water*	1¼ cups
	sugar, see method	
	lemon juice, see method	

Halve the fruit, scoop out and weigh the pulp. Put this into the preserving pan with the water and simmer until soft. Strain through a jelly bag or muslin. To each 600 ml/1 pint (2½ cups) allow 450 g/1 lb (2 cups) sugar and 2 tablespoons (2½ tablespoons) lemon juice. Heat the juice, add the sugar and stir over a low heat until the sugar has dissolved. Add the lemon juice, bring to the boil and cook rapidly until setting point is reached. Pour into hot jars and seal down. Do not give a second boiling.

Variations

Custard Apple (Sour Sop) Jelly: use the same weight of custard apple pulp as guava and follow either the recipe above or the Guava and Apple Jelly below.

Guava and Apple Jelly: to give a slightly sharper taste to the jelly use 675 g/1½ lb guava pulp and 225 g/8 oz (½ lb) cooking apples. Prepare the guava pulp and dice the apples without peeling or coring them. Simmer together in 450 ml/¾ pint (scant 2 cups) water then strain as usual. Allow the same amount of sugar and lemon juice as in the Guava Jelly.

Mango Jelly: make sure the fruit is really ripe. Cut a slice of fruit and skin from the side of each mango; scoop out the pulp from the slice and from around the stone. Weigh the pulp and follow the recipe for Guava Jelly or Guava and Apple Jelly above.

Guava Butter: prepare the fruit pulp as instructed in Guava Jelly. Cook this then rub through a sieve. Measure the pulp and to each 600 ml/1 pint (2½ cups) allow the same amount of sugar and lemon juice as for the jelly plus 25 g/1 oz (2 tablespoons) butter; add this with the sugar. Proceed as for jelly until setting point is reached. Spoon into hot containers and cover.

MEDLAR JELLY

Cooking time: 40 to 45 minutes • For yield see page 68

Medlars were better known many years ago than they are today. This may be because medlar trees become very large in size, so are not suitable for small modern gardens. The medlar belongs to the rose family and is a native to south-eastern Europe, although it was once quite well known in Britain. The fruits form small round balls, open at the top, and are only edible raw when the flesh becomes very soft and brown (they appear almost rotten). Jelly can be made with really ripe, or slightly under-ripe, fruit. Adjust the amount of water accordingly, see page 80.

Metric/Imperial	Ingredients	American
900 g/2 lb	*medlars*	2 lb
300 to 600 ml/¹/₂ to 1 pint	*water*	1¹/₄ to 2¹/₂ cups
	sugar, see method	
	lemon juice, see method	

Cut the fruit into pieces – do not peel or remove the seeds. Put into the preserving pan with the water. If really ripe use only 300 ml/¹/₂ pint (1¹/₄ cups) water but use the larger amount if the fruit is still firm. Simmer until soft then strain through the jelly bag or muslin. Allow 450 g/1 lb (2 cups) sugar to each 600 ml/1 pint (2¹/₂ cups) juice and stir over a low heat until dissolved. If the fruit was very ripe then add 2 tablespoons (2¹/₂ tablespoons) lemon juice to each 600 ml/1 pint (2¹/₂ cups) juice, but if fairly firm add just 1 tablespoon (1¹/₄ tablespoons) to the same amount of juice. Boil rapidly until setting point is reached then pour into hot jars and seal down. Do not give a second boiling to the fruit pulp.

Variations

- Medlars can be flavoured with lemon or orange rind in cooking, as described under Quince Jelly (see pages 81 to 82).

MULBERRY JELLY

Cooking time: 35 minutes • For yield see page 68

These berries make an excellent jelly, and they are even better if a small amount of cooking apple is included.

Metric/Imperial	Ingredients	American
2 medium	*cooking apples*	2 medium
300 ml/¹/₂ pint	*water*	1¹/₄ cups
900 g/2 lb	*mulberries*	2 lb
	sugar, see method	

Cut the apples into small pieces – do not peel or core them. Put into the preserving pan with the water and cook slowly for 10 minutes. Add the mulberries and continue cooking until a soft pulp. Strain through a jelly bag or muslin. Allow 450 g/1 lb (2 cups) sugar to each 600 ml/1 pint (2¹/₂ cups) juice. Heat the juice, add the sugar and stir over a low heat until dissolved, then raise the heat and boil rapidly until setting point is reached. Pour into hot jars and seal down. Do not give a second boiling.

Variation

Rose Hip Jelly: use the recipe above with rose hips instead of mulberries and 600 ml/1 pint (2¹/₂ cups) water.

Another recipe for this jelly uses 450 g/1 lb cooking apples and 450 g/1 lb rose hips. In this case cook the apples and the rose hips separately, each in 300 ml/¹/₂ pint (1¹/₄ cups) water. Strain the two lots of fruit pulp; blend the juices together then follow the recipe for Mulberry Jelly above.

ORANGE JELLY WITH CERTO

Cooking time: 20 to 25 minutes • Makes nearly 3 kg/nearly 6¾ lb jelly

This is a very refreshing jelly which can be melted and used as a glaze on sweet dishes or cakes. It is excellent with duck, pork or goose: a little can be added to sauces or gravy to serve with these foods.

Metric/Imperial	Ingredients	American
4 to 6	*large oranges*	4 to 6
1	*large lemon*	1
450 ml/³/₄ pint	*water*	scant 2 cups
1.125 kg/2½ lb	*sugar*	5¼ cups
250 ml/9 fl oz	*Certo*	1⅛ cups

Halve 4 of the oranges and the lemon, and squeeze out the juice from both fruits. Measure this: you should have 450 ml/³/₄ pint (scant 2 cups). If less than this, halve and squeeze one, or both, of the remaining oranges to give the required amount. Put the orange halves, free from pips, into a saucepan, add the water and bring the liquid to the boil. Cover the pan and simmer for 10 minutes. Remove the orange halves, then strain and measure the liquid. You should have 150 ml/¼ pint (²/₃ cup). If more than this return the liquid to the pan and boil vigorously until reduced to that amount. Add the fruit juice to the liquid in the pan, heat gently, then add the sugar and stir over a low heat until dissolved. Raise the heat and boil vigorously for 2 minutes only. Remove from the heat and stir in the commercial pectin. Return to the heat and boil again for 30 seconds only. Skim if necessary then pour into hot jars and seal down.

Variations

- Use 600 ml/l pint (2½ cups) unsweetened orange juice *less* 3 tablespoons (3³/₄ tablespoons). Add 3 tablespoons (3³/₄ tablespoons) fresh lemon juice. Heat the juices then add the sugar and continue as the recipe above.
- Use Seville oranges with the lemon then continue as above.
  This makes a more bitter jelly which is particularly good with hot or cold duck or goose.

QUINCE JELLY

Cooking time: 50 minutes • For yield see page 68

Quinces make a wonderful jelly – their rich flavour is delicious and the preserve is equally good to serve with scones, as a filling for sponge cakes or as an accompaniment to savoury dishes. The amount of water needed varies according to the ripeness of the fruit. It is possible to use really hard under-ripe fruit for the jelly. If it is very ripe you will need lemon juice to ensure a good set (see the method). This is not essential with under-ripe fruit, although the flavour of lemons blends very well with quinces.

Metric/Imperial	Ingredients	American
900 g/2 lb	quinces	2 lb
900 ml to 1.5 litres/ 1½ to 2½ pints	water	3¾ to 6¾ cups
	sugar, see method	
	lemon juice, see method	

Cut up the quinces – do not peel or core them but cut away any bruised parts. Put into the pan with the right amount of water: use the smaller amount if the fruit is really ripe and the maximum quantity if very hard. Simmer gently until the fruit becomes a soft pulp. Put through the jelly bag or muslin and measure the juice. Allow 450 g/1 lb (2 cups) sugar to each 600 ml/1 pint (2½ cups) juice. Heat the juice, add the sugar and stir over a low heat until dissolved. If the fruit was very ripe the juice will contain less pectin so allow 2 tablespoons (2½ tablespoons) lemon juice to each 600 ml/1 pint (2½ cups) quince juice. Boil rapidly until setting point is reached. Pour into hot jars and seal down. If the fruit was very ripe do *not* give a second boiling; if it was firm and under-ripe you could do this. Use only 600 ml/l pint (2½ cups) water with the fruit pulp.

Variations

Quince and Apple Jelly: this combination of fruit has an excellent flavour. Use 450 g/1 lb quinces and 450 g/1 lb cooking apples or crab apples. Add 750 ml/1¼ pints (generous 3 cups) water if the fruit is ripe and 900 ml/1½ pints (3¾ cups) water if firm. Add the usual amount of sugar to the juice and just 1 tablespoon (1¼ tablespoons) lemon juice to each 600 ml/1 pint (2½ cups) of `juice if the quinces were ripe. This combination of fruit blends very well with cinnamon: add a 3.5 cm/ 1½ inch stick of cinnamon to the fruit when cooking and remove before straining the fruit pulp.

Quince and Lemon Jelly: pare the rind from 3 large lemons (make sure there is no bitter pith), and add to the quinces when boiling them. Use 150 ml/¼ pint (⅔ cup) lemon juice instead of this amount of water when cooking the quinces. The lemon juice will add the necessary pectin to the fruit, so the extra 1 tablespoon (1¼ tablespoons) lemon juice mentioned above can be omitted.

Quince and Orange Jelly: use the rind from 3 oranges instead of the lemon rind above and 300 ml/½ pint (1¼ cups) orange juice instead of the same amount of water.

RHUBARB JELLY

Cooking time: 25 to 30 minutes • For yield see page 68

Rhubarb by itself makes a rather dull jelly with not a lot of flavour or colour. It is improved by the addition of oranges, as in the following recipe. Rhubarb blends well with a number of soft fruits to make jellies (see Variations).

Metric/Imperial	Ingredients	American
900 g/2 lb	rhubarb	2 lb
3	large oranges	3
	sugar, see method	
	lemon juice, see method	

Cut the rhubarb into small pieces, taking care not to lose any skin, for this gives colour to the jelly. Grate the rind from the oranges, halve the fruit and squeeze out the juice. Simmer the rhubarb with the orange rind and juice until a smooth pulp. Strain through the jelly bag or muslin and measure the juice..To each 600 ml/1 pint (2½ cups) add 450 g/1 lb (2 cups) sugar and 2 tablespoons (2½ tablespoons) lemon juice. Heat the juice, add the sugar and lemon juice and stir over a low heat until the sugar is dissolved. Raise the heat and boil rapidly until setting point is reached. Pour into hot jars and seal down.

Variations

Rhubarb and Loganberry Jelly: omit the orange rind and juice. Simmer 450 g/1 lb rhubarb and 450 g/1 lb loganberries with 2 tablespoons (2½ tablespoons) water, then continue as the recipe above.

Rhubarb and Raspberry Jelly: omit the water but continue as Rhubarb and Loganberry Jelly. Mash the raspberries before adding the rhubarb to provide some moisture in which to cook the rhubarb, or cook in the top of a double saucepan to avoid any possibility of the fruit sticking to the pan. Continue as Rhubarb Jelly.

Rhubarb and Strawberry Jelly: simmer 450 g/1 lb rhubarb and 550 g/1¼ lb strawberries as described in Rhubarb and Raspberry Jelly. Measure the juice and add 450 g/1 lb (2 cups) sugar and 3 tablespoons (3¾ tablespoons) lemon juice to each 600 ml/1 pint (2½ cups) juice. Continue as Rhubarb Jelly.

ROWAN JELLY

Cooking time: 30 to 35 minutes • For yield see page 68

The rowan, or mountain ash, tree is found throughout Britain but mostly in the north of England, Scotland and Wales. Birds love the red berries when ripe, so you must pick these quickly when they reach this stage, otherwise there will be no fruit for jelly. Used by themselves the berries have a faintly bitter taste, which some people may not like. Combined with apples you have a milder taste. Either version of the jelly makes an excellent accompaniment to game dishes.

Metric/Imperial	Ingredients	American
900 g/2 lb	rowanberries	2 lb
300 ml/½ pint	water	1¼ cups
	sugar, see method	

Wash the fruit well then put into the pan with the water and simmer slowly until very soft. Press the berries from time to time to extract the juice. Strain through a jelly bag or muslin, measure the juice and add 450 g/1 lb (2 cups) sugar to each 600 ml/1 pint (2½ cups) juice.
Heat the juice, add the sugar and stir over a low heat until this has dissolved, then boil rapidly until setting point is reached. Pour into hot jars and seal down.

Variations

Rowan and Apple Jelly: use 450 g/1 lb rowanberries and 450 g/1 lb acid cooking apples or crab apples. The latter blend particularly well with rowanberries. Cut large apples into pieces and halve crab apples, so they will soften at the same speed as the rowanberries. Put into the pan with 450 ml/¾ pint (scant 2 cups) water. Continue as the recipe above.
A second boiling can be done with this jelly and for the Rowan Jelly too. Use just 150 ml/¼ pint (⅔ cup) water.

Sloe and Apple Jelly: sloes are the blackish fruit from the blackthorn; they have a very sour taste but with apples make an interesting jelly. Cut 900 g/2 lb cooking apples into small pieces, put into the pan with 100 g/4 oz (1 cup) sloes and 450 ml/¾ pint (scant 2 cups) water. Simmer until a purée then continue as Rowan Jelly, above.

TAMARILLO JELLY

Cooking time: 30 minutes • For yield see page 68

The other name for tamarillo is 'tree tomato'. As this indicates, the plant belongs to the same family as the tomato and recipes using tomatoes can be made with this lesser known egg-shaped fruit. There are three types of fruit – yellow, red and dark red. The yellow tamarillo has the best flavour. The skin of the fruit is very bitter so it must be removed. Tamarillo jelly can be used as a sweet spread but, like the tomato jellies below, it is also an excellent accompaniment to pâtés, meat or fish dishes.

Metric/Imperial	Ingredients	American
900 g/2 lb	tamarillos	2 lb
900 ml/1½ pints	water	3¾ cups
	sugar, see method	
	lemon juice, see method	

Put the fruit into a bowl, add boiling water and allow to stand for 5 minutes – this is necessary for the skins are very tough. Remove the fruit from the water and pull away the skins. Place the skinned fruit in the preserving pan with the water and simmer gently until a pulp. Strain through the jelly bag or muslin and measure the juice. Allow 450 g/1 lb (2 cups) sugar and 2 tablespoons (2½ tablespoons) lemon juice to each 600 ml/1 pint (2½ cups) juice. Heat the juice, add the sugar and stir over a low heat until dissolved. Bring to the boil and cook rapidly until setting point is reached. Pour into hot jars and seal down. Do not give a second boiling.

Variations

- For a slightly sharper flavour pare the rind from 2 or 3 lemons and add to the fruit while simmering. Remove all the pith from the rind.

Persimmon Jelly: use persimmons in place of tamarillos in the recipe. It is not essential to skin the fruit before making the jelly, for although the skin is quite tough it does not give a bitter taste.

Tomato Jelly: either red or green tomatoes can be used for this jelly, which is excellent as an accompaniment to savoury dishes. There is no need to skin the tomatoes before use. If using red tomatoes allow 300 ml/½ pint (1¼ cups) water to each 900 g/2 lb fruit.
  If using green tomatoes allow 600 ml/1 pint (2½ cups) water. Add the same amount of sugar and lemon juice to the strained juice as in the Tamarillo Jelly.
  About 6 basil leaves can be added to the tomatoes while simmering, or add about 1 to 2 tablespoons grated fresh ginger.
  The extra lemon rind, recommended for Tamarillo Jelly, adds a pleasant flavour to Tomato Jelly too.

HERB JELLIES

A number of herbs can be combined with the jellies in this section to give an interesting preserve to accompany meats, poultry, fish or vegetarian dishes. The jellies can be tinted green by adding a little colouring. Among the most popular herb jellies are the following.

MINT JELLY

Use the Apple Jelly recipe on page 72 (cooking or crab apples can be used) or the Gooseberry Jelly on page 77. Strain the pulp and measure the juice. To each 600 ml/1 pint (2½ cups) allow the usual 450 g/1 lb (2 cups) sugar plus 2 tablespoons (2½ tablespoons) white malt or wine vinegar and 2 to 3 tablespoons finely chopped mint. Heat the juice, add the sugar and stir over a low heat until dissolved, then allow the jelly to boil rapidly for a few minutes. Add the vinegar and continue boiling until the setting point is reached. Stir the mint into the jelly then spoon into hot jars and seal down. Mint Jelly blends well with lamb, cold fish dishes, cheese dishes or with liver pâté. There is a Pineapple and Mint Jelly on page 86 and Mint Marmalade on page 94.

ROSEMARY OR SAGE JELLIES

For this use the Apple Jelly or Gooseberry Jelly (pages 72 and 77), or the Apple and Lemon Jelly on page 73. An unusual, but very pleasant, combination of flavours is made by using the Blackcurrant Jelly on page 76 with sage, and the Tomato Jelly above or the Quince Jelly on page 81 with either sage or rosemary. Strain the pulp and add the usual amount of sugar, as given above. Both sage and rosemary have a strong flavour so you may prefer to use just 1 to 2 tablespoons only of finely chopped leaves and only 1 tablespoon (1¼ tablespoons) white vinegar to each 600 ml/1 pint (2½ cups) juice. The vinegar could be omitted, but it adds a pleasing sharpness to the jelly. Rosemary Jelly is an excellent accompaniment to chicken or turkey, lamb or vegetable dishes. Sage Jelly blends well with ham, duck, goose, pork and casserole dishes using lamb.

THYME JELLY

For this use the Apple Jelly or the Apple on page 72 and Elderberry Jelly on page 73 or the Gooseberry Jelly on page 77. A very interesting combination of flavours is made by using the Rowan Jelly or Rowan and Apple Jelly on pages 83 to 84. Strain the pulp and add the usual amount of sugar plus just 1 tablespoon (1¼ tablespoons) chopped thyme to each 600 ml/
1 pint (2½ cups) juice. Although you could add 1 tablespoon (1¼ tablespoons) vinegar, this could be omitted for the thyme gives an excellent flavour to the jelly. Thyme Jelly blends well with chicken, turkey, veal dishes or with fish dishes.

PINEAPPLE AND MINT JELLY

Cooking time: 15 minutes • Makes 750 g/²⁄₃ lb jelly

This is an easily made mint jelly using canned or bottled pineapple juice. There is no vinegar in the recipe but it could be added, see under Variations. This version of Mint Jelly is an excellent alternative to those given on page 85.

Metric/Imperial	Ingredients	American
600 ml/1 pint	unsweetened pineapple juice	2½ cups
450 g/1 lb	sugar	2 cups
4 tablespoons	lemon juice	5 tablespoons
1½ tablespoons or to taste	finely chopped mint	scant 2 tablespoons, or to taste

Heat the pineapple juice, add the sugar and stir over a low heat until dissolved. Pour in the lemon juice, raise the temperature and boil rapidly until setting point is reached. Add the mint, stir briskly to distribute this then pour into hot jars and seal down.

Variations

- If using sweetened pineapple juice add 350 g/12 oz (1½ cups) sugar.
- Add 1 tablespoon (¼ tablespoons) white wine vinegar or malt vinegar just before setting point is reached.
- Finely chopped rosemary, sage or thyme can be added – use only half the quantity of these chopped herbs as given for mint.

Dill or Fennel Jelly: depending on personal taste, add 1 to 2 tablespoons finely chopped dill or fennel leaves to the jelly in place of mint. This is an excellent jelly to serve with cold fish dishes.

MARMALADE

Marmalade is undoubtedly the most popular breakfast-time preserve in Britain and one that it is well worth making, for 450 g/1 lb oranges, or alternative fruits, provides a good batch. One suggestion is that marmalade was first made in Britain thanks to an enterprising housewife. In the eighteenth century a ship carrying a cargo of oranges sheltered from a storm off the east coast of Scotland at Dundee. The Spanish ship (although some reports claim it was from Portugal) disposed of the oranges to a local shopkeeper, a Mr Keiller. When he came to sell them his customers were not pleased, for they were bitter, not sweet as had been expected. Rather than wasting the produce, in true Scottish thrifty fashion Mrs Keiller decided to try her hand at making a preserve, and so marmalade was created. Seville (bitter) oranges are by far the most popular citrus fruit for marmalade although, over the years, other varieties of this preserve have become better known. Recipes for all types of marmalade are given on the following pages. The information on pages 6 to 19 will help you to produce perfect marmalade but there are a few points special to this particular preserve, as follows:

1. When preparing the citrus fruit never discard the pith or pips – these are ingredients that add flavour to the preserve and they are essential for helping the marmalade to set. There are various ways of incorporating these into the different kinds of marmalade. This is explained in the recipes.
2. Simmer the peel very slowly to make sure it is tender, unless doing this in a pressure cooker (see pages 13 to 14 and 89).
3. Check that the peel really *is* soft, for it will not tenderize once the sugar has been added; in fact, it tends to become somewhat tougher. To test if adequately cooked, take a piece of peel between your forefinger and thumb – you should be able to rub it almost to nothing if adequately cooked.
4. However, having said that the peel must be adequately cooked, there is no virtue in over-cooking it, for that destroys the flavour and colour of the marmalade.
5. Always stir in the sugar over a low heat to make sure it has been dissolved, then raise the heat and allow the preserve to boil rapidly until setting point is reached. This is explained on page 18.
6. Marmalade has only a brief period when it is at setting point, so it is *imperative that you test early*. Once this setting point has passed the marmalade will *never* set.
7. Allow the cooked preserve to cool for a time in the preserving pan so that it thickens slightly, then stir briskly. In this way the peel is evenly distributed.
8. Spoon into hot jars and seal down as instructed on page 19.

PREPARING THE FRUIT FOR MARMALADE

Although there are other fruits used in marmalade, it is mostly citrus fruits that form the basis of this preserve. Always wash citrus fruits well for much of the fruit sold today has a wax coating to help it last, and this should be removed before cooking.

Using the pips: the pips of citrus fruit help the marmalade to set so these are very important. In the recipes the instructions state these should be tied in muslin and soaked, then simmered with the fruit to extract the maximum amount of pectin. If you don't have any muslin, put the pips into the amount of water given in the recipe and simmer for 10 to 15 minutes, then strain and measure the liquid. You will find it is now less than the amount given in the particular recipe so add sufficient cold water to make up the quantity. The pips can then be discarded.

CUTTING UP THE PEEL

Cutting the peel for marmalade does take a long time. If doing this by hand, use a really sharp knife and a firm board on which to place the peel. It is, however, very easy if you put the peel and pulp through the shredding equipment of an electric mixing machine or food processor. Make sure all the juice has been squeezed out first, for the firmer the pulp and peel the easier it is to shred neatly. The peel and pulp can also be put through a mincer or mincing attachment – this is very successful if a fine-cut peel is required.

COVERING THE PAN

Most recipes for marmalade use a fairly high quantity of water to allow for evaporation as the peel softens. This means that if you leave the heat under the pan sufficiently low covering is not essential. If, however, you find that the liquid is evaporating too quickly then do cover the pan. Many preserving pans do not have lids, so use a thick piece of aluminium foil over the top.

FLAVOURING MARMALADE

All the various kinds of marmalade in this section can be flavoured with brandy or whisky to make a more exciting preserve. Allow 1 to 2 tablespoons whisky for every 450 g/1 lb (2 cups) sugar used. Add the whisky just before the preserve has reached setting point. Another interesting variation to marmalade recipes is to use some apple juice instead of water. This is particularly good with tangerine or kumquat marmalades where the flavour of apple juice blends very well. It can be used with the other citrus fruits too. Use half water and half apple juice. As an alternative, use still, not sparkling, dry cider mixed half and half with water.

MARMALADE IN A PRESSURE COOKER

The pressure cooker can be used to soften citrus fruit for marmalade within a very short time. Since the cooking time is so brief; compared with the conventional method, use just half the amount of water given in the marmalade recipes. The comments on pages 13 to 14 provide basic information on using a pressure cooker for preserving, and on the limitations on the quantity that can be cooked at one time. The instruction book with your particular cooker will give detailed information, but on the whole you will find that the peel of oranges is softened within 10 minutes at 10 lb (medium) pressure and that of lemons within 8 minutes.

MARMALADE IN A MICROWAVE OVEN

This method of cooking citrus fruit is less satisfactory than when using a pressure cooker for the peel does not become as soft as it should. It is better, therefore, to use either a conventional method of cooking the fruit or a pressure cooker when dealing with small quantities.

If the peel or skin in marmalade is still tough when the preserve is cooked, is there any way of softening it?
Sadly there is not. The peel or skin must be softened before adding the sugar; that is why gentle simmering in the first stage of cooking the peel for marmalade or the fruit for jam is so important.
   When making a conserve, in which sugar is generally added to the uncooked fruit, it important to choose only fruits that have no skin or a very tender skin.

BANANA MARMALADE

Cooking time: 1½ to 2 hours • Makes 2.25 kg/5 lb marmalade

The inclusion of bananas in a lemon marmalade makes a very pleasant preserve. The dry sherry is not essential but does make it more interesting. Be sure to use bananas that are very firm and not too ripe.

Metric/Imperial	Ingredients	American
450 g/1 lb	lemons	1 lb
1.35 litres/2¼ pints	water	5²/₃ cups
6 medium	bananas	6 medium
1.35 kg/3 lb	sugar	6 cups
150 ml/¼ pint	dry sherry	²/₃ cup

See Lemon Marmalade on page 93 for how to prepare, soak and simmer the lemons. Peel the bananas and cut into 1.5 cm/½ inch slices, add to the lemon preserve with the sugar and sherry, stir over a low heat until the sugar has dissolved then raise the heat and boil rapidly until setting point is reached. Stir to distribute the fruit then spoon into hot jars and seal down.

- Omit the sherry and use 150 ml/¼ pint (⅔ cup) extra water.

Banana and Orange Marmalade: use 450 g/1 lb sweet oranges or half sweet and half Seville oranges with the bananas. Using only Seville oranges will overwhelm the flavour of the bananas. Add 3 tablespoons (3¾ tablespoons) lemon juice with the sugar.

GINGER MARMALADE

Cooking time: 40 to 45 minutes • For yield see page 68

Although called a marmalade, this is really an apple, gooseberry or rhubarb jelly with pieces of preserved ginger added. Rather less water is used than for Apple Jelly, so you have a more concentrated juice that blends well with the ginger. Cooking apples are better than crab apples for this preserve.

Metric/Imperial	Ingredients	American
1.35 kg/3 lb	*cooking apples*	3 lb
600 ml/1 pint	*water*	2½ cups
	sugar, see method	
	preserved ginger, see method	

Cut up the apples – do not peel or core them – add them to the water and cook until a smooth purée. Strain through a jelly bag or muslin, as described under Apple Jelly (pages 70, 72-3). Measure the juice and to each 600 ml/1 pint (2½ cups) allow 450 g/1 lb (2 cups) sugar and 3 tablespoons (3¾ tablespoons) preserved ginger cut into 1.5 cm/½ inch dice. Heat the juice, add the sugar and stir over a low heat until the sugar has dissolved, then add the ginger, with any ginger syrup adhering to it. Raise the heat and boil until setting point is reached. Cool for a short time, then stir to distribute the pieces of ginger. Spoon into hot jars and seal down.

Variations

- Use 900 ml/1½ pints (3¾ cups) water to give a less strongly flavoured jelly.
- Use green gooseberries and treat them as apples.
- Use rhubarb but add 1½ tablespoons (nearly 2 tablespoons) lemon juice to every 450 g/1 lb (2 cups) sugar.

GRAPEFRUIT MARMALADE

Cooking time: 1½ to 2 hours • Makes 1.8 kg/good 4 lb marmalade

Grapefruit marmalade makes a most pleasant preserve. Although grapefruit has a sharp flavour, the preserve will set better if some lemon juice is included. Pink grapefruit have become much more plentiful and these make a most attractive-looking marmalade as well as one with an exceptionally good flavour.

Metric/Imperial	Ingredients	American
2 medium*	grapefruit	2 medium*
1.5 litres/2½ pints	water	6¾ cups
1.125kg/2½ lb	sugar	5 cups
4 tablespoons	lemon juice	5 tablespoons

*total weight of about 450 g/1 lb

Cut the grapefruit into halves and scoop out the pips – tie these in muslin. Squeeze out the grapefruit juice and put this on one side. Shred the peel and pith finely and soak in the water with the bag of pips for several hours or overnight. Simmer the fruit gently with the bag of pips until soft then remove the pips and add the sugar, grapefruit juice and lemon juice. Stir over a low heat until the sugar has dissolved then boil rapidly until setting point is reached. Cool slightly then stir to distribute the peel. Spoon into hot jars and seal down.

Variations

- If the grapefruit are much bigger or smaller than average weigh them and increase or decrease the amounts of water, sugar and lemon juice in proportion.

Pomelo Marmalade: these fruits are not particularly plentiful; they look like a very large grapefruit and their flavour is not dissimilar although much sweeter. To 450 g/1 lb fruit use the same amount of water and sugar as for Grapefruit Marmalade but as the fruit has very little natural pectin increase the amount of lemon juice to 150 ml/¼ pint (⅔ cup).

Ugli Fruit Marmalade: these fruits are becoming more plentiful. The flavour is like a mixture of grapefruit and orange. Use the same proportions of fruit, water and sugar as for Grapefruit Marmalade but increase the amount of lemon juice to 6 tablespoons (7½ tablespoons) to 450 g/1 lb fruit.

JELLY MARMALADES

Cooking time: 1½ hours • For yield see below

While the recipe below is based on Seville oranges, any citrus fruits can be made into jelly marmalades. These are ideal for those people who like the flavour of the fruit but not the peel. Because the peel is not included – or only a little top rind, often called zest, is used – the marmalade does tend to taste sweeter. Do not waste any part of the fruit, otherwise the marmalade will not set.

Metric/Imperial	Ingredients	American
450 g/1 lb	Seville oranges	1 lb
1.8 litres/3 pints	water	7½ cups
1.35 kg/3 lb	sugar	6 cups
4 tablespoons	lemon juice	5 tablespoons

If you want a jelly marmalade with some peel, pare the top rind from 1 or 2 of the fruits and cut this into very thin shreds. Do not include any pith, but do retain this. Halve the oranges, squeeze out the juice and put this on one side. Remove the pips. If you do not want any peel at all then simply halve all the oranges, remove the juice and pips. Tie the pips with all the pith and pulp into a strong thick piece of muslin to form a bag. Put this into the water and soak overnight. The shredded peel, if used, should be soaked at the same time. Simmer the peel with the bag of oranges, pith, pulp and pips until the peel is tender. Remove the bag of fruit, which can then be discarded. Follow this method even if not using the shredded top zest but see under Variations. Add the sugar with the orange and lemon juice and stir over a low heat until the sugar has dissolved. Boil rapidly until setting point is reached. If there is peel in the jelly marmalade allow this to cool slightly and stiffen, then stir to distribute the peel before spooning into the hot jars. If there is no peel the jelly can be poured immediately into hot jars and sealed down.

Variations

- If no peel is required in the jelly marmalade, first halve the fruit and squeeze out the juice then soak all the chopped up oranges and pips in the water as above. There is no need to tie them in muslin. After soaking, simmer gently in the water for 1½ hours, then strain the liquid and discard all the oranges. Add the sugar with the orange and lemon juice and proceed as above.

Other Jelly Marmalades: use the proportions for any of the citrus fruit marmalades in this chapter but follow the method given for the Sweet Seville Orange Marmalade above.

Yield

This will depend on the particular recipe. Each 450 g/1 lb (2 cups) of sugar used should produce 750 g/1²⁄₃ lb marmalade.

KIWIFRUIT MARMALADE

Cooking time: 1¼ to 1½ hours • Makes 2.25 kg/5 lb marmalade

Sweet oranges are better in this preserve, as the flavour of Seville (bitter) oranges rather overwhelms the taste of the kiwifruit.

Metric/Imperial	Ingredients	American
2 large	oranges	2 large
1 large	lemon	1 large
900 ml/1½ pints	water	3¾ cups
900 g/2 lb	kiwifruit pulp, see method	2 lb
1.35 kg/3 lb	sugar	6 cups

Halve the oranges and lemon and squeeze out the juice – put this on one side. Take out any pips and put them into a muslin bag. Shred the pulp and peel of the oranges and lemon very finely and soak in the water overnight with the bag of pips. Simmer gently until the citrus peel is absolutely tender. Halve the kiwifruits and scoop out the pulp. Weigh this and dice it neatly, then add to the pan, together with any juice that may have flowed on to the chopping board. Add the orange and lemon juice and simmer gently for 5 to 10 minutes, or until the kiwifruit is very hot. Add the sugar and stir over a low heat until dissolved. Raise the heat and boil rapidly until setting point is reached. Allow the preserve to cool for a time in the pan, then stir to distribute the peel and pieces of kiwifruit and spoon into hot jars. Seal down.

KUMQUAT MARMALADE

Cooking time: 1 to 1¼ hours • Makes 1.5 kg/3⅓ lb marmalade

These small fruit, which look like miniature oranges, have become very popular during the last few years. People who like bitter flavours are quite happy to eat them raw. Although kumquats look like citrus fruits, and are in fact related to them, they belong to a different genus known as Fortunella. *They are grown mainly in the Far East and Australia.*

Metric/Imperial	Ingredients	American
675g/1½ lb	kumquats	1½ lb
900 ml/1½ pints	water	3¾ cups
900 g/2 lb	sugar	4 cups
2 tablespoons	lemon juice	2½ tablespoons

Slice the kumquats and cover with the water. Allow to stand for several hours or overnight. Simmer in the water until tender then add the sugar and lemon juice. Stir over a low heat until the sugar has dissolved then raise the heat and boil rapidly until setting point is reached. Cool for a short time in the pan then stir to distribute the peel. Spoon into hot jars and seal down.

LEMON MARMALADE

Cooking time: 1½ to 2 hours • Makes 1.8 kg/good 4 lb marmalade

Lemons make an excellent marmalade; they are better cut up before cooking, as in the recipe below, rather than boiled whole.

Metric/Imperial	Ingredients	American
450 g/1 lb	lemons	1 lb
15 litres/2½ pints	water	6¼ cups
1.125kg/2½ lb	sugar	5 cups

Halve the lemons, remove the pips and tie these in muslin. Squeeze out the lemon juice and put it on one side. Cut up the lemon peel and pith and soak in the water, with the bag of pips, for several hours or overnight. Simmer the peel in the water with the pips until tender. Check carefully that the peel is tender (see page 87) for lemon peel is often fairly tough. Remove the bag of pips and then add the sugar and lemon juice.

Stir over a low heat until the sugar has melted then raise the heat and boil rapidly until setting point is reached. Allow the marmalade to cool for a short time in the pan then stir to distribute the peel. Spoon into hot jars and seal down.

Variations

Chunky Lemon Marmalade: use only 1.2 litres/2 pints (5 cups) water with the same amount of sugar; this gives a slightly thicker marmalade. The peel can be cut into somewhat larger pieces.

Lime Marmalade: use limes instead of lemons in either of the recipes above. Since limes have relatively little juice compared with lemons it is a good idea to allow 1 tablespoon (1¼ tablespoons) lemon juice or extra lime juice to each 450 g/1 lb limes. Add the lemon or extra lime juice with the sugar.

Lemon and Lime Marmalade: use 225 g/8 oz (½ lb) lemons and 225 g/ 8 oz (½ lb) limes in the first Variation recipe.

Lemon or Lime Jelly Marmalade: follow the directions on pages 91 to 92.

MINT MARMALADE

Cooking time: 1½ to 2 hours • Makes 1.5 kg/3⅓ lb marmalade

This is an unusual marmalade but one that takes the place of a chutney. It blends very well with hot or cold lamb.

Metric/Imperial	Ingredients	American
	as Lemon Marmalade, page 93	
3 tablespoons	*finely chopped mint*	3¾ tablespoons

Make the Lemon Marmalade as described. When setting point has just been reached add the mint and stir to distribute. Cool a little in the pan so the marmalade thickens slightly then stir again to distribute both the peel and the mint. Spoon into hot jars and seal down.

MARMALADE WITH CERTO

Cooking time: 1¼ hours • Makes nearly 4 kg/9 lb marmalade

This recipe makes a marmalade with finely shredded peel and no bitter flavour. It would not set easily without the commercial pectin.

Metric/Imperial	Ingredients	American
8 to 10	*Seville oranges**	8 to 10
2	*lemons**	2
1.2 litres/2 pints	*water, plus any extra required, see method*	5 cups
2.25 kg/5 lb	*sugar*	10 cups

15 to 25 g/½ to 1 oz	**butter, optional**	1 to 2 tablespoons
250 ml/9 fl oz	**Certo**	1⅛ cups

the oranges and lemons together should weigh 1.35 kg/3 lb

Remove the peel from the fruit in quarters, cut away and discard half of the white pith from this peel, leaving just the orange and lemon rind (zest). Shred this very finely and place in the preserving pan with the water. Bring to the boil, cover tightly and simmer until the peel can be easily crushed (see page 87). Stir from time to time. Meanwhile squeeze out the juice from the oranges and lemons and cut up the pulp from the peeled fruit. Discard the pips and any tough pith in this particular recipe. Add the fruit pulp and juice to the tender peel and simmer, without covering the pan, for a further 20 minutes. Measure all the cooked pulp – it should be 1.75 litres/3 pints (7½ cups); if less, add a little water. Return to the pan and heat gently. Add the sugar and stir gently over a low heat until dissolved. At this stage add the butter if desired, for this lessens the formation of scum. Raise the heat and boil rapidly for 5 minutes. Remove the pan from the heat and stir in the Certo. Stir and skim alternately for 7 minutes, until the marmalade starts to thicken, then spoon into hot jars and seal down.

MARROW MARMALADE

Cooking time: 40 minutes • Makes 1.5 kg/3⅓ lb marmalade

It is important to use a mature autumn marrow for this preserve as these have very much more flavour than young spring marrows.

Metric/Imperial	Ingredients	American
900 g/2 lb	**marrow, weight when peeled and seeds removed**	2 lb
3 large	**oranges**	3 large
2 medium	**lemons**	2 medium
3 tablespoons	**orange juice**	3¾ tablespoons
4 tablespoons	**lemon juice**	5 tablespoons
900 g/2 lb	**sugar, see method**	4 cups

Cut the marrow flesh into 2.5 cm/1 inch dice. Finely grate the rind from the oranges and lemons. Halve one orange and squeeze out the 3 tablespoons (3¾ tablespoons) juice required, then halve one or both of the lemons and squeeze out the amount of juice in the ingredients. Add the grated rinds and juice to the marrow together with the sugar. In this particular marmalade you can use either granulated sugar or a soft, light brown sugar for extra flavour and colour. Cover the container and leave the marrow soaking for 2 hours then heat gently, stirring all the time, until the sugar has dissolved. Raise the heat and boil steadily until the marrow is tender, but the dice still unbroken, and setting point is reached. Cool slightly, stir to distribute the whole pieces of marrow then spoon into hot jars and seal down.

- Instead of using just the juice, halve the three oranges, carefully scoop out the orange pulp, making sure it is free from skin and pips, and add to the marrow.

ORANGE PEEL AND APPLE MARMALADE

Cooking time: 1½ hours • Makes 2.25 kg/5 lb marmalade

This is a recipe that became quite famous during the Second World War. Very few oranges were brought into the country during that period and those that were imported were sold only on ration for small children. Mothers would save the peel to make this preserve. Although it looks cloudy, like a jam, it has a very good flavour.

Metric/Imperial	Ingredients	American
peel from 450 g/1 lb sweet oranges		
1.2 to 1.8 litres/ 2 to 3 pints	water	5 to 7½ cups
450 g/1 lb	cooking apples, weight when peeled and cored	1 lb
1.35 kg/3 lb	sugar	6 cups

Shred the orange peel as finely as desired – do not remove any of the pith. Soak for several hours in the water; use the smaller amount if the peel is very finely shredded for it will not take as long to soften. Simmer the orange peel in the water until nearly tender. Weigh the peeled and cored apples – you can tie the parings and cores in muslin to give more flavour and setting quality to the marmalade. Dice the apples and add to the orange peel. Continue simmering, with the bag of apple parings and cores, until the peel is really tender and the apples have formed a soft purée. Remove the bag of parings and cores if using. Add the sugar and stir over a low heat until dissolved. Raise the heat and boil rapidly until setting point is reached. Cool for a short time then stir to distribute the peel, spoon into hot jars and seal down.

Variations

- For a less sweet preserve use only 1.2 kg/2½ lb sugar.
- Add 2 tablespoons (2½ tablespoons) lemon juice with the sugar for a firmer set and more flavour.

SWEET ORANGE MARMALADE (1)

Cooking time: 1¼ to 1½ hours • Makes 1.5 kg/3⅓ lb marmalade

Sweet oranges can be cooked whole without soaking, just as the Chunky Seville Orange Marmalade on page 98. A generous amount of lemon juice is necessary to ensure the preserve sets well. Oranges from different parts of the world are available throughout the year, so this is a preserve that can be made at any time. Choose large juicy fruit that is as fresh as possible to ensure the best results. Because sweet oranges cook more rapidly than Seville oranges, the amount of water should be less, and less sugar is needed for a good flavour.

Metric/Imperial	Ingredients	American
450 g/1 lb	sweet oranges	1 lb
1.2 litres/2 pints	water	5 cups
900 g/2 lb	sugar	4 cups
4 tablespoons	lemon juice	5 tablespoons

Follow the method of making marmalade as given on page 98.

SWEET ORANGE MARMALADE (2)

Cooking time: 1¼ to 1½ hours • Makes 1.5 kg/3⅓ lb marmalade

This recipe enables you to make as fine or as chunky a cut marmalade as desired.

Metric/Imperial	Ingredients	Amer:can
450 g/1 lb	sweet oranges	1 lb
1.2 litres/2 pints	water	5 cups
900 g/2 lb	sugar	4 cups
4 tablespoons	lemon juice	5 tablespoons

Follow the method of making marmalade as given on page 98.

Variations

Orange and Lemon Marmalade: use 2 large oranges and 2 large lemons with 1.5 litres/2½ pints (6¼ cups) water and 1.125 kg/2½ lb (5 cups) sugar plus 3 tablespoons (3¾ tablespoons) extra lemon juice. Follow the method of making Sweet Seville Marmalade on page 98. In this variation 1.125 kg/2½ lb (5 cups) sugar makes 1.8 kg/good 4 lb marmalade.

Orange and Tangerine Marmalade: use 225 g/8 oz (½ lb) sweet oranges and 225 g/8 oz (½ lb) tangerines or similar fruit with the same amount of water and sugar as the first recipe but add 5 tablespoons (6¼ tablespoons) lemon juice. Follow the recipe for Sweet Seville Marmalade on page 98.

SWEET SEVILLE ORANGE MARMALADE

Cooking time: 1½ to 2 hours • Makes 2.25 kg/5 lb marmalade

This recipe gives a pleasantly sweet preserve with the distinctive flavour of Seville oranges.

Metric/Imperial	Ingredients	American
450 g/1 lb	**Seville oranges**	1 lb
1.8 litres/3 pints	**water**	7½ cups
1.35 kg/3 lb	**sugar**	6 cups
4 tablespoons	**lemon juice**	5 tablespoons

Halve the oranges and remove the pips – tie these in muslin. Squeeze out the orange juice and put this on one side. Cut the peel and pith as finely as desired and soak in the water for several hours or overnight, together with the bag of pips. Simmer the peel in the water with the bag of pips until tender, then remove the pips. Add the sugar, orange and lemon juice and stir over a low heat until the sugar has dissolved. Raise the heat and boil rapidly until the setting point is reached. Allow the marmalade to cool for a short time in the pan until it begins to stiffen then stir to distribute the peel. Spoon into hot jars and seal down.

Variations

• Use only 1.5 litres/2½ pints (6¼ cups) water with 1.125 kg/2½ lb (5 cups) sugar and the same amount of lemon juice. This gives a slightly thicker and less sweet marmalade.

Sweeter Seville Orange Marmalade: use 1 sweet orange to every 2 Seville oranges. Weigh the fruit and follow the proportions in the first recipe or the variation given above.

CHUNKY SEVILLE ORANGE MARMALADE

Cooking time: 2 hours • Makes 1.5 kg/3⅓ lb marmalade

In this recipe the fruit is not cut up but the oranges are simmered whole until tender. They are not soaked first. The main recipe below is for traditional bitter marmalade. If the fruit is very fresh, lemon juice is not necessary, but see under variations.

Metric/Imperial	Ingredients	American
450 g/1 lb	**Seville oranges**	1 lb
1.2 litres/2 pints	**water**	5 cups
900 g/2 lb	**sugar**	4 cups

Put the whole fruit in the pan with the water. Simmer slowly for about 1½ hours, or until a wooden skewer or knitting needle pierces the skin with ease. Remove the fruit from the water and cool until it can be handled. Halve the fruit, remove the pips and put these pips back into the pan with the liquid. Boil steadily for 10 minutes then strain the liquid and return it to the pan. Cut up the fruit into small chunks and add to the liquid. Bring the pulp to the boil then add the sugar. Stir over a low heat until the sugar has dissolved then raise the heat and boil rapidly until setting point is reached. Allow to cool in the pan until slightly stiffened then stir to distribute the peel. Spoon into hot jars and seal down.

Variations

- If you have had the Seville oranges for some days then add 2 tablespoons (2½ tablespoons) lemon juice. This is also important if the fruit has been frozen and then defrosted. The lemon juice should be added with the sugar.

Dark Chunky Marmalade: use half white and half dark brown sugar, or use 825 g/1¾ lb (3½ cups) white sugar and 100 g/4 oz (scant ⅓ cup) black treacle or molasses. This should be added with the sugar.

For a darker marmalade which is much milder in flavour use the amount of sugar given in the first recipe plus 1 level tablespoon (1¼ tablespoons) treacle or molasses.

QUINCE AND LEMON MARMALADE

Cooking time: 1 hour • Makes 2.25 kg/5 lb marmalade

The Spanish name for quince is 'marmelo' and as this fruit is frequently made into various preserves in that country this may be the origin of the word 'marmalade'. Quinces do make a splendid breakfast preserve.

Metric/Imperial	Ingredients	American
450 g/1 lb	lemons	1 lb
1.35 kg/3 lb	ripe quinces	3 lb
1.5 litres/2½ pints	water	6¼ cups
1.35 kg/3 lb	sugar	6 cups

Finely grate the peel from the lemons or cut away the top rind (zest) and then slice this into narrow shreds. Halve the fruit and squeeze out the juice. Put this on one side. Keep the pulp, pips and pith from the lemons. Peel and core the quinces. Put the parings and cores with the lemon pith, pips and peel and tie securely in muslin. Cut the quince pulp into small dice or narrow strips, add half the lemon juice and cover the container so the fruit remains a good colour. Put the grated or shredded lemon rind and the muslin bag of quince parings and lemon pith, etc., into the water and simmer for 20 minutes. Add the diced quinces and simmer until soft. Remove the muslin bag and add the sugar and remainder of the lemon juice. Stir over a low heat until the sugar has dissolved then boil rapidly until setting point is reached. Cool slightly, then stir to distribute the whole pieces of quince. Spoon into hot jars and seal down.

Variations

Quince and Orange Marmalade: use sweet oranges in place of lemons and the same amount of water and sugar together with 4 tablespoons (5 tablespoons) lemon juice. Grate or shred the orange rind (zest) then halve the oranges and squeeze out the juice. Prepare the quinces as above. Put half the lemon juice and all the orange juice over the quinces and allow these to stand while simmering the quince parings and orange pulp, pips and pith. Put the quinces and their juice into the preserving pan and simmer until tender then add the sugar and remaining lemon juice and continue as the recipe above.

Pear and Lemon Marmalade: use firm dessert pears in place of quinces in the main recipe above.

TANGERINE MARMALADE

Cooking time: 1¼ to 1½ hours • Makes 1.125 kg/2½ lb marmalade

There are many small citrus fruits that are somewhat similar to tangerines. Many of these, like satsumas and clementines, are seedless. This makes them excellent to eat as dessert fruit, but means that they lack pectin, so a generous amount of lemon juice is essential if using them to make preserves.

Metric/Imperial	Ingredients	American
450 g/1 lb	tangerines or similar	1 lb
900 ml/1½ pints	water	3¾ cups
675g/1½ lb	sugar	3 cups
5 tablespoons	lemon juice	6¼ tablespoons

Halve the fruit, take out the pips (if there are any) and tie these in muslin. Squeeze out the juice and put on one side. Cut up the peel, pulp and pith and soak for several hours, or overnight, in the water, adding the bag of pips. Simmer in the water until tender, then remove the pips. Add the sugar, the juice from the fruit and the lemon juice. Stir over a low heat until the sugar has dissolved then boil rapidly until setting point is reached. Cool for a short time, then stir to distribute the peel and spoon into hot jars and seal down.

The marmalade I made with Sevllle oranges did not set properly. I used fruit that I had frozen as I had no time to make the preserve when the oranges were in season. I have never had any problems with marmalade before, why this time?
Freezing fruit destroys a little of the natural setting quality in the fruit and therefore it is necessary to add extra lemon juice or to use slightly more fruit to increase the pectin content. This is explained on page 14.

THREE FRUIT MARMALADE (1)

Cooking time: 1¼ hours • Makes 1.5 kg/3⅓ lb marmalade

The preserve made using this particular combination of fruits is often known as Scotch Marmalade. The three fruits should give a total weight of about 500 g/1 lb 2 oz.

Metric/Imperial	Ingredients	American
1 medium	**grapefruit**	1 medium
1 medium	**sweet orange**	1 medium
1 medium	**lemon**	1 medium
1.2 litres/2 pints	**water**	5 cups
900 g/2 lb	**sugar**	4 cups
2 tablespoons	**lemon juice**	2½ tablespoons

Halve the three fruits, remove the pips and tie them in muslin. Squeeze out the juice from the fruits and put this on one side. Cut up the pulp – do not discard any pith. Put the pulp to soak in the water with the bag of pips and leave overnight. Simmer the fruits in the water with the bag of pips until the peel is really soft. Remove the pips, then add the sugar and stir over a low heat until this has dissolved. Raise the heat and boil rapidly until setting point is reached. Allow to cool in the pan for a short time, stir to distribute the peel then spoon into hot jars and seal down.

Variations

Three Fruit Marmalade (2): use 1 medium grapefruit with 2 sweet oranges and 2 lemons and prepare the fruit as in the recipe above. This marmalade does not have such a pronounced grapefruit flavour. Use the amount of fruit in Three Fruit Marmalade (1) or (2).

For a fairly chunky marmalade add 1.5 litres/2½ pints (6¼ cups) water to the fruit and pips and simmer until tender.

For a less chunky marmalade use 1.8 litres/3 pints (7½ cups) water. In this particular recipe the pulp is measured after cooking. After this, choose between the fairly sweet or less sweet marmalade below.

For a fairly sweet marmalade use 550 g/1¼ lb (2½ cups) sugar and 1½ tablespoons (nearly 2 tablespoons) lemon juice to each 600 ml/1 pint (2½ cups) fruit pulp.

For a less sweet marmalade use 450 g/1 lb (2 cups) sugar and 2 tablespoons (2½ tablespoons) lemon juice for each 600 ml/1 pint (2½ cups) pulp. Heat the pulp, add the sugar and lemon juice and continue as the first recipe.

Four Fruit Marmalade: use the three fruits in the first recipe plus 2 bitter oranges with 1.6 litres/2¾ pints (scant 7 cups) water and 1.25 kg/2¾ lb (5½ cups) sugar and 3 tablespoons (3¾ tablespoons) lemon juice.

Five Fruit Marmalade (1): use the three fruits given in the first recipe plus 1 lime and 1 bitter orange with the same proportions of water, sugar and lemon juice as in the Four Fruit Marmalade.

Five Fruit Marmalade (2): use the three fruits given in the first recipe plus 1 bitter orange and 2 clementines or tangerines with the same proportions of water, sugar and lemon juice as for the Four Fruit Marmalade.

Yield

In these variations each 500 g/1 lb 2 oz (2¼ cups) sugar will make 800 g/nearly 1¾ lb marmalade.

TOMATO MARMALADE

Cooking time: 1½ hours • Makes 2.62 kg/5¾ lb marmalade

This is one very pleasing way to use up green tomatoes. It makes a good breakfast preserve for the lemons add flavour to the tomatoes.

Metric/Imperial	Ingredients	American
3	lemons*	3
900 ml/1½ pints	water	3¾ cups
1.35 g/3 lb	green tomatoes	3 lb
1.57 kg/3½ lb	sugar	7 cups

these should weigh about 350 g/12 oz (¾ lb)

Halve the lemons, remove the pips and tie these in muslin, then squeeze out the juice and put this on one side. Cut up the peel and pith of the lemons finely and soak for several hours or overnight in the water. Simmer gently, with the bag of pips, until the peel is almost tender. Meanwhile quarter the tomatoes if small or cut into wedges if large, add to the lemons and continue cooking until the tomatoes are soft but not broken into smaller pieces. Remove the bag of pips. Add the sugar and lemon juice, stir over a low heat until the sugar has dissolved then raise the heat and boil rapidly until setting point is reached. Cool until the marmalade stiffens slightly, then stir to distribute the peel and pieces of tomato. Spoon into hot jars and seal down.

FRUIT BUTTERS, CHEESES AND CURDS

These preserves have many purposes, for they can be served instead of jams or conserve but they are equally good as accompaniments to main dishes or as quick snacks with cheese. Some of them are ideal for rather unusual desserts.

A fruit butter is very like jam except it is stiffer and smoother in texture. It forms a thicker topping on bread or filling for tarts and cakes. As the name suggests a small amount of butter is often added to the fruit and sugar. Spoonfuls of fruit butter make an excellent change from chutneys or sweet pickles with savoury dishes.

A fruit cheese is almost the same as a butter except it should be stiffer, so it can be cut into neat slices. This makes it an excellent preserve to garnish open sandwiches or to serve as an elegant accompaniment to cheese and other savoury ingredients.

All fruits used for jams could be made into butters or cheeses, if the fruit is cooked until very stiff, then sieved or liquidized to make an absolutely smooth purée. Liquidising is not suitable if the mixture contains tough skins and hard pips or stones. The refreshing fruits are the best, however, and they are used in a number of recipes in this section.

When sieving fruit for a butter or cheese, or for any purpose, use a nylon, or hair sieve, *not* a metal sieve. Metal is inclined to flavour the fruit and it can spoil the colour slightly.

Some butters and cheeses are made with a relatively low amount of sugar, so these should not be treated as preserves that keep for a long time. Cover the mixture carefully to exclude the air and retain the pleasantly soft texture. Store in the refrigerator or freeze the mixture in the containers for long-term keeping.

Fruit curds are richer in flavour than either butters or cheeses, for they are made with fruit and sugar plus a generous amount of butter and eggs. Strangely enough, the alternative name for Lemon Curd is Lemon Cheese, which is not quite correct, since a good curd should be the consistency of lightly whipped cream and not too stiff. Although citrus fruits are generally chosen for curds, other rather acid fruits, such as gooseberries, could be used. If made with the full amount of sugar and covered to exclude the air, curds should keep like jam or similar preserves.

MAKING FRUIT SYRUPS

During the Second World War, citrus fruits were unobtainable, apart from very infrequent supplies of oranges which were rationed to small children (see page 96). Rose hip syrup was made by many mothers to ensure that their families would have an adequate amount of Vitamin C. Fruit syrups keep well if sterilized after filling the containers. Now that coulis of various kinds are served instead of thickened sauces with ice cream, cold desserts and meat, fish and poultry dishes, many of the fruit syrups could form a basis for these.

CONTAINERS FOR FRUIT BUTTERS AND CHEESES

These preserves make splendid gifts, and they look very attractive when packed in ornamental containers. The fruit butters or cheeses can be put into heated jars, just like jam, after cooking but as they are thicker in consistency this makes it more difficult to remove neat portions. It is, therefore, better to use bowls or wide bottling jars from which it is easy to spoon or cut the preserve. The containers must be sterilized in exactly the same way as jam jars (see page 15).

If the butter or cheese contains a high percentage of sugar then the preserve will keep like a jam, but if a relatively small proportion of sugar is used then it must be frozen, or stored for a limited time only in the refrigerator. Make sure the containers used are suitable for freezing. If you intend to freeze the preserve, allow a good air space at the top of the container, for although the fruit will appear thick in texture, it contains a high amount of water which will expand during freezing.

Curds can be put into heated jam jars and covered just like jam if made with the full amount of sugar. If a lower amount is used then the preserve must be frozen, or kept in the refrigerator for a limited time.

ADDING FLOWERS TO BUTTERS AND CHEESES

Some edible flowers or leaves can be added to the fruit butters and cheeses that follow to give a subtle flavour and, in some cases, an interesting decoration. Make quite sure they are well washed before using. Add the flowers or leaves to the fruit before cooking. Although they are particularly good with fruit butters and cheese, flowers are an excellent way to add flavour to fruits in jellies, jams and conserves. Choose flowers or leaves that will enhance, not overwhelm, the natural flavour of the fruit. Here are some suggestions:

- Cook 1 or 2 small bunches of elderflowers with the blackberries, damsons, or quinces on pages 105 to 107 and 111 to 112.
- About 12 blue borage flowers or the same number of individual cowslip flowers blend well with the quantity of grapes used in the recipe on pages 107 to 108 for Grape Butter or Cheese. The preserve looks attractive if several blossoms are placed at the bottom of each container before filling it with the hot mixture. When turned out the preserve is topped with the flowers.

- Scented geranium leaves blend well with Guava Butter on page 79. Add only 2 or 3 to the quantity of fruit given for their flavour is very strong.
- Saffron strands or powder (these are dried stamens from special crocuses) are ideal for colouring and flavouring Pumpkin Butter and the other fruits on pages 110 to 111. Use about 10 to 12 strands or ¼ to ½ teaspoon of the powder to the quantity of fruit in the recipe.

ADDING ALCOHOL TO BUTTERS AND CHEESES

Mention is made of the special choice of alcohol in some of the recipes in this section, but a little wine, spirit or liqueur can be added to all the butters or cheeses that follow.

Use 1 to 2 tablespoons to each 600 ml/1 pint (2½ cups) fruit pulp. Add this with the sugar.

- Port wine is excellent with dark or red fruits, like blackberries, damsons, loganberries and boysenberries (see pages 105 to 106 and 108 to 109).
- Dry or sweet sherry enhances the flavour of Pumpkin Butter and the other fruits on pages 110 to 111.
- Whisky or brandy blends well with most fruits.
- Apricot brandy is a natural choice for the Apricot Butter on page 110 and cherry brandy for the Sharp Cherry Cheese on page 107.

BLACKBERRY AND APPLE CHEESE

Cooking time: 40 minutes • For yield see end of recipe

This makes an excellent accompaniment to roast game or duck or goose. It is also good with cheese or can be adapted as a dessert, see under Variations.

Metric/Imperial	Ingredients	American
900 g/2 lb	cooking apples	2 lb
675 g/1½ lb	blackberries	1½ lb
4 tablespoons	water	5 tablespoons
	butter, see method	
	sugar, see method	

Cut the apples into small pieces – do not peel or core. Put into the pan with the blackberries and water. Simmer gently until a thick pulp. Rub through a sieve and then measure the purée. To each 600 ml/1 pint (2½ cups) allow 25 g/1 oz (2 tablespoons) butter and 400 g/14 oz (1¾ cups) sugar. Return the fruit purée to the pan, heat this gently then add the butter and sugar. Stir over a low heat until the butter and sugar have dissolved then raise the heat and boil steadily, not too rapidly, until setting point is reached and the mixture is very thick. Spoon into hot containers and seal down.

Yield

Each 450 g/1 lb (2 cups) sugar makes 750 g/1²⁄₃ lb fruit cheese.

Variations

Blackberry and Apple Butter: use 150 ml/¼ pint (²⁄₃ cup) water in which to cook the fruit. If the purée seems very thick after sieving add a little more water. The butter should be the consistency of a thick jam.

Blackberry and Apple Dessert: cut the cheese into thick slices or the butter into neat spoonfuls. Top with chopped hazelnuts and serve with ice cream or fromage frais.

Spiced Blackberry and Apple Cheese: add 1 teaspoon ground cinnamon and about 4 cloves when cooking the fruit.

Banana and Apple Cheese: omit the blackberries in the recipe. When the apples are nearly tender add 450 g/1 lb peeled bananas, mashed with 2 tablespoons (2½ tablespoons) lemon juice and 3 teaspoons finely grated lemon rind. Continue cooking until the apples are quite soft then sieve as the recipe above. Measure the purée and allow 25 g/1 oz (2 tablespoons) butter and 225 g/8 oz (1 cup) sugar to each 600 ml/1 pint (2½ cups). Continue as the recipe. This cheese must be stored in the refrigerator or frozen as the sugar content is low. The smaller amount of sugar makes a preserve with a very good sharp flavour.

DAMSON CHEESE

Cooking time: 25 to 30 minutes • For yield see end of recipe

This is an excellent way of using damsons, for the stones are removed when sieving but the thick cheese retains all the rich flavour of the fruit. It is particularly good as an accompaniment to cold duck or pork. It can, however, be served as a dessert, see under Quince Butter, page 111.

Metric/Imperial	Ingredients	American
1.35 kg/3 lb	**damsons**	*3 lb*
300 ml/¹⁄₂ pint	**water**	*1¹⁄₄ cups*
	butter, see method	
	sugar, see method	

Put the fruit into the pan with the water and cook slowly until a thick pulp. This is a very small amount of water for the quantity of damsons, so cover the pan tightly and check that it does not boil dry. If necessary, add a little more water but try and keep the pulp as thick as possible. Rub the fruit through a sieve and measure the pulp. To each 600 ml/1 pint (2½ cups) allow: 25 g/1 oz (2 tablespoons) butter and 450 g/1 lb (2 cups) sugar. Damsons have such a sharp flavour that this is a cheese where butter mellows the taste and the full amount of sugar gives the best result. Heat the pulp gently, stirring well over a low heat. Add the butter and sugar and continue stirring until these have dissolved. Raise the heat and boil steadily until setting point is reached. Spoon into hot containers and seal down.

Yield

Each 450g/1 lb (2 cups) sugar makes 750 g/1²/₃ lb fruit cheese.

Variations

Sharp Cherry Cheese: use cooking cherries, not the dessert type. Follow the directions for the Damson Cheese. Rub most of the cherries through a sieve but save about a quarter as whole fruit. Remove the stones from these when cooked. Heat the purée, add the butter and sugar. Stir until these have dissolved then add the whole cherries and continue as the Damson Cheese.

Mulberry Cheese: substitute mulberries for the damsons and follow the main recipe.

Mulberry and Apple Cheese: use 900 g/2 lb mulberries with 450 g/1 lb cooking apples. Simply cut the unpeeled apples into small dice and cook with the mulberries.

Plum and Almond Cheese: use cooking plums instead of damsons – do not use ripe dessert plums, for their flavour is not sufficiently strong. Rub the fruit through a sieve and measure the pulp. Add the same amount of butter and sugar as for Damson Cheese for a preserve that keeps well, or reduce the amount of sugar to 225 g/8 oz (1 cup) for a preserve that must be refrigerated or frozen. In addition to the butter and sugar add 50 to 100 g/2 to 4 oz; (½ to 1 cup) finely chopped blanched almonds to each 600 ml/1 pint (2½ cups) purée. Add the nuts when the butter and sugar have dissolved.

GRAPE BUTTER

Cooking time: 25 to 30 minutes • For yield see end of recipe

Both Grape Butter and Grape Cheese have a very refreshing flavour, especially if made with a lower amount of sugar, as given under Variations below.

Metric/Imperial	Ingredients	American
1.35 kg/3 lb	*grapes*	*3 lb*
4 tablespoons	*red or white wine*	*5 tablespoons*
	sugar, see method	
	lemons, see method	
	butter, see method	

Simmer the grapes with the wine until a very thick purée. Rub through a sieve then measure. To each 600 ml/1 pint (2½ cups) allow 450 g/1 lb (2 cups) sugar. Add 2 teaspoons finely grated lemon rind plus 1 tablespoon (1¼ tablespoons) lemon juice, or use 2 tablespoons (2½ tablespoons) if the grapes were very ripe and sweet. To each 600 ml/ 1 pint (2½ cups) purée add 25 g/1 oz (2 tablespoons) butter. Heat the fruit pulp, add the sugar, lemon rind and juice and the butter. Stir over a low heat until the sugar has dissolved then boil rapidly until setting point is reached. Spoon into hot containers and seal down.

Yield

Each 450 g/1 lb (2 cups) sugar makes 750 g/1²⁄₃ lb fruit butter.

Variations

- Reduce the amount of sugar used to 350 g/12 oz (1½ cups). The butter will then keep less well so should be stored in the refrigerator or frozen.
- Grape Butter or the cheese below can be flavoured with mixed spice, or other spices, used sparingly.

Grape Cheese: omit the butter in the recipe above and boil until the mixture is very firm.

LOGANBERRY CHEESE

Cooking time: 25 to 30 minutes • For yield see end of recipe

Of all the popular berry fruits, loganberries are probably the most suitable for a fruit cheese, for they have a very definite flavour and a firmer texture than raspberries or strawberries. Boysenberries, cranberries and tayberries are also extremely good. These particular cheeses are excellent as a dessert, see Quince Butter and Cheese on pages 111 to 112. They also blend well with roast game or poultry.

Metric/Imperial	Ingredients	American
900 g/2 lb	loganberries	2 lb
	water, see method	
	sugar, see method	

Put the loganberries into the pan with the water. If the fruit is very ripe use only 150 ml/¼ pint (²⁄₃ cup) to the quantity above; if the fruit is very firm then use 225 ml/7½ fl oz (scant cup). It is important to have as firm a mixture as possible for a cheese. Simmer the fruit in the water until a purée then rub through a sieve. Measure the pulp. To each 600 ml/1 pint (2½ cups) allow 450 g/1 lb (2 cups) sugar. Heat the purée, add the sugar and stir over a low heat until dissolved. Raise the heat and boil rapidly until setting point is reached. Spoon into hot containers and seal down.

Yield

Each 450 g/1 lb (2 cups) sugar makes 750 g/1²⁄₃ lb) fruit butter.

Variations

- Use only 300 g/10 oz (1¼ cups) sugar to each 600 ml/1 pint (2½ cups) pulp. The cheese must then be kept in the refrigerator or frozen.

- Add 2 to 3 tablespoons chopped hazelnuts or pinenuts to each 600 ml/1 pint (2½ cups) purée. These should be added just before setting point.

Boysenberry Cheese: follow the recipe using ripe boysenberries.

Cranberry Cheese: use 300 ml/½ pint (1¼ cups) water if the fruit is very ripe but up to 450 ml/¾ pint (scant 2 cups) water if firm and less ripe. Cover the pan tightly when simmering and do not raise the lid until the cranberries cease 'popping' – they tend to jump out of the pan until tenderised. For an interesting flavour simmer the cranberries in red wine or half red wine and half water. Follow the recipe for Loganberry Cheese.

Tayberry Cheese: follow the recipe using ripe tayberries.

PRUNE BUTTER (1)

Cooking time: 35 to 50 minutes • For yield see end of recipe

The first butter keeps well, just like the jam on which it is based (see pages 54 to 55). The second butter must be stored for a limited time in the refrigerator or frozen. Both go well with savoury dishes, especially cooked beef, or can be used as a filling for cakes and pastries or a topping for ice creams.

Metric/Imperial	Ingredients	American
450 g/1 lb	tenderised dried prunes	1 lb
600 ml/1 pint	water or weak China tea	2½ cups
	lemons, see method	
	sugar, see method	
	grated or ground nutmeg, see method	

Put the fruit into the pan with the water or tea. Grate enough lemon rind to give 2 tablespoons (2½ tablespoons) and add to the liquid. Simmer the fruit until soft, rub through a sieve then measure the purée. To each 600 ml/1 pint (2½ cups) allow 450 g/1 lb (2 cups) sugar and ½ teaspoon grated or ground nutmeg, with 2 tablespoons (2½ tablespoons) lemon juice. Heat the prune purée, add the sugar, lemon juice and nutmeg and stir over a low heat until the sugar has dissolved. Raise the heat and boil rapidly until setting point is reached. Spoon into hot containers and seal down.

Yield

450 g/1 lb (2 cups) sugar makes 750 g/1⅔ lb fruit butter.

Variations

Prune Butter (2): cook 450 g/1 lb tenderised dried prunes until just tender then strain well and put into a saucepan with the finely grated rind of 2 large oranges, 4 tablespoons (5 tablespoons) orange juice, ½ teaspoon ground cinnamon, 225 g/8 oz (generous 1 cup) soft brown sugar and

1 tablespoon (1¼ tablespoons) maple syrup. Stir over a low heat until the sugar has dissolved then add 25 g/1 oz (2 tablespoons) butter and continue cooking until thick. Spoon into hot containers and seal down.

Apricot Butter: use 450 g/1 lb dried apricots with 2 tablespoons (2½ tablespoons) lemon juice, the finely grated rind of 1 lemon and 1 litre/1¾ pints (nearly 4½ cups) water. Simmer the fruit with the lemon juice, rind and water until tender. Rub through a sieve and measure the purée. To each 600 ml/1 pint (2½ cups) allow 450 g/1 lb (2 cups) sugar and a further 2 tablespoons (2½ tablespoons) lemon juice with 25 g/1 oz (2 tablespoons) butter. Heat the apricot purée and add the sugar, lemon juice and butter. Stir over a low heat until the sugar has melted then raise the heat and boil rapidly until setting point is reached. Spoon into hot containers and seal down. You could add 50 g/2 oz (½ cup) chopped almonds to each 600 ml/1 pint (2½ cups) purée. Add these just before setting point is reached.

PUMPKIN BUTTER

Cooking time: 35 minutes • Makes nearly 900 g/2 lb butter

This particular butter can be served instead of a jam or as a filling in a sponge cake. By steaming the pumpkin you prevent it becoming too watery and soft.

Metric/Imperial	Ingredients	American
450 g/1 lb	pumpkin, weight when peeled and seeds removed	1 lb
pinch	salt	pinch
2 teaspoons	finely grated lemon rind	2 teaspoons
3 tablespoons	lemon juice	3¾ tablespoons
450 g/1 lb	sugar	2 cups
50 g/2 oz	butter	¼ cup

If you intend to use a food processor to make a purée allow slightly over 450 g/1 lb since a little may be wasted in the processor. Peel and dice the pumpkin. Place it in a steamer, add a very small amount of salt, then cover and cook over boiling water until tender. Either mash the vegetable or process until smooth. Do not over-process, for this would make the pumpkin sticky. Put the mashed pulp into the preserving pan with the lemon rind, juice, sugar and butter. Stir over a low heat until the sugar and butter have dissolved then simmer gently for 20 minutes or until very thick. Spoon into hot jars and seal down.

Variations

- Cook in the top of a double saucepan over boiling water for 25 to 30 minutes. This prevents any possibility of the mixture sticking to the pan or burning.
- Use a microwave oven, as described on page 12.
- Flavour the pumpkin with grated lime rind and juice instead of lemon.

Marrow Butter: use marrow instead of pumpkin with the same flavourings or add about 2 tablespoons (2½ tablespoons) finely chopped preserved ginger or 1 to 2 teaspoons ground ginger. In this case use only half the lemon rind and juice.

Melon Butter: use the same quantity of ripe melon as given for Pumpkin Butter. This does not need pre-cooking or salting; simply sieve or mash the fruit or put it into the food processor until smooth. Heat with the ingredients and continue as the recipe. The ginger flavouring recommended for Marrow Butter above could be included.

Papaya (Pawpaw) Butter: use the same quantity of uncooked ripe papaya as for Pumpkin Butter. Make a smooth purée of the fruit then add the ingredients given in the recipe, heat these and continue as above.

QUINCE BUTTER

Cooking time: 1 hour • For yield see end of recipe

The flavour of quinces blends well with sweet ingredients, so this butter can be served as a dessert with sweet biscuits, see under Variations, or as an accompaniment to cheese and biscuits or crusty bread.

Metric/Imperial	Ingredients	American
900 g/2 lb	ripe quinces, weight when peeled and cored	2 lb
450 ml/³/₄ pint	water	scant 2 cups
	lemons, see method	
	sugar, see method	

Peel and core the quinces, then weigh them. Cut the pulp into small dice and simmer in the water until soft and a thick purée. Either mash, sieve or liquidize this to make it very smooth. Measure the purée and to each 600 ml/1 pint (2½ cups) allow the finely grated rind of 1 lemon plus 3 tablespoons (3¾ tablespoons) lemon juice and 450 g/1 lb sugar (2 cups). Return the purée to the pan, add the lemon rind and juice and sugar, then stir over a low heat until the sugar has dissolved. Boil steadily until the mixture is very thick and smooth. Spoon into a large bowl or individual dishes and cover tightly. To serve, turn out of the dishes or serve with a spoon.

Yield

Each 450 g/1 lb (2 cups) sugar gives about 750 g/1²/₃ lb fruit butter.

Variations

- Add 25 g/1 oz (2 tablespoons) butter to the hot purée before adding the sugar.

For a Dessert: turn the quince butter out of the dish or dishes on to serving plates. Dredge with sifted icing sugar or top with blanched almonds and then add the icing sugar. The butter is delicious served with a light yoghurt or single cream or fromage frais. The butter also makes an excellent filling for tarts or sponge cakes.

Quince Cheese: this must be sufficiently stiff to cut into slices, so cook the purée until very stiff before adding the lemon rind, juice and sugar. Omit the butter, which tends to soften the texture.

Apple Butter: use cooking apples, or for a sweeter butter use the kind of dessert apples that cook well. Apples cook quicker than quinces so allow only 300 ml/½ pint (1¼ cups) water. When the apples are cooking they can be flavoured with lemon rind and juice as before, or omit the lemon rind, but not the juice, and add 1 to 2 teaspoons ground ginger or finely chopped ginger. Allow the same amount of lemon juice and sugar as for Quince Butter. Apple Butter is excellent as a dessert or with cheese or cold pork or duck.

Apple Cheese: make the consistency thicker, as described in Quince Cheese.

Pear Butter: use fairly firm dessert pears and only 300 ml/½ pint (1¼ cups) water. Pears can be flavoured with a little ground cinnamon or a piece of cinnamon stick or ginger (as under Apple Butter). Proceed as for Quince Butter.

LEMON CURD

Cooking time: 30 minutes • Makes approximately 450 g/1 lb curd

Lemon curd and the variations given are some of the most delicious of all spreads. Because of the mixture of acid fruit juice and eggs, care must be taken that the ingredients do not become too hot, otherwise they will curdle (separate).

Metric/Imperial	Ingredients	American
3 large	lemons	3 large
225 g/8 oz	sugar	1 cup, but see method
115 g*/4 oz	fresh butter	½ cup
2 large	eggs	2 large

*use this metrication

Wash and dry the lemons well. The best way to remove the rind is to use loaf (lump) sugar and rub this over the lemons until all the top rind (zest) has been removed and the lumps of sugar are completely coated with yellow zest. This makes quite sure that no bitter white pith is included. If this is not possible grate the lemon rind finely and carefully, taking just the yellow part. Halve 2 of the lemons and squeeze out the juice – you need 4 tablespoons (5 tablespoons) but this will depend upon personal taste; more can be added later if desired. Put the lemon rind, juice, sugar and butter into the top of a double saucepan or basin. Stand this over a pan of hot, but not boiling, water and whisk until the butter and sugar have melted. Beat the eggs and add to the warm mixture then stir continually until the curd is sufficiently thick to coat the back of a wooden spoon. Do not cook for too long for the curd thickens when cold. Spoon into hot jars and seal down. See page 104 for information on storing curds.

Variations

Economical Lemon Curd: use only 50 g/2 oz (¼ cup) butter.

Apple and Lemon Curd: use the ingredients as the curd above, plus 2 medium to large cooking apples. Bake these until soft, remove the peel and cores and mash the pulp. Add to the lemon rind and juice and continue as above. This particular curd does not have a sufficiently high percentage of sugar to keep well so should be stored in the refrigerator. To make a preserve that keeps well use 450 g/1 lb (2 cups) sugar. Follow the method as for Lemon Curd.

Grapefruit Curd: use the grated rind from 2 small or 1 very large grapefruit plus 4 tablespoons (5 tablespoons) grapefruit juice or a little more if desired. Follow the method for Lemon Curd.

Marrow and Lemon Curd: steam sufficient diced marrow to give 225 g/ 8 oz (1½ cups) when cooked. Sieve or liquidize to make sure this is absolutely smooth. Add to the lemon rind and juice then continue as Lemon Curd. This curd does not have sufficient sugar to keep well, so store in a refrigerator or use 450 g/1 lb (2 cups) sugar to make a preserve that keeps well.

Orange Curd: use the same quantity of orange rind and juice as for the Lemon Curd. The mixture has a little more flavour if 1 tablespoon (1¼ tablespoons) lemon juice is added to the other ingredients. Another way of introducing more bite into this curd is to use 2 tablespoons (2½ tablespoons) juice from Seville oranges and 2 tablespoons (2½ tablespoons) juice from sweet oranges plus 1 tablespoon (1¼ tablespoons) lemon juice if desired. Use the rind from 3 sweet *not* Seville oranges.

Tangerine Curd: use the grated rind from 4 to 6 tangerines or similar fruits plus 5 tablespoons (6¼ tablespoons) juice from the fruit. This curd has a very mild flavour and it is improved if 1 to 2 tablespoons lemon juice is added.

When I bottle plums and damsons in syrup I find the fruit has not absorbed the fruit syrup, why is this?
Plums and damsons have a tough skin so it is advisable to prick the fruit in several places with a needle or very fine skewer before covering with syrup so this can penetrate and flavour the fruit.
   This is particularly important when using alcohol, as in the method on pages 153 to 154.

GOOSEBERRY CURD

Cooking time: 35 minutes • For yield see end of recipe

Really sour green gooseberries make an excellent curd; it is not necessary to use lemons.

Metric/Imperial	Ingredients	American
900 g/2 lb	gooseberries	2 lb
300 ml/½ pint	water	1¼ cups
	butter, see method	
	sugar, see method	
	eggs, see method	

Wash the fruit but do not top or tail it. Simmer with the water until a thick purée then rub through a nylon sieve and measure. To each 600 ml/1 pint (2½ cups) allow 115 g*/4 oz (½ cup) unsalted butter, 450 g/1 lb (2 cups) sugar, 3 large eggs or 6 egg yolks (this is a good recipe in which to use left-over egg yolks).

Put the gooseberry purée with the butter and sugar into the top of a double saucepan or a large basin over hot, not boiling, water and heat until the butter and sugar have melted. Whisk the eggs or egg yolks and add to the gooseberry purée. Cook slowly until sufficiently thick to coat the back of a wooden spoon. Spoon into hot jars and seal down.

Yield

Each 600 ml/1 pint (2½ cups) gooseberry purée makes 1 kg/2¼ lb curd.

Variations

Apple Curd: use cooking apples instead of gooseberries. These can be baked in a conventional or microwave oven to make a thick purée that does not need sieving. Discard the skins and cores and measure the pulp, then follow the recipe above.

Apricot Curd: use fresh apricots and cook these as the gooseberries above. It is advisable to add 1 or 2 tablespoons lemon juice when cooking the apricots to make sure they keep a good colour.

*use this metrication

FRUIT SYRUPS, JUICES AND COULIS

MAKING FRUIT SYRUPS

It is wise to prepare fruit syrups when there is an abundance of fresh fruits and they are at their cheapest. These can then be used in winter time when the fruit is out of season. Choose fruits that have a refreshing flavour and plenty of natural juice. Syrups are easy to prepare for, like fruit jellies, there is no need to remove the peel and cores from apples or top and tail gooseberries. The method of making all fruit syrups is rather simpler than the special method for Rose Hip Syrup on page 117. Far less water is required for other fruits, since their taste is less strong than that of rose hips. Syrups should have sufficient flavour so they can either be diluted and served as hot or cold drinks or form the basis for jellies, ice creams, sorbets or other desserts. Cook the fruit for the minimum length of time and with the smallest amount of water to give the strongest flavour. The fruit can be cooked in a preserving pan, or in the top of a double saucepan, or in a bowl in a microwave oven. Strain the purée through a jelly bag, exactly as though making a fruit jelly (see pages 70 to 71), then heat the juice for a very short time with the sugar. In the past, 225 to 350 g/8 to 12 oz (1 to 1½ cups) sugar was added to each 600 ml/1 pint (2½ cups) juice, but nowadays, with the emphasis on using less sugar, you may like to reduce this or use honey as the sweetener. Fruit syrups can be frozen, as suggested on page 117, or sterilized in bottling jars as described on pages 126 to 127.

MAKING FRUIT JUICES

Prepare the fruit as for a fruit syrup but omit the sugar. This is ideal for those on a diabetic diet or for people who want to lose weight and are anxious to avoid using extra sugar. The method of preservation is exactly the same as for a fruit syrup. An idea of the amount of water needed with each 450 g/1 lb fruit is given on page 116.

SUITABLE FRUITS FOR SYRUPS
OR FRUIT JUICES

To 450 g/1 lb fruit	Water content and any flavouring
Apples – choose juicy cooking or dessert fruit	300 ml/^{1}/2 pint (1^1/4 cups) A little lemon juice can be added to dessert apples, or simmer them with a small amount of lemon zest.
Apples and Cranberries – use twice as many apples as cranberries	300 ml/^{1}/2 pint (1^1/4 cups) See comments about cooking cranberries on pages 32 to 33.
Apricots – choose very ripe fruit	150 ml/^{1}/4 pint (^{2}/3 cup) Add a little lemon juice to improve both colour and flavour.
Blackberries	4 tablespoons (5 tablespoons)
Blackberries and Apples – use equal quantities	175 ml/6 fl oz (^{3}/4 cup)
Boysenberries	5 tablespoons (6^1/4 tablespoons)
Cherries – choose very ripe red or black fruit	150 ml/^{1}/4 pint (^{2}/3 cup)
Damsons – choose ripe fruit	300 ml/^{1}/2 pint (1^1/4 cups)
Gooseberries – choose ripe fruit	225 ml/7^1/2 fl oz (scant cup)
Grapes	No water
Lemons, Limes or Grapefruit	600 ml/1 pint (2^1/2 cups) Pare top zest from lemons, avoid any pith; halve the fruit and remove the pulp; discard the pips but thin skin does not matter; simmer fruit and zest in water for 15 minutes.
Loganberries	5 tablespoons (6^1/4 tablespoons)
Mulberries – one cooking apple to each 450 g/1 lb mulberries gives a good flavour	5 tablespoons (6^1/4 tablespoons)
Oranges	300 ml/^{1}/2 pint (1^1/4 cups) Follow method as for lemons
Raspberries	No water
Tayberries	5 tablespoons (6^1/4 tablespoons)

ROSE HIP SYRUP

Cooking time: 5 minutes • For yield see end of recipe

Rose hips are the fruit of the wild rose. It was discovered that they contain a very high percentage of Vitamin C (ascorbic acid), so they were particularly valuable during the Second World War. The method given below is the way to retain the very maximum vitamin content of the fruit. Even if the full amount of water is used, the syrup is so strong in flavour that it needs to be diluted before it is served. In view of the convenience of being able to freeze the syrup you will find a method that takes up far less space in the freezer below. The old method of storing the syrup was to sterilize it, and details of sterilizing are on pages 125 to 126.

Metric/Imperial	Ingredients	American
450 g/1 lb	rose hips	1 lb
1.2 to 1.8 litres/ 2 to 3 pints	water	5 to 7½ cups
	sugar, see method	

Wash the hips then chop or grate them while bringing the water to the boil. Do not let the fruit stand after preparation for valuable vitamins will be lost. Use the smaller amount of water if you are anxious to save space in bottling jars or in the freezer. Simmer the fruit and liquid for 5 minutes only, then allow to stand for 15 minutes – during this time more of the flavour is extracted from the fruit. Keep the pan covered during the standing period. Strain the liquid and measure this. If only 1.2 litres/ 2 pints (5 cups) of water was used then allow 300 g/10 oz (1½ cups) of sugar to each 600 ml/1 pint (2½ cups). If the larger amount – i.e. 1.8 litres/3 pints (7½ cups) – of water was used the juice will be less concentrated so only 225 g/8 oz (1 cup) sugar could be added, but the amounts given are purely a matter of personal taste. In this recipe the sugar is a flavouring and not a means of preservation. Heat the juice, add the sugar and heat only until the sugar has dissolved. Do not continue boiling, for the longer the mixture is boiled the more Vitamin C is lost.

If sterilizing: pour into hot sterilized jars and proceed as directed on page 125.

If freezing: follow the recommendations below.

Yield

Each 600 ml/1 pint (2½ cups) juice, plus the sugar, will give just over 600 ml/1 pint (2½ cups) syrup.

FREEZING FRUIT SYRUPS AND JUICES

Fruit syrups and juices (with or without sugar), as well as the mixtures that form the basis of a coulis, freeze extremely well. It is important to freeze the mixture in the right amounts for your use; for if you defrost a large container you should not re-freeze any that is left. Some of the mixtures that follow contain a high percentage of water, but even if extra water is not added, the fruit itself has a high moisture content. That is why it is essential to leave a good 1.5 to 2.5 cm/½ to 1 inch of air space at the top of any container in which the ingredients are packed.

Freezing in ice trays: another good idea is to freeze the mixtures in the container used for making ice. In this way you make flavoured ice cubes. Remove the cubes from the ice trays and pack into polythene freezer bags. This method of freezing is particularly useful in the case of Rose Hip Syrup, which has such a concentrated flavour. Simply take one cube, put it in a tumbler, then add water, soda water or milk. The iced syrup cools the drink and provides the flavouring.

Reducing the water content: the amount of water given in the recipes can be reduced a great deal if you are anxious to save space in the freezer. Use only enough to stop the mixture from sticking when heating the ingredients. The juice or purée will then be extremely concentrated but you can dilute this with the right amount of liquid when it is being served or used to make a coulis.

COULIS MIXTURES

The term 'coulis' is used to describe a modern sauce that is not thickened with flour or cornflour or arrowroot; the thickening comes from the fruit or vegetable purée. The coulis should be clear and not too thick in consistency. It is very useful to make coulis mixtures in advance and store them for future use.

Fruit Coulis

When preparing a fruit coulis choose those fruits that have a very definite flavour and are good partners to other fruits and a variety of desserts. Ideal fruits to select are apples (with a sharp flavour), apricots, black and redcurrants, blueberries, boysenberries, gooseberries, loganberries, raspberries and tayberries (a fairly new fruit created by crossing a blackberry with a raspberry). Use raw fruit wherever possible. If you do cook the fruit, give the minimum of heating time, so the fresh flavour remains. A little flavouring, such as cinnamon, ginger or lemon juice, could be added. Often it is better to leave these additions until serving the coulis so you can decide just what extra flavours would enhance the dish. Since a coulis should not be too sweet, there is insufficient sugar in the mixture to act as a preservative, so the prepared sauce must be frozen or sterilized in bottling jars as directed on pages 125 to 126. When freezing the coulis, pack the mixture into small containers so you have just enough for a meal and allow 1.5 to 2.5 cm/½ to 1 inch headroom in a polythene bag or box to allow for expansion during freezing, due to the high water content of fruit.

Vegetable Coulis

Various vegetables can be made into a coulis, the most appropriate being asparagus, carrots, cucumber, mushrooms and spinach. All can be flavoured with various fresh herbs during preparation. Fruits such as avocado, green, red and yellow peppers, and tomatoes are often used with savoury dishes. These can be frozen or sterilized as other fruits, see page 124. A vegetable coulis can be frozen or sterilized. In order to be certain of satisfactory results it *must* be sterilized in a pressure cooker, as described on page 126.

PREPARING A FRUIT COULIS

Choose really ripe fruit, especially if it is a type that does not need cooking to extract the juice. Rub through a hair or nylon sieve, *not* a metal one which could spoil both colour and flavour a little. A liquidizer could be used for fruits that are without skin and pips. If the fruit needs cooking, prepare as usual (there is no need to peel and core apples or top and tail gooseberries). Cut large fruits into small pieces so they cook in the minimum of time. Put into a small quantity of water or fruit juice, such as lemon or orange or redcurrant (excellent with boysenberries, raspberries and tayberries). Cook for the shortest possible time then rub through a sieve or liquidize. Add a little sugar to the uncooked or cooked fruit – about 50 g/2 oz (¼ cup) to each 600 ml/1 pint (2½ cups) of purée – to give a slight sweetness. It may be best to use this small amount and add a little more sugar, if desired, when serving, for if it is to accompany a rich or very sweet dessert the coulis needs to be sharp to provide a good contrast in flavour. If serving within a day or so, store in the refrigerator, otherwise freeze or sterilize. Details and timing for sterilizing fruit are on page 125.

PREPARING A SAVOURY COULIS

Choose young vegetables that need the minimum of cooking. Prepare them as usual and cut larger vegetables into small pieces, so they cook in the shortest possible time. Either steam the vegetables or cook in a little boiling salted water. Do not cook in any form of fat, for that would spoil the clarity of the purée. Parsley, chives, thyme, sage and other fresh herbs should be added to the vegetables. When cooked, rub through a hair or nylon sieve or liquidize to give a 100% smooth texture. Extra seasoning can be added but wait until serving the coulis to adjust this so the sauce complements the other ingredients. The vegetable purée may seem too thick for a sauce but can be diluted when serving the coulis.

Fruits such as avocados, peppers and tomatoes can be used for a savoury coulis. Avocados blend well with savoury foods, especially fish. They should be sieved or liquidized and blended immediately with lemon juice to prevent discolouration. Season lightly if desired. Deseed peppers, dice and simmer until just soft then sieve or liquidize. Season to taste. Tomatoes should be heated gently, without water, or used raw and rubbed through a sieve. Season lightly and add 1 to 2 teaspoons of sugar to enhance the flavour. If serving within a day or so, store in the refrigerator, otherwise freeze or sterilize vegetables in a pressure cooker, as described on page 126. Avocados, peppers and tomatoes should be treated like the other fruits described on page 118.

FREEZING FRUIT

Many fruits are excellent when frozen, particularly raspberries and other berry fruits with the exception of strawberries, which tend to lose both flavour and texture (they are better frozen as a purée). The general points about freezing, given under Vegetables (page 122), are just as important when freezing fruit.

1. The fruit should be just ripe but not over-ripe. If you need to wash it in cold water, drain well as fruit has a high water content and, if damp, you are freezing unnecessary water.
2. Many fruits are excellent frozen without liquid but some fruits have a better flavour when frozen in syrup or water. Details of the best way of freezing individual kinds of fruit follow.

To Prepare Fruit for Freezing

If freezing in syrup prepare this beforehand and allow it to become quite cold. The recipe for various strengths of syrup is given on page 125.

Apples: choose good cooking apples or the kind of dessert apples that can be cooked. Peel, core and slice. Drop into boiling water to blanch for 12 minutes. Cool, drain well then pack tightly without liquid. If preferred the sliced apples can be simmered in syrup, allowed to cool then packed.
   As a purée: one of the best ways of freezing apples is to cook them (without sugar) until a purée, then cool and freeze. The amount of sugar required can be added when using the purée.

Apricots: these discolour easily. The best way to prepare them is to halve the fruit, remove the stones, then simmer for a short time in lemon-flavoured syrup. Cool and pack. Use 2 tablespoons (2½ tablespoons) lemon juice to each 600 ml/1 pint (2½ cups) of syrup. Apricots can be frozen as a purée too. Add lemon juice when cooking the fruit to retain the colour, or ascorbic acid (see greengages, page 120). To prevent halved apricots darkening in colour during freezing, place thick crumpled paper over the fruit before adding the lid of the container, so they are pushed under the syrup. Bottling is better for preserving apricots than freezing.

Bananas: do not freeze.

Blackberries: open-freeze either with or without sugar. Arrange the fruit on trays lined with paper and freeze. When firm lift off the paper and pack into bags with or without sugar to taste. In this way the fruit is frozen individually and does not form a solid mass. It also defrosts more quickly. If preferred the fruit can be packed into containers and covered wih cold syrup before freezing.

Blueberries, boysenberries, loganberries, raspberries, tayberries: these should all be treated in the same way as blackberries.

Black and redcurrants: treat in the same way as blackberries.

Cherries: better packed in a light syrup.

Damsons: the skins are inclined to become tough in freezing, especially if the fruit is not pre-cooked. Either simmer the damsons in a light syrup until tender, or, even better, cook until a purée. Sieve to remove the stones then cool and pack.

Figs: fresh figs freeze well either by packing them whole or halved in containers, or by covering the uncooked fruit in cold syrup then freezing.

Grapefruit and other citrus fruits: halve and remove the segments of fruit. Before removing the segments, grate the top zest from the fruit and freeze this in small containers, ready to use for cakes, biscuits and desserts. Pack the fruit either with a sprinkling of sugar, without sugar or in a light cold syrup. Citrus fruit juices freeze well, either in small boxes or as frozen ice cubes. Whole fruit can be frozen – this is especially useful for Seville oranges which are in season for such a short period of the year.

Grapes: freeze in a light cold syrup. If they have pips remove these first.

Greengages: follow the instructions for apricots. Greengages lose colour if no lemon juice is added. Instead of lemon juice, you could add a 300 mg ascorbic acid tablet to each 600 ml/1 pint (2½ cups) syrup.

Mangoes: cut the pulp into neat pieces and pack in cold syrup using lemon juice or ascorbic acid to retain the colour (see under apricots and greengages).

Melons: do not freeze watermelon, but other melons freeze fairly well. They do, however, lose some of their firm texture. Dice the fruit and pack in cold syrup or pack dry with or without a little sugar.

Peaches and nectarines: follow the instructions for apricots. The peaches should be skinned before freezing and halved or cut into slices. These fruits are rather better bottled, see page 124.
Pears: follow the instructions for apples. Pears make a good purée, but they are better bottled, see page 124.

Pineapple: the texture is disappointing; it is better bottled, rather than frozen. If freezing, pack in cold syrup.

Plums: as apricots and greengages.

Rhubarb: wash well, then cut into neat pieces. Blanch in boiling water for 1 minute if young or 2 minutes if older rhubarb. Drain, cool and pack dry or in cold syrup.

Strawberries: if you do want to freeze them whole choose the smallest fruit possible. Tiny wild strawberries freeze better than cultivated ones. However the best way to freeze strawberries is to make a purée of the uncooked fruit; this can be frozen with or without sugar.

Storage Times in the Freezer

The maximum storage time for fruits packed in syrup or with sugar is up to 1 year; if packed in water use within 8 to 9 months. Fruit purées should be used within 8 months. Fruit juices should be used within 5 months. If fruits are kept frozen longer than these times they lose colour, flavour and texture.

Serving Frozen Fruit

All frozen fruit is at its best when it is just defrosted, so do not allow it to thaw out for too long a period before serving. This applies particularly to strawberries which collapse when 100% thawed; they are nicer if slightly frozen. If cooking frozen fruit, allow a very short cooking time, for the process of freezing does soften the fruit. They can be cooked from the frozen state, unless the recipe states otherwise. If putting frozen fruit into a tart or flan, allow it to defrost and drain well, for the amount of juice that comes from defrosted fruit would spoil the layer of pastry under the fruit.

FREEZING VEGETABLES

In order to achieve good results there are certain points to consider.

1. Never try to freeze too large a quantity of vegetables at one time. It is essential *not* to freeze more than one-tenth of your freezer capacity, i.e. a 6 cu. ft. freezer holds 54 kg/120 lb, so the maximum amount that should be frozen at one time is 5.4 kg/12 lb.

2. The ideal temperature for quick freezing is -24°C/-11°F and most freezers have a cold control that should be turned to the lowest setting well before placing the food in the freezer. The faster the food is frozen, the better the results. When the food is frozen, return the indicator to the normal setting.

3. Vegetables for freezing should be very fresh, young and in first-class condition. It is not worthwhile freezing indifferent produce, for the process will not improve it in any way.

4. Use the correct packing material, i.e. boxes or bags made specially for freezing. Foods that are not well packed lose flavour and moisture. Freezer packaging is readily available: buy a selection of sizes so you can store enough vegetables for various occasions. The vegetables should fit into containers fairly snugly, after allowing about 1.5 cm/ ½ inch air space for expansion during freezing because of the water content of the vegetables. The less air space there is in packages of frozen food the better the food will keep.

5. Vegetables should be blanched before freezing – this means lightly cooking them in boiling water. This destroys harmful enzymes and helps to retain colour and flavour during freezing. Never try to blanch too many vegetables at the same time. Blanch about 450 g/1 lb, allow to cool, then blanch another batch. The table on page 128 gives advice on blanching in a saucepan or in a pressure cooker.

6. After blanching immediately plunge the vegetables into ice-cold water to prevent over-cooking. Drain very well and when cold pack into the bags or containers and seal tightly. If using bags, stand these in empty sugar, or other, boxes. When the food is frozen remove from the box and you will find the bag of food has formed a neat shape that is easy to pack in the freezer.

7. Label containers and bags clearly with the kind of food and the date frozen, for it is so easy to become confused with an assortment of unlabelled packages. It is important to use food within the specified

time. It will not go bad in the freezer but after a certain period it tends to lose both colour and flavour.

8. When cooking frozen vegetables remember they have been partially cooked during blanching and therefore their final cooking time should be shortened accordingly.
9. Frozen vegetables do not need defrosting before the final cooking, unless you are following a recipe that specifically instructs you to allow them to thaw.

Storage Times in the Freezer

The maximum storage time for most vegetables is 10 to 12 months but any vegetables frozen as a purée should be used within 6 to 7 months.

FREEZING HERBS

All herbs freeze well and it is extremely useful to have these available in winter-time when home-grown herbs are no longer flourishing and fresh herbs are expensive to buy. Pick the herbs when young and at their best. Parsley is the most satisfactory herb to freeze in sprigs – other herbs are slightly less good frozen this way, although you may like to try it. They are better treated as (a) and (b) below.

Parsley sprigs: wash the sprigs of parsley and let them drain, then put into the freezer without covering them. When frozen they can be placed in plastic bags but do not tie the bags tightly and take care not to crush the leaves. When you want parsley, bring out a few sprigs, use before they have defrosted for garnish or crush the frozen leaves with your fingers the moment they come from the freezer. They are so crisp that they crumble without the bother of chopping.

Chopped herbs: wash and dry the herbs and chop finely. Freeze using either of the methods given below.
a) Pack into small freezer bags and then put into a clearly labelled freezer box. These herbs can be added to salads or most other dishes.
b) Put the herbs into ice-making trays, then cover with water and freeze. This means you can use the herbs for flavouring stews, soups and sauces. The frozen herb flavoured ice cubes can be packed into boxes or large freezer bags. Frozen herbs do not need defrosting before being used with hot ingredients.

Mint: freeze as method (a) or (b) or pack with a little sugar, ready to make Mint Sauce. You could freeze the mint with sugar and vinegar but this takes up more space in the freezer and needs longer to defrost. The frozen mint, or mint and sugar, defrosts very rapidly when vinegar is added.

Storage Times for Herbs in the Freezer

Use all herbs within 6 months to enjoy the flavour at its best.

BOTTLING AND STERILIZING FRUIT

To a large degree freezing has made the bottling and sterilization of fruit unnecessary but there are certain fruits that are better bottled and details about these are given below. The fruits that are extremely successful when bottled, and less so when frozen, are pears, peaches and nectarines. Other fruits freeze well and berry fruits are infinitely better frozen (see pages 120 and 121) for they retain more flavour and a good texture.

To Prepare Bottling Jars

Wash the jars if they are new or have been used before. Put the jars, plus rubber rings and lids, into a large container of cold water. Slowly bring the water to boiling point. Remove from the heat and leave the jars in the water until required.

To Prepare Pears, Peaches and Nectarines

These fruits can be bottled in a syrup or just in water.

Pears: ideally you should choose firm but ripe dessert pears. The fruit should be peeled, halved lengthways and then cored. If using cooking pears, simmer these until just tender, either in a light syrup, see below, or in water. Pears turn brown very quickly, so it is advisable to keep them in a salt solution during preparation. Use 1 level tablespoon (1¼ tablespoons) kitchen salt to each 1.2 litres/2 pints (5 cups) cold water. Put the pears in the salted water and place a plate on top of the fruit so they are kept under the liquid. Rinse well in cold water before bottling or cooking to soften the fruit.

Peaches: lower the fruit gently into boiling water and leave for about 30 seconds, then place in cold water to cool. Remove the skins, halve and stone the fruit.

Nectarines: prepare in the same way as peaches.

To Bottle Fruit

Pack the fruit into the jars as tightly as possible without damaging the flesh. Fill the jars to the top with cold water or cold syrup. A little lemon juice could be added to the syrup, especially for pears in order to maintain their white colour. Place the rubber rings in position then put on the lids and screw bands. Give the bands half a turn back to loosen them slightly, for the glass expands during sterilizing and if the bands were too tight the bottles could crack. If using bottling jars with clips, and not screw bands, move the clips slightly to the side of the lids so the pressure on the jars is not so great.

Syrup for Bottled Fruits

Dissolve the sugar in the water (see measurements below) and allow this to become quite cold before using. Sometimes the syrup looks a little cloudy – this does not detract from the flavour, only from the appearance of the fruit, so strain through fine muslin. Fruit looks better in a light syrup and today, when there is such emphasis on low sugar intake, this is more popular.

For a light syrup: use 50 to 100 g/2 to 4 oz (¼ to ½ cup) sugar to each 600 ml/1 pint (2½ cups) water.

For a medium syrup: use 100 to 175 g/4 to 6 oz (½ to ¾ cup) sugar to each 600 ml/1 pint (2½ cups) water.

For a heavy syrup: use 175 to 300 g/6 to 10 oz (¾ to 1¼ cups) sugar to each 600 ml/1 pint (2½ cups) water.

TO STERILIZE BOTTLED FRUIT

If using a proper sterilizer place the bottles on the rack at the bottom. If using a deep pan pad the bottom with a thick layer of cloth or paper. This prevents the bottles cracking, as they might if placed in direct contact with the metal base of the pan, which will become very hot over the heat of the cooker. Make sure the jars do not touch each other. Fill the sterilizer or pan with cold water to come right up to the neck of the bottles, then cover with a lid. If no lid is available use a thick layer of foil. This keeps the steam in the sterilizer or pan. Take 1½ hours to bring the water to simmering, i.e. 74 to 79.5°C/165 to 175°F when bottling peaches or nectarines but a slightly higher temperature, i.e. 82 to 87.5°C/180 to 190°F, for pears. Maintain the temperature for 30 minutes. Carefully remove the hot jars from the sterilizer or pan. This is easier to do if some of the very hot water is ladled out first. Stand the hot jars on a wooden surface *not* on a cold one. Tighten the screw bands or move the clips into the centre of the lids. Leave for 24 hours then remove the screw bands or clips and test if the lids are tightly sealed. If so, the jars are properly sterilized and the fruit will keep. If the lids are not tight then the fruit is not safe to keep. It should be eaten very soon or the jars resterilized. Store in a cool place.

Sterilizing Other Fruits

If you decide to bottle other fruits (tomatoes are counted as a fruit) then follow the directions above. All fruits should be brought to the temperature given for peaches and maintained at this temperature for 10 minutes. Tomatoes, which can be covered with cold water plus a very little salt and sugar, or simply packed with seasoning and a pinch of sugar but no liquid, should be sterilized at the higher temperature given for pears and the water should be held at this setting for 30 minutes.

To Sterilize Low-Sugar Jams

Spoon or pour the very hot jam into sterilized and heated bottling jars. Seal down as for fruit, loosening the screw bands and moving the clips slightly to one side of the lids. Lower the very hot jars on to the rack of a sterilizer or padding in a deep pan. In this case the sterilizer or pan should be filled with *boiling water* up to the neck of the bottling jars. Let the water come to a good rolling boil, then cover. Maintain the water at boiling point for at least 10 minutes. Ladle some of the boiling water out of the pan and remove the jars on to a wooden board. Tighten the screw bands or move the clips into position. Leave for 24 hours then test to see if the jars have sealed.

To Sterilize Fruit Syrups, Juices etc.

Follow the directions for sterilizing low-sugar jams above.

Sterilizing Fruit in a Pressure Cooker

A pressure cooker is excellent for sterilizing fruit. Prepare the jars and fruit as directed on page 124. Stand the jars on the inverted trivet (rack) in the pressure cooker. Take care the jars do not touch each other or the sides of the cooker (see note below). Add 600 ml/1 pint (2½ cups) hot water to the cooker. Put on the lid with a 5 lb (low) weight and slowly bring the water to pressure. Maintain this pressure for 3 to 4 minutes. If bottling maintain the pressure for 7 minutes. Turn off the heat but do not lift the pressure cooker off the hob, simply slide it away from the electric hotplate. Allow to stand at room temperature until the pressure drops then take off the lid and carefully transfer the very hot jars to a wooden board. Tighten the screw bands or move the clips into position and leave for 24 hours then test as directed on page 125.

NOTE: Aluminium pans tend to darken when sterilizing. Add 1 tablespoon vinegar or lemon juice to the water to stop this happening. Put wads of paper between the jars in a sterilizer or deep pan or pressure cooker if you are afraid they will touch each other.

Storing Bottled Foods

Store bottled produce in a cool dark cupboard.

BOTTLING AND STERILIZING VEGETABLES

It is important to appreciate that vegetables *must not* be bottled, except in a pressure cooker. Using an ordinary sterilizer does not ensure that harmful enzymes are destroyed. The vegetables are sterilized at 10 lb (medium) pressure. Choose young vegetables that are in excellent condition. Prepare them as for cooking then blanch them in boiling water using the timings given on page 128. If preferred, the vegetables can be blanched in the pressure cooker. This must be at 10 lb (medium) pressure; the timings are given in the table on page 128. Prepare the bottling jars by sterilizing them (see page 125). Pack the vegetables into the jars then cover them with hot salted water. The amount of salt will be to personal taste but most people like about ½ to 1 teaspoon to each 600 ml/1 pint (2½ cups) water. The salt is not essential if you are trying to omit this from your diet.The salt and water should be brought to the boil before adding it to the jars. Work out any air bubbles that might occur by twisting the jars around. The salt water, or ordinary hot water, should come to within 2.5 cm/1 inch of the top of the jars. Put on the rubber rings, lids and the screw bands but loosen the bands half a turn to allow for expansion of the glass during heating. If using jars with clips, move the clips to one side of the lids to release the extra pressure. Sterilize the jars of vegetables *immediately* after filling. Place these on the inverted rack in the pressure cooker, then add 600 ml/1 pint (2½ cups) hot water to the pressure cooker. Fix the lid and bring slowly to 10 lb (medium) pressure. Maintain this pressure for the time given in the table on page 128. Make quite sure the pressure does not drop at any time. Turn off the heat and move the pressure cooker away from the electric hotplate but do not lift off the hob. Allow the pressure to drop at room temperature. Transfer the hot jars from the pressure cooker to a wooden board. Tighten the screw bands or move the clips into the centre of the lids. Leave for 24 hours then remove the screw bands or clips and check that the lids have sealed. If they have not sealed then use the vegetables at once. It would spoil the flavour to re-sterilize them and be unsafe to keep them for any length of time. Store in a cool dark cupboard. (See the note on page 126 about aluminium pans and how to keep jars separate during sterilisation.)

Blanching Vegetables

Blanching (lightly cooking) is a process that is necessary before bottling or freezing vegetables. This destroys harmful enzymes and also helps the vegetables keep a good colour, texture and flavour. If blanching vegetables in a large saucepan, lower fairly small batches into the boiling water, leave for the time indicated below, then bring them out and immediately lower into ice-cold water. This prevents them becoming overcooked. As soon as the vegetables are sufficiently cool to handle, drain and pack into the bottling jars. Continue like this until all jars are filled.

If blanching vegetables in a pressure cooker use the trivet if the column is marked **T**; if there is no **T** then place the vegetables in the cooker or in separators, if you have these. Before adding the vegetables pour 300 ml/½ pint (1¼ cups) water into the pressure cooker. Bring this to the boil then add the vegetables. Fix the lid and bring the pressure cooker to 10 lb (medium) pressure as quickly as possible. Maintain at this pressure for the short time indicated in the table on page 128. Release the pressure at once then remove the vegetables from the cooker and place in ice-cold water. Drain and proceed as above. In some cases in the table there is an asterisk (*) after the words 'Bring just to 10 lb'. This means you allow the cooker to come just to 10 lb (medium) pressure then immediately turn of the heat and release the pressure.

Times for Sterilizing Vegetables

The pressure cooking times begin when the cooker has reached 10 lb (medium) pressure. The blanching time is when the vegetables are placed in boiling water. The slight variation in times is to allow for different sizes of vegetables use the longer duration for larger vegetables. Bottling is not suitable for all vegetables and the table indicates those that are unsatisfactory (they become badly over-cooked).

Vegetables and preparation	Blanching in pan *minutes*	Blanching in pressure cooker *minutes*	Cooking times at 10lb pressure *minutes*
Artichokes: globe	5	1 T	35
Jerusalem	7-10	1 T	35
Asparagus	3-4	Bring just to 10 lb*	30-35
Aubergines (Eggplant) – slice (peel if preferred)	4	1 T	35
Beans: broad – podded	3	Bring just to 10 lb*	40
French – string, keep whole	3	Bring just to 10 lb*	40
runner – string, slice thickly	3	Bring just to 10 lb*	40
Beetroot (Beets): young whole, scald and rub off skins – slice	15-20	15-20	40
	12	6	40
Broccoli – trim to tight heads	3	Bring just to 10 lb*	Better frozen
Brussels sprouts – trim	2-3	1-2	Better frozen
Carrots – scrape, leave whole if young or slice if older	5- 6	2	40
Cauliflower – florets	3	1 T	Better frozen
Celery – heart	6	1 T	Better frozen
Chicory (Endive) – whole head	4	1 T	Better frozen
Corn on Cob – remove leaves	4-6	1 T	45
Courgettes (Zucchini) – slice	1	1 T	Better frozen
Mixed root vegetables – dice	5-6	1 T	40
Mushrooms, see note A	1	Bring just to 10 lb*	35-40
Peas – podded	2	1 T	35
Peppers (Bell peppers), see note B	–	–	40
Potatoes: new – scrape	5	2	45
old – peel and dice	6	4 minutes at 15 lb	45
Spinach, see note C	1	Bring just to 10 lb*	Better frozen
Turnips, parsnips, swedes (Rutabaga) pressure	5-6	1-2	45

NOTE A: cook until liquid flows instead of blanching, then bottle.

NOTE B: these are really fruits, so can be bottled like fruit, see page 124. Alternatively, halve and put the rounded sides under a hot grill until the skins turn black, then remove the skins. Deseed the peppers and slice, pack tightly into bottling jars without liquid and sterilize for 40 minutes.

NOTE C: Blanch only 225 g/8 oz: (½ lb) at a time.

DIABETIC PRESERVES

People who follow a diabetic diet appreciate the fact that preserves of all kinds have a high sugar content. Many companies make reduced-sugar jams and 'pure fruit spreads', which although not totally sugar-free do have a lower sugar content. These are perfectly acceptable if you have diabetes. It is also possible to make your own preserves at home following the guidelines given by Diabetes UK. These are the alternatives:

1. You can use smaller amounts of sugar than usual. There is detailed information about this on page 15, together with facts on the correct storage of preserves that contain less than the standard amount of sugar. If following this method you can adapt all the recipes in this book. In addition, you will find below a low-sugar marmalade recipe, taken from the Diabetes UK's book of preserves.
They point out that the small proportion of sugar present in a portion of jam or marmalade is unlikely to affect the sugar glucose of a diabetic person. Sugar that contains pectin is quite acceptable for diabetic preserves.

2. You can omit sugar entirely and use an artificial sweetener (see the recipe for Lemon Curd on page 130).

3. You can use gelatine or fruit juice or liquid pectin, like Certo, which are available from supermarkets, or use concentrated apple juice, which is sold by health food shops. Special diabetic recipes based on the ingredients mentioned in this alternative are on pages 130 and 132. There is a diabetic chutney recipe on page 132 and one for pickles also on page 132. The following recipes came from the *British Diabetic Booklet on Preserves*, which is now no longer in print.

DIABETIC GRAPEFRUIT AND LEMON MARMALADE

Cooking time: 2 to 2¼ hours • Makes 1.575 kg/3½ lb marmalade

This is a very good sweet marmalade made with a low proportion of sugar. It is not recommend for freezing.

Total per 100 g/4 oz = 60 g CHO/270 calories

Metric/Imperial	Ingredients	American
1 kg/2¼ lb	grapefruit	2¼ lb
350 g/12 oz	lemons	¾ lb
1.8 litres/3 pints	water	7½ cups
1 kg/2¼ lb	sugar with added pectin	4½ cups

Scrub the fruit and cut in half; squeeze out the juice and extract the pips. Cut the peel into fine shreds. Place the shredded peel, soft pulp and the juice in a preserving pan with the water. Tie the pith, pips and any fibrous tissue into a muslin bag and hang in the pan. Bring to the boil, then lower the heat and cook gently for nearly 2 hours or until the peel is soft. Squeeze the muslin bag, then remove it. Add the sugar and stir over a low heat until dissolved. Raise the heat and boil rapidly for at least 4 minutes, or until setting point is reached (it is important to test early with marmalade, see page 87). Remove from the heat and allow to cool, then stir to distribute the peel. Spoon into hot jars and seal down. This lower-than-average sugar content marmalade should be stored in the refrigerator.

DIABETIC LEMON CURD

Cooking time: 30 minutes • Makes 625 g/nearly 1½ lb curd

This curd uses low-fat spread instead of butter, and an artificial sweetener instead of sugar.

Total per 100 g/4 oz = Neg CHO/150 calories

Metric/Imperial	Ingredients	American
4 large	lemons	4 large
1	orange	1
3	eggs	3
100 g/4 oz	low-fat spread	½ cup
8 tablespoons	granular artificial sweetener	10 tablespoons

Finely grate the lemon and orange rind and squeeze out the juice. Beat the eggs then put all the ingredients into the top of a double saucepan or bowl over a pan of hot, but not boiling, water. Stir until the low-fat spread has melted then whisk or stir briskly until the mixture is thick. Do not allow it to boil – see the recipe on page 112. Pour into hot jars and cover. This keeps for up to 2 weeks in the refrigerator. Do not freeze.

DIABETIC KIWI AND STRAWBERRY JAM

Cooking time: 50 minutes • Makes 800 g/generous 1¾ lb jam

This is an example of a jam without any sugar. It does not set to a very firm consistency but the flavour is excellent. Certo and Set are both commercial pectins.

Total per 100 g/4 oz = 10 g CHO/60 calories

Metric/Imperial	Ingredients	American
50 g/2 oz	dried pears	⅓ cup
2 tablespoons	lemon juice*	2½ tablespoons

5	kiwi fruit	5
450 g/1 lb	strawberries	1 lb
150 ml/¼ pint	unsweetened apple juice	²/₃ cup
150 ml/¼ pint	Certo or Set	²/₃ cup

*or the juice from 1 good-sized lemon, whichever is the greater amount

Purée the dried pears with the lemon juice in a food processor or liquidizer. Place in a preserving pan. Peel and slice the kiwi fruit and chop the strawberries. Add to the preserving pan with the apple juice. Cook gently for 15 to 20 minutes until the fruit is soft and pulpy. Purée again. Return to the pan and boil rapidly for approximately 30 minutes or until setting point is reached. Add the Certo and boil for a further 2 minutes. Pour into hot jars and seal down. Store in the refrigerator for up to 2 weeks. Do not freeze.

DIABETIC RASPBERRY JAM

Cooking time: 20 minutes • Makes 450 g/1 lb jam

This recipe relies on gelatine to set the jam. It will be a fairly solidly set preserve.

Total per 100 g/4 oz = Neg CH0/50 calories

Metric/Imperial	Ingredients	American
3 tablespoons	water (for gelatine)	3³/₄ tablespoons
11 g/0.4 oz (1 sachet)	gelatine	1 envelope
150 ml/¼ pint	water	²/₃ cup
450 g/1 lb	raspberries	1 lb
150 ml/¼ pint	orange juice	²/₃ cup
3 tablespoons	granular artificial sweetener	3³/₄ tablespoons

Put the 3 tablespoons (3³/₄ tablespoons) water into a basin, add the gelatine and leave on one side. It will become soft and spongy. Put 150 ml/¼ pint (²/₃ cup) water with the raspberries and orange juice into a pan and cook gently until soft. Stir from time to time. Remove from the heat, add the softened gelatine and stir until dissolved. Leave for a few minutes then stir in the granulated sweetener. Pour into a hot jar and seal down. Store in the refrigerator for up to 2 weeks. Do not freeze.

DIABETIC DATE CHUTNEY

Cooking time: 50 minutes • Makes 800 g/1³/₄ lb chutney

This recipe is sweetened naturally with dried dates. It has a very good flavour.

Total per 100 g/4 oz = 30 g CHO/130 calories

Metric/Imperial	Ingredients	American
100 g/4 oz	onions	1 cup
2	garlic cloves	2
450 g/1 lb	dates, weight when stoned	2¹/₂ cups, when pitted
1 to 2 teaspoons, or to taste	salt	1 to 2 teaspoons or to taste
300 ml/¹/₂ pint	unsweetened apple juice	1¹/₄ cups
600 ml/1 pint	white malt vinegar	2¹/₂ cups

Peel and finely chop the onions; peel and crush the garlic. Remove the stones from the dates if necessary and finely chop the fruit. Put all the ingredients, except the vinegar, into the pan and simmer gently for 20 minutes, or until tender. Add the vinegar and simmer until the mixture thickens. Spoon into hot jars and seal down. When opened store in the refrigerator. Do not freeze.

DIABETIC MUSTARD PICKLE

Cooking time: 25 to 35 minutes • Makes 800 g/1³/₄ lb pickle

In this recipe from the Diabetes UK they state that the vegetables in the pickle contain very little carbohydrate and therefore have not been counted.

Total 100 g/4 oz = Neg CHO/40 calories

Metric/Imperial	Ingredients	American
	Wet brine, see page 141	
225 g/8 oz	onions	2 cups
225 g/8 oz	cucumber	2 cups
100 g/4 oz	red pepper	1 cup
100 g/4 oz	peas, weight when shelled	³/₄ cup
225 g/8 oz	cauliflower florets	2 cups
1 teaspoon	turmeric	1 teaspoon
2 teaspoons	dry English mustard powder	2 teaspoons
350 ml/12 fl oz	vinegar, see page 138	1¹/₂ cups
2 teaspoons	flour	2 teaspoons
15 g/¹/₂ oz	sugar	1 tablespoon, firmly packed

Make the brine as directed on page 141 and pour this into a container. Peel and finely chop the onion, dice the cucumber and the pepper (discard the core and seeds from this). Put the vegetables into the brine and leave soaking for 24 hours. Remove from the brine and wash thoroughly under cold water then drain well. Put the vegetables with the turmeric and mustard into a pan with most of the vinegar and simmer for 20 minutes or until just tender; do not over-cook. Blend the flour and sugar with the rest of the cold vinegar and add to the vegetables. Bring to the boil, and boil rapidly for 2 to 3 minutes. Spoon into hot jar(s) and cover as instructed on page 139. Store in a cool place. Leave for 6 to 8 weeks before opening the jar(s). Once opened, store in the refrigerator or a cool place. Do not freeze.

CRYSTALLIZED FRUITS

Commercially crystallized ingredients are prepared with enormous skill and the benefit of specialist equipment. The density of the sugar is measured with a hydrometer and the rooms in which the fruits, and other items for crystallisation, are prepared will be at exactly the correct temperature and humidity. These special conditions are not available in the home and therefore the results may not look quite as perfect as those you buy. However, with care and patience (the process takes 8 days) it is possible to produce very acceptable results.

1.   Only certain fruits are suitable. All those chosen must be perfect, without any bruises or imperfections. They should be just ripe but not over-ripe. Before coating with the sugar mixture the fruits should be prepared as below.
2.   In the case of apricots, greengages and dessert plums, choose fairly small fruits so they can be crystallized whole.

TO PREPARE THE FRUIT

Apricots: carefully remove the stones, without damaging the fruit. If not quite ripe poach in a little water (without sugar) until just soft. A few drops of lemon juice can be added to keep the fruit a good colour. When ready, strain and use the water as part of the liquid in the syrup recipe on page 135.

Cherries: choose large dessert fruit. Remove the stones without damaging the fruit.

Grapes: slit and carefully remove the pips with the tip of a knife. Keep the fruit whole. The skins could be removed if desired.

Greengages: prepare in the same way as apricots.

Oranges: divide into segments and remove all skin and pith. Clementines can be prepared in the same way.

Pears: peel and core without damaging the shape of the fruit and sprinkle with a little lemon juice to keep the flesh white. If large then halve or quarter the fruit lengthways.

Peaches: skin by immersing in boiling water for a few seconds, then putting into cold water. Pull away the skin and cut into halves or quarters. Sprinkle with a little lemon juice.

Pineapple: peel the fruit, remove the hard core and cut the pulp into neat segments. Poach for a short time in water as for apricots.

Plums: use dessert plums and follow the directions for apricots.

Strawberries: these can be a disappointment for the fruits tend to deteriorate quickly and are not suitable for long term storage.

PROCESS OF CRYSTALLIZING

The process of coating the fruit takes 8 days. Choose a time of dry weather and avoid having any steam in the kitchen while coating the fruit and leaving it to dry.

Metric/Imperial	Ingredients	American
450 g/1 lb	prepared fruit, see above	1 lb
175 g/6 oz	granulated sugar	3/4 cup
	plus	
400 g/14 oz	extra sugar needed for days 2 to 7	1 3/4 cups
300 ml/1/2 pint	water	1 1/4 cups

Day 1 Place the prepared fruit in a shallow dish in a single layer. Put the 175 g/6 oz (3/4 cup) of sugar and water into a saucepan. Stir over a low heat until the sugar has dissolved then pour the hot syrup over the fruit. Leave for 24 hours.

Day 2 Carefully drain the syrup from the fruit into a saucepan using a nylon sieve. Return the fruit to the original dish. Add another 50 g/2 oz (1/4 cup) of sugar to the pan. Stir over a low heat until dissolved then pour the hot syrup over the fruit. Leave for 24 hours.

Day 3 Repeat Day 2.

Day 4 Repeat Day 2.

Day 5 Repeat Day 2.

Day 6 Repeat Day 2, but this time add 75 g/3 oz (3/8 cup) of sugar to the syrup.

Day 7 Repeat Day 2, but once again add 75 g/3 oz (3/8 cup) sugar.

Day 8 Drain off any thick syrup. Preheat the oven to 100°C/approximately 200°F, Gas Mark 1/4 (or the lowest setting). Place the fruit on a fine-meshed wire cooling tray with a large baking tray underneath to catch the drips. Keep the oven door slightly ajar and leave the fruit for about 45 minutes or until the outside is slightly crisp.

To store Cool the fruit and place in sweetmeat cases or small paper cases then transfer to a tightly covered box or tin.

TO CRYSTALLIZE CANNED FRUIT

Canned fruits crystallize well. Choose the best quality possible. From the point of view of flavour it is better to use the ones that have been canned in natural juice, but you save a little time in preparation if you buy those canned in syrup. The fruit should be weighed after draining away the juice or syrup and you should use 450 g/1 lb fruit if following the above proportions.

If Canned in Natural Juice

Strain all the juice from the fruit. Use this instead of all, or part of, the water in the recipe on page 135. Make the syrup, pour over the fruit and proceed as Day 1 in the recipe.

If Canned in Syrup

Strain all the syrup from the fruit, measure this and if necessary add a little more water and sugar to make it up to the quantity on page 135. It will not be possible to know exactly how much sugar was used in canning the fruit but the proportions are usually very much those of the syrup in the recipe on page 125. Bring the syrup to the boil, pour over the fruit and proceed as Day 1 in the recipe.

TO CRYSTALLIZE ANGELICA

This perennial plant is quite easy to grow. After preparation, as given below, it is crystallized in exactly the same way as fruit on pages 134 to 135. Like all forms of crystallizing, coating angelica is a fiddly job as I well remember, for in the late 1950s I did a programme for BBC Television on crystallizing flowers (see page 137), angelica and peel (see below). I felt decidedly sticky by the end of the programme.

To Prepare Angelica

Choose young tender stems. Cut these into convenient lengths (7.5 to 10 cm/3 to 4 inches are ideal to handle). Wash and dry the stems then put them into a large mixing bowl. Dissolve 1 tablespoon (1¼ tablespoons) sea salt or block kitchen salt in 2.25 litres/4 pints boiling water, pour over the angelica and leave for just 10 minutes to draw out the excess moisture. Strain the angelica and rinse very thoroughly in cold water. Put into a saucepan of boiling water and simmer for 10 minutes, then cool and strip away the outer skin, leaving just the soft fleshy part underneath. Weigh the prepared angelica and make up the syrup in proportion to the weight of the stems (see page 135). Proceed as the recipe on that page.

TO CRYSTALLIZE PEEL

Home-made crystallized peel is well worth preparing, for you make use of the part of citrus fruits that may otherwise be wasted. The process of crystallizing peel is not as prolonged as that of fruit. Use the peel from oranges, clementines and similar fruit, lemons, limes and grapefruit. Make sure the peel is perfect and take great care to remove all the excess bitter pith. Leave the peel in fairly large pieces so it is easier to handle.

Metric/Imperial	Ingredients	American
450 g/1 lb	**citrus peel, weight when excess pith removed**	1 lb
15 g/½ oz	**bicarbonate of soda (baking soda)**	1 tablespoon
2.4 litres/4 pints	*water*	10 cups

600 ml/1 pint	liquid from simmering peel	2½ cups
675 g/1½ lb	granulated sugar	3 cups

Day 1 Place the peel in a large casserole in a fairly flat layer. Put the bicarbonate of soda into a bowl. Bring the water to the boil, add to the bicarbonate of soda and make sure it is well dissolved. Pour over the peel and leave for 20 minutes only, to tenderise. Drain thoroughly then rinse the peel in several lots of cold water. Tip the peel into a large saucepan and add enough fresh cold water to cover. Put on the lid and simmer gently until tender then strain the liquid and reserve 600 ml/1 pint (2½ cups). Pour this liquid into a saucepan, add 450 g/1 lb (2 cups) of the sugar, stir over a low heat until the sugar has dissolved then pour the syrup over the peel and leave for 48 hours.

Day 3 Drain the syrup from the peel, pour into a saucepan, add the remaining 225 g/8 oz (1 cup) of sugar and stir over a low heat until dissolved. Add the peel to the saucepan and simmer gently until transparent. Strain the syrup from the peel and reserve this. Place the peel on a wire cooling tray with a large baking tray underneath and proceed as Day 8 on page 135. Reboil the syrup until very thick, dip each piece of peel in this and leave in the air to harden and dry again. Cut it into small pieces before it becomes too hard.

To store Place the peel in tightly sealed tins or jars.

TO CRYSTALLIZE FLOWERS

Flower petals make very attractive decorations on trifles and other cold desserts. Rose and violet petals are the most popular but the blossom of apple, cherry, plum and pear trees could be used, as can primrose flowers. Never use flowers from bulbs – most of these are poisonous. Pick the flowers on a dry day but do not gather them until you have prepared the gum arabic solution. As you will see from the recipe, this has to stand for 24 hours before using. Rose water and gum arabic are obtainable from most chemists. Keep the stems on the flowers, where possible, for this makes them easier to hold. You need a very fine paintbrush to coat the petals with the solution.

Metric/Imperial	Ingredients	American
25 g/1 oz	gum arabic	1¼ tablespoons
4 tablespoons	triple-strength rose water	5 tablespoons
	flower petals	
	caster (superfine) sugar, for sprinkling	

Put the gum arabic into a container, add the rose water and blend thoroughly then leave for 24 hours to melt. Dip a fine paintbrush in the solution and paint on both sides of the petals. Sprinkle caster (superfine) sugar over the petals while the solution is damp. Leave to dry on sheets of greaseproof paper or baking parchment, then store in airtight containers.

PICKLING FOODS

Pickling is one of the oldest of all methods of preservation, for in days past, before so much food was imported in winter and when canning and refrigerators were unknown, families in Britain and elsewhere had to prepare for wintertime by preserving those foods that were plentiful in summer.

Vinegar is the essential preservative for many pickles, used either by itself or in partnership with sugar (as in pickled fruits and chutneys) or with salt. Spices have been appreciated in Britain for centuries, and these form a part of the flavouring in pickled food. In order to produce good pickles there is one golden rule to follow. *Buy good ingredients.* The four most essential are:

Vinegar: this must be of good quality and contain the right amount of acetic acid. Most bottled vinegars are ideal for they have between 5 and 6%, which is perfect. If buying draught vinegar, which can have a lower acidity content, it must be boiled well, often with the pickling spices, until reduced to approximately half the original volume. Malt vinegars are generally chosen for pickling vegetables and other foods. Brown vinegar is the usual choice, but white malt vinegar is better when pickling fruits, so the colour of the fruit is not impaired. In chutneys you can select the colour you feel will enhance the look of the finished product, for the flavours are very similar. Both red and white wine vinegar, cider vinegar or distilled vinegar (very popular in Scotland) can be used. Wine and cider vinegars are more expensive than malt vinegars and have a more delicate flavour, which may be lost when cooked with other fairly strong tasting ingredients, as in many chutneys.

Salt: this is essential when pickling vegetables, which are first put into a wet or dry brine. The purpose of this is to draw out the high water content and so enable the vinegar to be of sufficient strength. Recipes for brine are given on page 141. The brining will also add to the clarity of the pickles. As explained on page 141, it is better to use pickling salt or sea salt for brining instead of the free-flowing table salt because table salt has additives which cloud the brine.

Sugar: this is used in pickling fruit and in chutneys, so is an additional preservative with the vinegar. White or brown sugar can be used according to personal taste. In a few recipes the kind of sugar is specified, when tests have shown this to be the best for that particular recipe.

Spices: these are an essential ingredient in good flavoured pickles. Often the recipe simply states 'mixed pickling spices' and these can either be bought ready for use, or you can prepare your own mixture. There is more information about these mixtures on pages 139 to 140. Spices should be treated with great respect for they can turn dull dishes into interesting ones and produce pickles of all kinds that are full of subtle flavours. They also contain certain oils which help destroy harmful bacteria. Spices, however, do deteriorate with storage – they lose flavour and some are inclined to develop a rather musty taste. Never buy vast quantities of a certain spice unless you know you are going to use it regularly. In the old days grocers stored spices in drawers, so they excluded both air and light. It is advisable to keep spices away from the light whenever possible, so if you buy them in glass jars, put these in a closed cupboard rather than on show. That seems a pity for they look so attractive but it will preserve their flavour.

UTENSILS FOR PICKLING

The utensils used in the preparation, cooking and storage of pickles are very important.

Basins and bowls: glassware and china are ideal, but do not use copper bowls at any stage of the preparation if the vinegar is likely to come into contact with the container.

Sieves and strainers: the old-fashioned hair sieves are rarely obtainable today but nylon sieves are ideal when handling acid fruits or ingredients containing vinegar. Metal sieves or strainers could adversely affect both the flavour and colour of the food.

Preserving pan: it is stressed on page 6 that when pickling fruits, vegetables, or making chutney the preserving pan or saucepan used is of great importance since it comes into contact with vinegar. Aluminium and stainless steel are very satisfactory, and so is enamel, provided it is not chipped. Do not use brass, copper, iron or zinc pans.

Jars: bottling jars are excellent for pickles of various kinds and the glass lids are ideal for covering the pickle. If using ordinary jars with metal lids the inside of the lid must be covered with a thick layer of cardboard or paper, for if the metal comes into contact with vinegar the lid will rust. This is detrimental to the flavour and look of the pickle. Before use the jars and lids must be well sterilized and heated, as for jam jars (see page 7).

PICKLING SPICES

If you decide to buy a jar or packet of mixed pickling spices read the label carefully, for individual makes vary in the mixture of spices included and it is quite easy to find a blend you like. It is very possible, and undoubtedly better, to blend your own spices to achieve exactly the flavour you prefer in each type of pickle. Suggestions for the kind of spices to include in mixed pickling spices are given overleaf. You could use about 1 teaspoon of each to begin with. Having tasted the spiced vinegar, you can then assess what alterations you may require in future. You may have other favourite spices that you'd like to include.

Allspice: a berry that combines the flavours of a range of sweet spices.

Bay leaves: a dried herb, not a spice, which gives an aromatic taste.

Cardamon: tiny seeds or pods that give a sweet, yet hottish flavour.
Cassia: in rolls and seeds; rather like cinnamon in flavour.

Chilli: small pieces or whole dried seed pods of hot red peppers.

Cinnamon: small pieces of cinnamon bark; gives a very good strong flavour.

Cloves: dried flower buds that have a very strong flavour, so use sparingly; excellent with fruits.

Coriander: seeds which impart a slightly orange smell and flavour.

Ginger: dried root, very hot in flavour.

Mace: dried outer coating of nutmeg; has much the same flavour.

Mustard: dried seeds, which can be black or white or even brown and red in colour. These add a hot and piquant flavour.

Peppercorns: these give a hot flavour. Black peppercorns come from the fruit before it is quite ripe, whereas white peppercorns come from the ripe fruit. You may like to add freshly ground black or white pepper to pickles, or even cayenne pepper, which is ground hot chillies.

Pimento: dried seeds or the flesh of sweet peppers (pimentos). Sometimes also used as an alternative name for allspice.

A few cloves of garlic could also be included with the pickling spices. These are particularly pleasant with vegetable pickles.

SPICED VINEGAR

The average quantity of the mixed pickling spices required varies from a total of 1 teaspoon to 1 tablespoon to each 600 ml/1 pint (2½ cups) vinegar. Obviously this is a matter of personal taste. It is not only the amount of spice that dictates the flavour of the vinegar, but also the boiling time. For well-spiced vinegar pickles you should boil the vinegar and spices steadily for up to 15 minutes. For pickled fruits, where a fairly small amount of spice is required, 5 minutes' boiling may be sufficient. Sometimes a few spices are tied in muslin and cooked with the other ingredients; this is quite usual in chutney recipes. The cooking time extracts the maximum flavour from the spices. The size of the spices also determines the flavour. If they seem to be finely chopped more flavour is extracted, so a smaller amount and a shorter boiling time will be required.

The first time you prepare spiced vinegar use the minimum amount of spices and a short boiling time. Check the flavour and if necessary continue boiling or add more spices. Having made the pickles, and been satisfied with the flavour, do not add a few extra spices to the jars before sealing them. This is often done to make the jars look more pleasing. But remember that during the whole storage time the flavour of those extra ingredients will permeate the contents of the jar, so you will alter the original perfectly satisfactory taste. If you want to add spices then use some of those that come from the spiced vinegar *after* boiling and straining. Reduce the boiling time to compensate for the extra flavour given by the spices during storage.

USING PICKLED VINEGAR

Never waste the vinegar from the jars of pickles, for this has absorbed some of the flavour of the foods as well as the spices. The vinegar can be used in all forms of cooking and for salad dressings. The vinegar from pickling fennel, horseradish, lemons, nasturtium seeds and walnuts is particularly good in sauces. Never add this to a *boiling* sauce in which cream or eggs or milk are included, for the sauce would curdle.
Make sure the ingredients are only *hot*, then whisk in the required amount of vinegar. Simmer over a low heat to blend, whisking all the time.

USING A BRINE

On page 138 you will find the explanation for using a brine before pickling foods. There is a choice of a wet brine (salt dissolved in water) or a dry brine, where the salt is simply sprinkled over the food. Once every grocer's shop sold large blocks of salt and this was used for making both kinds of brine. This type of salt is now a rarity and sea salt or pickling salt is the usual successor. But if you cannot obtain either of these kinds then you must use ordinary table salt.

Wet Brine

Unless stated to the contrary, allow 50 g/2 oz (scant ¼ cup) salt to each 600 ml/1 pint (2½ cups) water. Simply mix the salt with the cold water. This is used where a softer result is required, as in Mustard Pickles (see page 149).

Dry Brine

Simply sprinkle the food with a good layer of salt and leave overnight or for the time stated in the recipe. The salt is then rinsed away in plenty of cold water. This is used when one wants a crisp result, such as in Pickled Red Cabbage (see page 144).

VINEGAR PICKLES

The following recipes give methods for pickling a variety of vegetables. Quantities are not given: the recommended proportions of pickling spices and vinegar are on page 140 and details of the wet brine and dry brine are given above. Herb-flavoured vinegars (see page 184) could be used instead of plain malt vinegar, which is the usual choice for these pickles.

PICKLED BEETROOT (BEETS)

Cut the cooked beetroot into slices or dice, according to personal taste. Put into boiling salted water – allow 1 level tablespoon (1¼ tablespoons) to each 600 ml/1 pint (2½ cups) water. This is a fairly high amount of salt but beetroot is not brined before being pickled. It can be reduced if desired, but then the beetroot does not keep as well. Simmer gently for 10 minutes then strain and pack into heated jars. While the beetroot is cooking, prepare the spiced vinegar as on page 140. Strain the boiling vinegar over the hot beetroot and seal the jars.

PICKLED CUCUMBERS

Wipe the cucumbers, but do not peel. If the cucumbers are small they can be left whole, otherwise cut into neat, even sized portions. If you prefer the cucumbers to remain fairly firm lay them on a flat dish and cover with a generous amount of salt. Leave overnight then drain away the salt and rinse in plenty of cold water. For a softer result place the cucumbers in wet brine, made as directed on page 141. Leave overnight, rinse in plenty of cold water then leave to drain very well. Pack into cold sterilized jars. Prepare the spiced vinegar as on page 140, allow to cool and strain. Pour the cold vinegar over the cucumbers and seal the jars. You could put 1 or 2 dried bay leaves into each jar.

SWEET PICKLED CUCUMBER

Use the recipe above but dissolve 2 teaspoons sugar, or as much as desired, in each 600 ml/1 pint (2½ cups) spiced vinegar.

PICKLED GHERKINS

Small gherkins can be pickled in exactly the same way as cucumbers.

PICKLED CAULIFLOWER

Use just the white head of the cauliflower and divide this into small neat florets. Place in wet brine (see page 141) and leave for 24 hours. Drain and rinse in plenty of cold water, then drain very well again. Pack into cold sterilized jars. Make the spiced vinegar as directed on page 140, allow to cool and strain. If there are any dried red chillies in the pickling spices retain a few of these. Pour the cold vinegar over the cauliflower, add one or two chillies and seal down. Do *not* use chillies that have not first been boiled in the pickled vinegar.

SWEET PICKLED CAULIFLOWER

Use the recipe above but dissolve 2 teaspoons sugar, or as much as desired, in each 600 ml/1 pint (2½ cups) vinegar.

PICKLED MUSHROOMS

Prepare the spiced vinegar as on page 140. The particular spices for mushrooms should include mace and a generous amount of peppercorns. Wipe the mushrooms well and remove the stalks – these could be trimmed and used in stews and soups. Put into well salted boiling water and cook for 5 minutes, then strain very thoroughly and pack into hot jars. Strain the boiling pickled vinegar over the hot mushrooms and seal down.

PICKLED ONIONS OR SHALLOTS

It is essential to use a stainless steel knife when preparing the onions or shallots to prevent the outsides darkening. Choose proper pickling onions or the very small silverskin onions. As their name suggests these have silver skins and a very mild flavour. A white wine vinegar could be used instead of malt vinegar. Put the onions into the wet brine (see page 141). It is often recommended that they are left for 36 to 48 hours, but for crisp onions leave for 24 hours only. Drain and rinse very thoroughly in cold water then drain again. Pack into cold sterilized jars. Prepare the spiced vinegar as directed on page 140, cool and strain. Pour the cold vinegar over the onions and seal down.

SWEET PICKLED ONIONS OR SHALLOTS

Use the recipe above but dissolve 1 tablespoon (1¼ tablespoons) sugar, or as desired, in each 600 ml/1 pint (2½ cups) spiced vinegar.

PICKLED MARROW (1)

Peel the marrow, remove all the seeds then dice the flesh. Place in a dish and sprinkle with salt. Leave for 24 hours then drain well. Rinse thoroughly in cold water then drain again.

Pack into hot sterilized jars. Make the spiced vinegar as on page 140 then strain over the marrow and seal down. A rather more interesting pickle using marrow is on page 148.

PICKLED COURGETTES (ZUCCHINI)

Use the same recipe as Pickled Marrow (1) above, or the second recipe on page 148, substituting courgettes for marrow. These do not need peeling, simply cut away the slightly tough ends. If very small, pickle whole; if larger, cut into even-sized portions.

MIXED VINEGAR PICKLE

Choose a good selection of vegetables, so there is a variety of colours, flavours and textures. This could include florets of cauliflower, small onions, diced cucumbers or gherkins and marrow or courgettes (zucchini) plus small green tomatoes and sliced green beans. With a selection of vegetables like this it is better to use dry brine, so arrange the vegetables in flat dishes in a single layer only. Sprinkle with a generous amount of salt and leave for 24 hours. Drain well and rinse very thoroughly in cold water, then drain again. Pack into cold sterilized jars, arranging the vegetables in an attractive pattern. Prepare the spiced vinegar as directed on page 140. Allow to cool and strain. You may like to take a few red chillies from this and put them in the jars. Pour the cold vinegar over the mixed vegetables and seal down. A softer pickle is made by using a wet brine (see page 141) and covering the vegetables with strained hot pickled vinegar.

PICKLED RED CABBAGE

Pickled red cabbage is one of the most popular of all pickles. The crisp cabbage blends well with many cooked dishes, such as Lancashire Hotpot and boiled beef, as well as being excellent with various cheeses and a good addition to an hors d'oeuvre. *Choose the cabbages carefully: they should be very firm and young, without any damaged leaves. Discard any tough outer leaves.*

With a stainless steel knife cut the cabbage leaves into fine shreds across the grain. Do not use any hard stalks. Put a layer of shredded cabbage into a dish then add a sprinkling of salt. Continue filling the dish or dishes like this, ending with a layer of salt. Leave for 24 hours then drain away the surplus moisture. If you like well-salted cabbage do not rinse in cold water. Many people try to avoid too much salt, in which case rinse well in cold water then drain again thoroughly. Make the spiced vinegar as instructed on page 140, allow this to cool then strain it. Return the cabbage to a large container, add the cold spiced vinegar and leave for several hours. During this time turn the cabbage around once or twice. Pack the cabbage fairly loosely into cold sterilized jars and completely cover with the vinegar then seal down. Allow the cabbage to mature for one week. Use within 2 to 3 months for the cabbage loses its crispness if kept longer.

Variation

- To add greater interest to the cabbage, put one or more layers of shredded raw onion into the jars between the layers of cabbage. These should be brined like Pickled Onions on page 143 in a separate dish from the cabbage.

PICKLING FOR FLAVOURING

Certain foods are good sources of flavour and it is worthwhile pickling them for use in cooking.

PICKLED FENNEL

Fennel is a wonderful ingredient in a salad and with fish dishes. It is not always available because good fennel does not grow well in Britain and has to be imported. Do not spice the vinegar for pickling fennel as the spices impair the delicate flavour of the plant. Use white malt or white wine vinegar. A sherry vinegar also gives an interesting taste. Trim the tough outer leaves from the white roots – save any perfect green leaves as these are wonderful in sauces and make the jars look attractive. If large, halve or quarter each fennel head; if small, pickle whole. Make the wet brine as on page 141 but in this case bring it to boiling point. Put in the fennel and leave in the brine until it has become quite cold. Make sure the plants are well under the liquid. Drain the fennel and pack into cold sterilized jars. Cover with the cold vinegar and seal down.

PICKLED HORSERADISH

The vinegar can be spiced if desired but white malt or white wine vinegar can be used without spicing, if you feel the flavour of the spices would spoil recipes in which horseradish is used. It is, however, essential to add salt to the vinegar since the horseradish is not brined before pickling.
To each 300 ml/½ pint (1¼ cups) of vinegar add 1 teaspoon salt.
This mixture does not need heating but make sure the salt is thoroughly dissolved. Peel fresh horseradish roots and finely shred or grate the flesh. Put into cold sterilized jars. Cover with the salted vinegar and seal down.

PICKLED LEMONS

There is presently great interest in dishes from the Arab world and various forms of pickled lemons are used in some of these. Pickled lemons are also an interesting accompaniment to salads and fish dishes.
I have always used an excellent recipe which I took from an old copy of *Mrs Beeton*. She gives an old-fashioned suggestion for assessing the right strength of a brine – it should be sufficiently strong to float an egg in it. The wet brine on page 141 is well salted (even if an egg does not float). Wash the lemons to remove any wax coating (this was not used in Mrs Beeton's day). Dry well then put in the wet brine as on page 141 Make sure the lemons are well immersed and stir them 2 or 3 times daily. Leave for 6 days. Remove from the brine but do not rinse. Put into a saucepan of boiling water and boil steadily for 15 minutes. Drain well and allow to become quite cold. Boil the vinegar with the spices. The spices suggested by Mrs Beeton are chillies, cloves, ginger, mace, mustard seed and peppercorns (see page 140). Add a little seasoning also. Put the lemons into hot jars. Pour the boiling spiced vinegar over the lemons. Mrs Beeton's recipe does not specify that the vinegar is strained before adding to the lemons. Personally, I do strain it but, if you like very highly spiced lemons, retain the spices in the jars. Seal down tightly and leave for 6 months to mature in flavour.

PICKLED NASTURTIUM SEEDS

Capers, the flower buds of a bush called Capparis sinosa *are grown in sunny Mediterranean climates but do not thrive in Britain.*
The alternatives are to buy pickled capers, which are quite expensive, or to preserve a surprisingly successful substitute – nasturtium seeds. Choose small jars in which to store the pickled seeds so the contents of each jar are used fairly quickly. Be fussy about the lids – they should fit

tightly, for the seeds deteriorate quite fast if exposed to the air or if the jars are left half full.

The nasturtium seeds must be picked when they are green and not left on the plants to become dry. Place in wet brine, made as directed on page 141, and leave for 24 hours. Drain the seeds; to avoid too salty a flavour, rinse in cold water and drain again thoroughly. Pack into hot jars. Prepare spiced vinegar as on page 140. Be fairly generous with the amount of peppercorns if selecting your own pickling spices, or add a few extra to the mixed pickling spice you buy if this contains a small amount of peppercorns. Strain the boiling spiced vinegar into a heated jug then pour over the nasturtium seeds and seal down. Make sure the seeds are well covered with the vinegar. A few peppercorns from the brine can be packed into the jars. Leave for 2 to 3 weeks to mature. The seeds keep well for months if covered properly, see above.

Variations

Another way of pickling the seeds is to boil vinegar with salt and peppercorns and any other spices you require (see page 140). Allow 1 tablespoon (1¼ tablespoons) salt and at least 6 peppercorns (more if possible) to each 600 ml/1 pint (2½ cups) vinegar. Be absolutely certain to pick the seeds on a dry day. Do not wash them or soak in brine. Boil the vinegar, peppercorns, or any other spices required, for 10 to 15 minutes. Strain into a measuring jug then add the right amount of salt. Heat again until the salt has dissolved. Pack the seeds into hot jars, cover with the boiling vinegar and seal down.

Pickled Capers: if you are able to obtain any real caper plants, pick the buds of the flowers when they are fully formed but still very tight. Put into a container and cover with a wet brine, made as page 141. Leave for 72 hours. Pack into hot jars. Prepare spiced vinegar as page 140, strain this and cover the capers with the boiling vinegar. Seal down the jars.

PICKLED WALNUTS

These have always been regarded as one of the most essential pickles. They are an ideal accompaniment to many cold dishes. The walnuts must be picked when the outer coatings (these become the hard brown shells) are green and soft: even if the coatings are only slightly hard you cannot pickle the nuts. Wear protective gloves when picking and handling the fruit, for the stain from walnuts is extremely difficult to remove from your hands. Use a silver fork or a long fine stainless steel needle for piercing the nuts.

Prepare the wet brine as directed on page 141. Prick each walnut all over then place in the brine. Leave for 3 days. Make sure the nuts are completely covered by placing a plate over them to push them below the solution. If it is not sunny (see below) it will not harm the pickle to leave for an extra day or two until the weather improves. Some experts recommend changing the brine and placing the nuts in a fresh batch for another 3 to 4 days. I have not found that necessary. Remove the nuts from the brine; do not rinse in water. Place in a single layer on a tray or cloth. It is good idea to pad the tray with plenty of white paper (not newspaper which would put newsprint on the nuts). Put the nuts in the sunniest place possible and leave until they turn black. It is not easy to give a time for this: if the weather is abnormally hot they may turn black within 2 hours, otherwise it will take several days. Prepare the spiced vinegar as described on page 140. Strain and allow to become cold. Pack the nuts (still wear gloves for this) into cold sterilized jars and cover with the cold vinegar. Seal down. Leave for a month at least before using. Pickled walnuts keep their flavour and texture extremely well, even for up to 2 years.

FRUIT AND VEGETABLE PICKLE

Cooking time: 1¼ hours • Makes 2.5 kg/good 5½ lb pickle

This is a slightly sweet yet savoury pickle. It goes well with all cold meats, pies and cheese.

Metric/Imperial	Ingredients	American
450 g/1 lb	cooking apples, weight when peeled and cored	1 lb
2 medium	lemons	2 medium
450 g/1 lb	green tomatoes	1 lb
450 g/1 lb	dates, weight when stoned	1 lb
900 g/2 lb	mixed vegetables, weight when prepared, see method	2 lb
600 ml/1 pint	brown malt vinegar	2½ cups
2 teaspoons	mixed pickling spices, see page 139	2 teaspoons
300 g/10 oz	sugar, preferably dark brown	1¼ cups
to taste	salt and freshly ground black pepper	to taste

Cut the apples into 6 mm/¼ inch dice. Grate the rind from the lemons; halve and squeeze out 3 tablespoons (3¾ tablespoons) of the juice. Blend the lemon rind and juice with the apples. Skin the tomatoes – this is fairly hard as green tomatoes are very firm, so they need to stand in boiling water for about 3 to 5 minutes. Cut into the same sized dice as the apples. Chop the dates into 6 mm/¼ inch pieces. Choose equal amounts of carrots, cucumber or gherkins, marrow, turnips and/or swedes (rutabaga). Weigh after cutting these into 6 mm/¼ inch dice to ascertain they make a total of 900 g/2 lb. Pour the vinegar into a preserving pan, add the pickling spices tied in muslin and the mixture of fruits, vegetables and lemon juice. Simmer steadily for 45 minutes. Add the sugar, stir over a low heat until dissolved then boil steadily until a thick mixture. Season to taste. Remove the bag of pickling spices. Spoon into hot jars and seal down.

Variations

- For a sweeter pickle increase the sugar to 450 g/1 lb (2 cups).
- You could tie 2 or 3 peeled garlic cloves in the muslin with the pickling spices.

Hot Fruit and Vegetable Pickle: add 2 or 3 finely chopped fresh hot red chilli peppers to the mixture. Slit the pods and remove the seeds to reduce the hot flavour. (Wear gloves when handling chillies.) Make sure there are plenty of mustard seeds in the pickling spice and also add about 3 teaspoons grated root ginger to the spices.

PICKLED MARROW (2)

Cooking time: 10 to 15 minutes • Makes 1 kg/2¼ lb pickle

This is a rather soft pickle, not unlike a chutney, except the marrow is kept in neat dice. Be careful not to over-cook the marrow in the vinegar.

Metric/Imperial	Ingredients	American
900 g/2 lb	marrow, weight when peeled and seeds removed	2 lb
	salt for dry brine, see method	
450 ml/³/₄ pint	brown malt vinegar or red wine vinegar	scant 2 cups
1 teaspoon, or to taste	ground ginger	1 teaspoon, or to taste
1 teaspoon, or to taste	curry powder	1 teaspoon, or to taste
2 teaspoons, or to taste	mustard powder	2 teaspoons, or to taste
6 to 8, or to taste	black peppercorns	6 to 8, or to taste
100 g/4 oz	sugar	¹/₂ cup

Cut the marrow into 2.5 cm/1 inch dice. Place on a flat dish and sprinkle with the salt. You need at least 75 g/3 oz (scant ³/₈ cup) salt for this particular dry brine. Leave for about 12 hours then drain away the liquid from the marrow. Rinse in several changes of cold water then allow to drain again. Blend a little of the cold vinegar with the ground ginger, curry powder and mustard powder to make a smooth paste. Heat the rest of the vinegar then blend in the spiced paste. Put in the peppercorns and sugar, stir over a low heat until the sugar has dissolved then simmer for 5 minutes. Put the marrow into the vinegar mixture and simmer until just tender – do not over-cook. Spoon into hot jars and seal down. The peppercorns can be left in the pickle.

Variations

- Use courgettes (zucchini) instead of marrow. These do not need peeling: simply cut into neat dice or slices.
- Diced pumpkin or squash can also be used in this pickle, or the recipe on page 143, instead of the marrow.

MUSTARD PICKLES

Cooking time: 45 minutes • Makes 1.35 kg/3 lb pickles

This is undoubtedly one of the most popular of all pickles. It should contain a good selection of vegetables in a smooth, thickened mustard sauce. The turmeric adds colour as well as flavour.

Metric/Imperial	Ingredients	American
900 g/2 lb	mixed vegetables, weight when prepared, see method	2 lb
	wet brine, see page 141	
600 ml/1 pint	spiced vinegar, see page 140	2½ cups
	plus	
3 tablespoons	vinegar	3¾ tablespoons
25 g/1 oz	plain flour	¼ cup
1 tablespoon, or to taste	mustard powder	1¼ tablespoons, or to taste
½ tablespoon, or to taste	turmeric	good ½ tablespoon, or to taste
2 teaspoons, or to taste	ground ginger	2 teaspoons, or to taste

Try to have as varied a selection of vegetables as possible, including cauliflower, cucumber or gherkins, green beans (French or young runners), marrow or courgettes (zucchini), small onions or shallots and small green tomatoes. Prepare the vegetables as though for cooking but cut them into small neat pieces about 2.5 cm/1 inch in size. Weigh them when prepared, so you have the right proportion of vegetables to mustard sauce. Make the wet brine as described on page 141; add the vegetables and leave for 24 hours. Prepare the spiced vinegar as directed on page 140 – in this case you could be fairly sparing with the mixed pickling spices as mustard, turmeric and ginger are being added. Boil the vinegar for 10 to 15 minutes. It will then be less than 600 ml/1 pint (2½ cups) but that will ensure the right consistency to the sauce. Blend the 3 tablespoons (3¾ tablespoons) plain vinegar with the flour, mustard powder, turmeric and ginger in a good-sized basin. Strain the spiced vinegar slowly on to this, stirring well. Pour the sauce into a saucepan and stir over a low heat until adequately thickened. This is important, for the sauce should be sufficiently thick to coat the spoon without running off rapidly. Lift the vegetables from the brine, drain well but do not rinse in cold water. Put into the mustard sauce and simmer for 5 minutes only. Stir lightly to ensure a good blend of vegetables then spoon into hot jars and seal down.

Variations

Sweet Mustard Pickles: follow the previous recipe but add 50 to 75 g/2 to 3 oz (¼ to ⅜ cup) sugar to the mustard sauce. Stir well to make sure it has dissolved.

Piccalilli: follow the recipe for Mustard Pickles but cut the vegetables into 1.5 cm/½ inch pieces or even slightly smaller. To prevent these becoming too soft add to the hot mustard sauce and simmer for 1 minute only, then spoon into hot jars and seal down.

Sweet Piccalilli: add the sugar to the Piccalilli, as in Sweet Mustard Pickles above.

Chow-Chow: follow the recipe for Mustard Pickles or Piccalilli above but include a generous amount of diced celery among the other vegetables. This is not usual in most Mustard Pickles but Chow-Chow always includes celery.

CARIBBEAN VEGETABLE PICKLE

Cooking time: 15 minutes • Makes 2.5 kg/good 5½ lb pickles

This is a highly spiced sweetish vegetable pickle that can be served with cold meats and poultry.

Metric/Imperial	Ingredients	American
1.35 kg/3 lb	mixed vegetables, weight when prepared, see method	3 lb
1.2 litres/2 pints	wet brine, see page 141	5 cups
2 or 3	red chilli peppers	2 to 3
1.2 litres/2 pints	white or red wine vinegar	5 cups
50 g/2 oz	plain (all-purpose) flour	4 tablespoons
2 teaspoons	tumeric	2 teaspoons
1 to 2 tablespoons	dry mustard powder	1¼ to 2½ tablespoons
300 g/10 oz	sugar	1¼ cups

Prepare the vegetables as though for cooking and cut into small neat pieces. In the Caribbean the selection would be made up of aubergines (eggplant), a small amount of breadfruit (used as a vegetable), cucumber, a small portion of pumpkin, a small cauliflower, a few green tomatoes, string beans and small onions. This selection can be varied according to the produce available. Soak overnight in the brine, drain and rinse in cold water, then drain again very thoroughly. Chop the chilli peppers into neat slices – for a milder taste remove the seeds before doing this to reduce the hot flavour. Wash your hands well after handling these hot chillies, see page 161. Put most of the vinegar into the preserving pan, bring to the boil, add the vegetables and simmer for 2 minutes only. Mix the flour, turmeric and mustard powder with the remaining cold vinegar. Spoon 2 to 3 tablespoons of the boiling vinegar over this and stir briskly then tip into the pan. Add the sugar and stir over a low heat until thickened then boil for 3 minutes only. Do not allow the vegetables to become too soft. Spoon into hot jars and seal down.

PICKLED HARD-BOILED (HARD-COOKED) EGGS

Cooking time: see method

These savoury eggs were once a feature of most public houses and snack bars. They have a very interesting flavour and deserve to be remembered. They form a good part of an hors d'oeuvre *or a light main dish served with salad.*

Hard-boil the eggs. There are various ways of doing this:

a) If large fresh eggs are placed in boiling water they need just 10 minutes' cooking time.
b) If they are placed in cold water and the water is heated, allow only 9 minutes from the time it comes to the boil.
c) Another method is to put the eggs into cold water, bring this to the boil, cover the pan. Turn off the heat and leave the eggs in the water for 15 minutes. This tends to give a lighter textured egg white which is excellent for pickling.

If using methods (a) or (b) put the eggs into cold water immediately they are cooked, so they cool rapidly. Crack the shells and carefully remove them with the white skin. Pack the eggs fairly loosely into jars. The eggs can be covered with cold unspiced malt vinegar but they have a better flavour with white or brown spiced vinegar (see page 140). The eggs can be used within 1 or 2 days but they develop a more interesting flavour if left for 2 to 3 weeks before using.

PICKLED FRUITS

A number of fruits are delicious if pickled in sweetened vinegar. They make excellent accompaniments to cold meats and poultry and other dishes. Use white wine vinegar or white malt vinegar, so the colour of the fruit is not impaired. Cider vinegar is very good with some fruits, as indicated in the recipes. Fruits, unlike vegetables, do not need brining before pickling.

Use pickling spices sparingly, for these must not overwhelm the flavour of the fruit. There are comments about these spices and information on how to spice the vinegar on page 140.

Traditional recipes use a high percentage of sugar, i.e. often 450 g/1 lb (2 cups) to approximately 300 ml/½ pint (1¼ cups) of vinegar, but this can be reduced if desired, although sufficient sugar should be used to balance the acid flavour of the vinegar. The recommended amount of sugar is given in the recipes with suggestions for reducing this where it will not spoil the flavour of the pickle. Use ordinary white granulated sugar or preserving sugar, without added pectin.

Take great care not to over-cook the fruit, for it must retain a firm texture. This is why the fruit should be kept whole or cut into fairly large pieces.

While ordinary jars with suitable lids, as described on page 139, can be used, pickled and spiced fruits are generally put into bottling jars. Use those with glass not metal lids. The temperature of the hot sweetened vinegar is sufficient to seal the jars, so the contents keep perfectly, even if a lower amount of sugar is used.

SPICED FRUITS

These are similar to pickled fruits, the only difference being that ordinary spices, such as cinnamon, are used instead of, or in addition to, pickling spice.

STORING PICKLED AND SPICED FRUITS

If possible, store the jars away from a sunny window or bright lights for this can cause the fruit to lose colour. Keep the bottles or jars of pickled or spiced fruits for at least 2 months before using them so the flavours mature. They can be kept for one year, but after this the fruits may become too soft from being in liquid so long.

DRAINING THE FRUIT

In the recipes for pickled and spiced fruits that follow, the fruit has to be removed from the vinegar before bottling, so this may be boiled with the sugar to make a syrup, see method below. Use a slotted (perforated) large spoon or a fish slice to remove the fruit, but hold this over the pan until all the drips cease. This method is better than tipping the fruit into a strainer for it avoids the possibility of breaking the cooked fruit.

SPICED APPLES

Cooking time: 30 to 35 minutes • Makes approximately 2.5 kg/5½ lb pickles

Apples are better preserved with sweet spices rather than pickling spices, although a slightly hotter flavour can be given to the fruit, see Variations below. Use a really sharp-flavoured apple to make a good contrast to the sweet syrup. It is essential to choose apples that will not become too soft during cooking. While the spices, except the allspice, can be tied in muslin and heated with the fruit, it is better to boil them in the vinegar first. This gives one a better chance to adapt the flavourings.

Metric/Imperial	Ingredients	American
750 ml/1¼ pints	white malt, white wine or cider vinegar	generous 3 cups
7.5 cm/3 inch length	cinnamon stick	3 inch length
about 10, or to taste	cloves	about 10, or to taste
½ to 1 teaspoon	allspice	½ to 1 teaspoon
1.35 kg/3 lb	cooking apples, weight when peeled and cored	3 lb
800 g/1¾ lb	sugar	3½ cups

Put the vinegar with the spices into a pan and bring to the boil. Lower the heat and simmer for 5 minutes. Check the flavour of the vinegar: if not sufficiently spiced either simmer for a little longer or increase the amount of cloves and allspice and simmer for a few minutes more. Strain the vinegar. Peel and core the apples. Leave whole if small or halve or quarter if large but do not cut into smaller pieces. Place in the hot vinegar and simmer gently until just tender. Lift the apples from the vinegar with a slotted spoon, draining them over the pan as you do so. Pack the apples into the hot sterilized jars (see page 125). Add the sugar to the vinegar, stir over a low heat until dissolved then boil steadily until a syrupy consistency. Pour the boiling vinegar syrup over the apples. Always make sure the fruit is covered with the vinegar and sugar syrup. Put on the lids and seal down immediately. The full amount of sugar given in the recipe produces the best result in Spiced Apples; this is not unduly generous for the amount of vinegar used, but see under Variations.

Variations

Reduced Sugar Spiced Apples: use just 550 g/1¼ lb (2½ cups) sugar to the amount of other ingredients in the recipe.

Ginger Spiced Apples: follow the recipe for Spiced Apples but add 2.5 to 5 cm/1 to 2 inches of chopped root ginger to the vinegar with the other spices or omit the cloves and allspice and use the larger amount of root ginger. Instead of root ginger substitute 1 to 2 teaspoons ground ginger. A few tablespoons thinly sliced or chopped preserved ginger could be heated in the vinegar and sugar syrup just before pouring this over the apples. In this case, use the smaller amounts of root or ground ginger to flavour the vinegar.

Chilli Spiced Apples: follow the recipe for Spiced Apples and use the spices given but add 2 to 3 green or red chilli peppers to the vinegar or a little chilli powder to taste.

Spiced Crab Apples: follow the basic recipe for Spiced Apples, or the variations above, but use the same weight of whole crab apples instead of peeled and cored cooking apples. Choose fruit that is just ripe and free from blemishes. Simmer carefully, so the fruit does not break.

Spiced Pears: use pears instead of apples in the recipe for Spiced Apples on page 152 or the variations that follow. Choose firm dessert pears and halve or quarter them. If the pears are very small just peel them and remove as much core as possible before cooking them in the vinegar. The thinly pared zest from 1 lemon could be added to the spices when flavouring the vinegar.

Spiced Quinces: use halved or quartered peeled quinces instead of the cooking apples. Because of the stronger flavour of quinces they are excellent if preserved in vinegar flavoured with pickling spices (see Pickled Gooseberries on page 156).

I understand that in the past some fruits were preserved by being covered with alcohol. How is this done?
Rather luxurious fruits are generally chosen for this method of preservation, such as dessert cherries, ripe damsons or dessert plums, peaches and dessert pears.

The alcohol used is generally brandy, although rum can be substituted. The uncooked fruit is packed into heated sterilized jars. The alcohol is heated just to boiling point, then poured over the fruit, and the jars are tightly covered. The alcohol can be lightly sweetened if desired by dissolving a little sugar in the alcohol.

A less extravagant method of using alcohol in bottling fruit is achieved by making a fruit syrup as on page 125. Allow it to become quite cold and add the required amount of alcohol. A good blend of flavour is achieved by using 75% syrup and 25% alcohol. Cover the fruit with the cold alcohol flavoured liquid and sterilize as pages 124 to 125.

PICKLED BLACKBERRIES

Cooking time: 25 to 30 minutes • Makes a good 2 kg/4½ lb pickles

The method for pickling blackberries is rather different from that for most other fruits. After the vinegar is spiced and strained the sugar is added and the blackberries cooked for a very short time in the flavoured syrup. Use this method for the other berries listed under variations.

Metric/Imperial	Ingredients	American
1.35 kg/3 lb	**ripe, firm blackberries**	*3 lb*
1½ to 2 teaspoons, or to taste	**mixed pickling spices, see page 139**	*1½ to 2 teaspoons, or to taste*
450 ml/³⁄₄ pint	**white or brown malt vinegar**	*scant 2 cups*
675 g/1½ lb	**sugar**	*3 cups*

If pickling wild blackberries they must be well washed in cold water. Put the fruit into a sieve and run the cold water gently over it. Allow at least 1 hour for the fruit to dry before making the pickles. Simmer the pickling spices in the vinegar for 5 minutes then strain and return the vinegar to the pan with the sugar. Stir over a low heat until the sugar has dissolved then add the blackberries. Cook gently for 3 to 4 minutes only until the fruit is soft but unbroken. Carefully lift the blackberries from the vinegar syrup with a slotted spoon. Hold over the pan so the fruit drains. Pack into warm sterilized jars. Boil the vinegar and sugar until a thicker syrup, pour over the blackberries, covering them completely. Put on the lids and seal down.

Variations

Spiced Blackberries: follow the recipe above but instead of the pickling spices substitute a 2.5 cm/1 inch piece of cinnamon stick or 1 to 2 teaspoons ground cinnamon, 4 to 5 cloves, or ¼ to ½ teaspoon ground cloves and 2 tablespoons (2½ tablespoons) grated root ginger or 1 teaspoon ground ginger. Simmer these in the vinegar, strain if using the cinnamon stick, whole cloves and root ginger, then proceed as the recipe above.

Pickled or Spiced Boysenberries: substitute boysenberries for the blackberries. They are a slightly firmer berry so may need 6 to 7 minutes' cooking in the vinegar and sugar. Loganberries and tayberries could be used instead. Raspberries are too soft and delicate in flavour for these particular recipes.

PICKLED DRIED FRUITS

Dried apricots, figs and prunes make excellent pickles. Rather less sugar is needed than when pickling fresh fruit, for the drying process accentuates the natural sugars in the fruits. The tenderised dried fruit obtainable today is ideal for pickling, since pre-cooking in water is not necessary. This means the flavour of the pickle is much better for the fruit has not been pre-soaked and cooked in water. Pickled and spiced dried fruits are excellent accompaniments to a variety of hot or cold meat and game dishes and delicious with all kinds of cheeses.

PICKLED DRIED APRICOTS

Cooking time: 45 minutes • Makes nearly 900 g/2 lb pickle

It is advisable to soak the apricots in the vinegar before cooking. This enables the vinegar flavour to permeate the fruit.

Metric/Imperial	Ingredients	American
450 g/1 lb	dried apricots	1 lb
600 ml/1 pint	white malt vinegar	2½ cups
1 teaspoon, or to taste	pickling spices, see page 140	1 teaspoon, or to taste
225 g/8 oz	sugar	1 cup

Place the apricots in the vinegar and allow to soak for 2 to 3 hours. Put into the pan and simmer for 30 minutes or until softened. The quality of dried fruits varies so test the fruit to make sure it really is tender before proceeding further. Lift the fruit from the vinegar; drain it very well and pack into hot sterilized jars. Add the pickling spices and sugar to the vinegar, stir over a low heat until the sugar has dissolved then boil steadily until a light syrup. Strain over the fruit. Put on the lids and seal down.

Variations

Spiced Apricots: use the recipe above but omit the pickling spices and add the pared zest of 1 lemon and a 2.5 cm/1 inch length of cinnamon stick to the vinegar instead.

Pickled Figs: substitute figs for the apricots in the recipe and add a 2.5 cm/1 inch length of cinnamon stick to the pickling spices. Soft dark brown sugar, instead of the usual white sugar, gives a good colour and flavour to the pickle.

Spiced Figs: substitute figs for apricots in the recipe. Omit the pickling spices and flavour the vinegar with a 5 cm/2 inch length of cinnamon stick, 3 or 4 cloves and 1 teaspoon allspice, or to taste.

Pickled Prunes: prunes are particularly good when pickled. Substitute prunes for apricots in the recipe. Brown malt vinegar can be used instead of white vinegar to enhance the darkness of the fruit, and light or dark brown sugar instead of the usual white sugar gives a better flavour in this particular pickle.

Spiced Prunes: follow the instructions for Spiced Figs above.

PICKLED GOOSEBERRIES

Cooking time: 35 minutes • Makes a good 2 kg/good 4½ lb pickles

Gooseberries make an excellent sweet pickle but, because the skins are fairly tough, it is better to spice the vinegar, then allow this to become quite cold before adding the fruit. The skins soften better if placed in a cold liquid. Choose fairly large green gooseberries that are firm in texture. For an alternative way of cooking gooseberries and some other fruits, see under Variations.

Metric/Imperial	Ingredients	American
600 ml/1 pint	**white malt or white wine vinegar,** see method	2½ cups
2 teaspoons, or to taste	**mixed pickling spices, see page 139**	2 teaspoons, or to taste
900 g/2 lb	**gooseberries**	2 lb
675 to 900 g/ 1½ to 2 lb	**sugar**	3 to 4 cups

Bring the vinegar and pickling spices to the boil and simmer for 3 to 4 minutes, or longer if a stronger taste is desired (see page 140). Strain and allow to cool or, for a more pronounced taste, leave the spice in the vinegar as it cools then strain. Top and tail the gooseberries then put into the cold spiced vinegar and simmer over a low heat until just tender but unbroken. Lift out of the vinegar and drain well, then pack into heated sterilized jars. Add the sugar to the vinegar, stir over a low heat until the sugar has dissolved then boil steadily until a syrup-like consistency. Pour over the gooseberries, put on the lids and seal.

Variations

Oven-cooked Fruits: gooseberries and the other fruits listed on page 157 can be cooked in the oven without liquid. Do not attempt this method for apples, pears or any fruit that discolours easily.

Pack the prepared gooseberries into the warm, but not hot, sterilized jars. Place glass lids in position on the jars to protect the top layer of fruit but do *not* put on screw bands for oven cooking.

Pad metal trays with a thick layer of paper or cardboard, so there is no fear of the jars cracking in the oven. Preheat the oven to 140°C/275°F,

Gas Mark 1 and cook the gooseberries for approximately 1 hour or until *just* softened. Wearing oven gloves, lift the jars one at a time out of the oven and stand them on a wooden surface. Do this when the vinegar and sugar syrup is quite ready: while the fruit is in the oven, heat the vinegar with the pickling spices, as described on page 140.

Strain and return the vinegar to the pan then add the sugar. Stir over a low heat until the sugar dissolves then boil steadily until a syrup-like consistency. Pour over the fruit. When the jar is full replace the lid and seal down. If the vinegar and syrup cool slightly after filling one or two jars bring them back to boiling point.

Spiced Gooseberries: gooseberries can be spiced rather than pickled. Omit the pickling spices in the vinegar as in the first recipe on the previous page and instead flavour this with 4 or 5 cloves, 5 cm/2 inches of cinnamon stick and ½ to 1 teaspoon allspice. The gooseberries can be cooked in the strained spiced vinegar, as in the recipe on page 156, or by the oven method described on page 156.

Pickled Cherries: use cherries instead of gooseberries in the recipe on page 156 with the same proportions of vinegar and sugar. It is better to cook cherries by the oven method on page 156 rather than simmering them in the vinegar, as in the first recipe on page 156. Make sure the fruit is not over-cooked. Both sharp cooking cherries and dessert fruit can be used. If using dessert cherries the amount of sugar in the recipe on page 156 can be reduced to 550 to 675 g/1¼ to 1½ lb (2½ to 3 cups) to the 600 ml/ 1 pint (2½ cups) vinegar, so giving a less heavy syrup.

Spiced Cherries: use cherries instead of gooseberries in the recipe on page 156 with the same proportions of vinegar and sugar but omit the pickling spices and flavour the vinegar with a 5 cm/2 inch stick of cinnamon, the pared zest from 1 orange and 1 lemon and 2 teaspoons grated fresh ginger. Cook the cherries by the oven method if possible, rather than simmering in the vinegar. Simmer the cinnamon, fruit zest and ginger in the vinegar for 5 to 10 minutes then proceed as for pickled fruit. If using sweet dessert cherries the amount of sugar can be reduced to 550 to 675 g/1¼ to 1½ lb (2½ to 3 cups) to the 600 ml/1 pint (2½ cups) vinegar to give a less heavy syrup.

Pickled Damsons: use ripe but firm damsons instead of gooseberries in the recipe on page 156. Damsons are better prepared by the oven method on page 156 rather than being simmered in vinegar. They are excellent as a pickled fruit. Do not try to stone the fruit. It is advisable to use the full amount of sugar, as given in the recipe on page 156, when pickling damsons.

Pickled Plums: use plums instead of gooseberries in the recipe on page 156 with the same amount of vinegar and sugar. Plums soften easily so choose very firm fruit. Small dark plums can be pickled by the oven method on page 156, but lighter coloured plums keep a better colour if cooked in the vinegar as the method given for gooseberries on page 156. If using sweet plums the sugar can be reduced to 675 g/1½ lb (3 cups) to the 600 ml/1 pint (2½ cups) of vinegar.

PICKLED PEACHES

Cooking time: 25 to 30 minutes • Makes 1.35 kg/3 lb pickles

Peaches and nectarines make wonderful luxury pickles; the fruit is excellent with many cold meat and poultry dishes. Choose yellow cling peaches, rather than the less plentiful white-fleshed fruit. Use pickling spices sparingly so they are not too strong for the delicate flavour of the fruit.

Metric/Imperial	Ingredients	American
900 g/2 lb	ripe peaches, weight when skinned and stoned	2 lb
300 ml/½ pint	white malt vinegar	1¼ cups
1 teaspoon, or to taste	mixed pickling spices, see page 139	1 teaspoon, or to taste
1	lemon	1
450 g/1 lb	sugar	2 cups

Lower the peaches into boiling water, leave for about 30 seconds then remove and put into cold water. Pull off the skins. Halve and remove the stones; these can be cracked and the kernels added to the pickle. Try to keep the peaches in halves but if very large quarter them. Do this just before cooking the fruit so it does not discolour. Put the vinegar and pickling spices into a saucepan, pare the top zest from the lemon and add to the pan then mix in the sugar. Stir over a low heat until the sugar has dissolved. Add the peaches and simmer gently until tender but unbroken. Turn around in the vinegar and sugar so the fruit becomes impregnated with the flavours. Lift the peaches into hot sterilized jars, draining them well. Boil the vinegar and sugar until a syrupy consistency, then strain over the fruit. Put on the lids and seal down. For a milder flavour boil the vinegar with the pickling spices first, strain it, then add the lemon zest, sugar and peaches. This pickle is nicer if sweet, but the sugar could be reduced to 350 g/12 oz (1½ cups).

Variations

Spiced Peaches: use the recipe above but omit the pickling spice and add a 2.5 cm/1 inch length of cinnamon stick and 4 to 5 cloves plus the lemon zest to the vinegar.

For a stronger flavour, 2 teaspoons whole allspice can be used too.

Using Canned Peaches: buy peaches that have been canned in natural juice. Drain well and weigh. Put into the very hot prepared syrup for pickling or spicing and simmer for 4 to 5 minutes only, then pack into jars. Simmer the syrup as in the recipe and pour over the fruit.

Pickled or Spiced Apricots: use apricots instead of peaches in the recipes. These can be left whole but in time the stones do add an almond flavour to the syrup. If you wish to avoid this then halve the fruit and remove the stones. It is not necessary to skin apricots.

Pickled or Spiced Mangoes: use the flesh from mangoes, cutting it into neat slices; weigh and use instead of peaches in the recipes above.

Pickled or Spiced Nectarines: use nectarines instead of peaches in the recipes.

PICKLED RHUBARB

Cooking time: 50 minutes • Makes nearly 1.8 kg/4 lb pickles

When pickled, as in this recipe, the rhubarb preserve has a fairly thick consistency almost like chutney. It makes a pleasant change from rhubarb chutney, though, for the flavour of the rhubarb is very definite. Use the mature garden, and not the delicate forced, rhubarb for this preserve.

Metric/Imperial	Ingredients	American
1 teaspoon, or to taste	**pickling spices,** *see page 140*	1 teaspoon, or to taste
2.5 cm/1 inch	**cinnamon stick, optional**	1 inch
2 tablespoons, or to taste	**grated root ginger**	2½ tablespoons, or to taste
450 ml/³/₄ pint	**white malt vinegar**	nearly 2 cups
900 g/2 lb	**rhubarb**	2 lb
675 g/1½ lb	**sugar**	3 cups

Put the spices with the cinnamon and ginger into the vinegar and simmer for 5 minutes, or a little longer if you prefer a slightly stronger flavour. Strain and return the vinegar to the pan. For a highly spiced pickle the spices can be tied in muslin and cooked with the rhubarb and removed just before potting the preserve. Cut the rhubarb into 3.5 to 5 cm/1½ to 2 inch pieces and add to the vinegar with the sugar. Stir over a low heat until the sugar has dissolved then simmer gently until the rhubarb is just tender. Lift from the vinegar and sugar syrup and drain well. Pack into hot sterilized jars. Boil the sugar and vinegar until a thick syrup then pour over the rhubarb. Put on the lids and seal down.

CHUTNEYS

Chutney is one of the most interesting of preserves for it combines both sweet and savoury flavours and can include both fruits and vegetables. It is an ideal accompaniment to a range of cold dishes, in addition to being the perfect partner for curry. The word chutney is derived from the Hindu 'chatni', which means strongly spiced, and the Indian chutneys, such as those on page 170, are full of the flavour of different spices. You can reduce or increase the spices as you desire.

The advice given on page 139 about the choice of cooking utensils when making pickles is just as important when preparing chutney. In addition, the following points should be remembered:

1. Do not cut down on the amounts of sugar and vinegar in the recipes, for these are the preservatives. If you do want to reduce the sugar content then the very hot chutneys must be put into bottling jars and sterilized, as for vegetables on page 126, since most chutneys contain onions. If the chutney is based on fruit only, then sterilize as for a fruit on page 126.

    Chutney can be frozen but always bring the jar out of the freezer some days before you want it so the flavours can mature.
2. If you have reduced the amount of sugar in a chutney, the opened jar must be stored in the refrigerator.
3. In a few of the recipes that follow the vinegar is added gradually to the ingredients. This is because in that particular chutney it allows the other flavours to prevail. Always use good-quality vinegar (see page 138). Where white vinegar is recommended this is to preserve the colour of the chutney.
4. When cooking chutney, do not cover the pan, unless the recipe states that this is important, for the chutney thickens by evaporation. As the mixture thickens, it is essential to stir from time to time to prevent it sticking to the pan.
5. Spoon the chutney into the hot jars as soon as possible after the end of the cooking period and cover it at once. A waxed circle, such as that used for jam, can be placed over the chutney but final jam covers are inadequate for any preserve containing vinegar. Use a glass lid if possible. If a metal cover is used it must be protected by cardboard or thick paper, since the vinegar would rust the metal (see page 139).
6. Most kinds of chutney take time to mature in flavour, so try to keep the jar for a month before opening it. There are, however, recipes for chutneys that can be made and eaten within a day or two (see pages 168, 177 and 178).
7. Store the chutney in a cool dry place, preferably away from a bright light for this can spoil the colour.

CHUTNEY INGREDIENTS

The choice of ingredients for making chutney is important, as with any preserve. Make sure all fruits and vegetables are fresh – the fruits should be just ripe, unless the recipe states to the contrary.

Vinegar is of great importance – giving a good flavour and acting as a preservative. There are guidelines about the choice of vinegar on page 138. You can vary the kind of vinegar you use, provided it is of sufficient strength to be a good preservative. Do *not* cut down on the quantity given in the recipe.

Sugar can be white or brown, though in some recipes a definite recommendation is given.

Onions are an important ingredient in most chutney recipes. Home-grown onions give a stronger taste than Spanish or red ones. In a few recipes the amount of onions is stressed by giving the weight when peeled and chopped. That is because in those specific recipes the balance of onions is of great importance.

Spices should be as fresh as possible. There is more about choosing and storing spices on pages 139 to 140, together with information on the use of pickling spices and on making your own mixtures.

Chillies are also very important, for they add a hot taste to a chutney. Dried chillies are included in most pickling spices, so to differentiate between these and fresh ones, which are easily obtained, I have called fresh chillies 'chilli peppers'. Handle these carefully for the pods and seeds can cause an unpleasant stinging feeling if your hands touch your face after preparing them.

Salt and pepper are needed in most chutneys, but it is better to season the mixture very lightly during cooking and to adjust the amount at the end of the cooking period, when all the flavours have blended together.

APPLE CHUTNEY

Cooking time: 40 minutes • Makes nearly 1.8 kg/4 lb chutney

Apple chutney is one of the most popular of all the fruit chutneys. Use a good cooking apple with plenty of flavour. The chutney can be varied in many ways, as indicated below. Apples are also an important ingredient in many other chutneys for they add flavour and a good consistency to the preserve. In this recipe, and in most of the fruit chutneys, the spices are tied in muslin and left in the pan until the chutney is cooked. If preferred, they can be simmered for 5 minutes, or longer, in the vinegar before making the chutney. The vinegar should then be strained. As there is a fairly small amount of vinegar in these particular chutneys, measure this after simmering with the spices and add a little more to make up the full quantity.

Metric/Imperial	Ingredients	American
450 g/1 lb	**onions, weight when peeled and finely chopped**	4 cups
300 ml/½ pint	**white malt vinegar**	1¼ cups

900 g/2 lb	cooking apples, weight when peeled and cored	2 lb
1 teaspoon	mixed pickling spices, see page 139	1 teaspoon
350 g/12 oz	soft light brown sugar	1½ cups
100 g/4 oz	raisins or other dried fruit	⁴/₅ cup
to taste	salt and freshly ground black pepper	to taste

Chop the onions and put into half the amount of vinegar and simmer gently for about 10 minutes. Cut the apples into 2 cm/¾ inch dice and add to the pan with the rest of the vinegar, the pickling spices (tied in muslin), the sugar, dried fruit and a little seasoning. Stir over a low heat until the sugar has dissolved then simmer steadily, stirring from time to time, until the consistency of a thick jam. Remove the bag of pickling spices. Spoon the chutney into hot jars and seal down.

Variations

Spiced Apple Chutney: omit the pickling spices in the recipe above and simply add 1 teaspoon ground mixed spice to the other ingredients. Taste the chutney before the end of the cooking time and increase the amount of mixed spice if desired.

Apple Ginger Chutney: add 1 to 2 tablespoons grated root ginger to the pickling spices or 1 teaspoon ground ginger to the other ingredients.
To make a more interesting chutney omit the dried fruit and add the same amount of diced preserved ginger. This should be blended with the other ingredients when the chutney is almost cooked.

Apple Mint Chutney: this makes an excellent accompaniment to mutton and lamb dishes. Follow the recipe for Apple Chutney and add 3 tablespoons (3¾ tablespoons) freshly chopped mint to the chutney when it is almost cooked.

Elderberry Chutney: follow the Apple Chutney recipe but if you are very fond of elderberries use 450 g/1 lb elderberries and 450 g/1 lb apples.
For a less strong flavour use only 225 g/8 oz (2 cups) elderberries and 675 g/1½ lb apples. In each case the weight of apples is when peeled and cored.

Green Tomato Chutney (1): use 900 g/2 lb green tomatoes plus 225 g/8 oz (½ lb) cooking apples (weight when peeled and cored) in the recipe for Apple Chutney or the variations that follow on page 161. The dried fruit can be omitted.

Gooseberry Chutney: either firm green gooseberries or riper fruit can be used. Follow the recipe for Apple Chutney on page 161 but substitute gooseberries for the apples.

Gooseberry and Orange Chutney: use firm green gooseberries instead of apples in the recipe for Apple Chutney on page 161. Add the finely grated zest of 2 large oranges plus the orange juice. These should be added with the gooseberries.

Papaya (Pawpaw) Chutney: use 675 g/1½ lb papaya (weight without skin and seeds) plus 450 g/1 lb cooking apples (weight when peeled and cored) in the recipe for Apple Chutney or the variations that follow on pages 161 to 162.

Melon could be used in the same way.

Plum and Apple Chutney: use 675 g/1½ lb plums with 450 g/1 lb apples (weight when peeled and cored) in the Apple Chutney recipe or the variations that follow on pages 161 to 162. Choose sharp cooking plums if possible, halve them and remove the stones. The kernels can be cracked and added to the chutney just before the end of the cooking time. Cook the plums and apples together.

Sultanas (seedless light raisins) are the best dried fruit to use with plums.

Rhubarb Chutney (1): use 6 75 g/1½ lb rhubarb and 450 g/1 lb apples in the recipe for Apple Chutney on page 161, adding 1 to 2 teaspoons ground ginger to the other ingredients. This proportion of rhubarb and apple could be used instead of all apples in the Apple Ginger Chutney on page 162.

How does one sterilize a chutney or purée?
- If the chutney is made only of fruit and does not include any vegetables then follow the method given on page 15 for sterilizing jam.
- Fruit purées can be sterilized in the same way.
- If the chutney contains vegetables then it is wise to use a pressure cooker. Put the hot chutney into hot sterilized bottling jars. Place on the rack in the pressure cooker with 600 ml/1 pint (2½ cups) boiling water. Fix the lid, bring to pressure, as detailed on page 126, and maintain for 10 minutes.
- Cooked vegetable purées,are sterilized in the same way, but allow 20 minutes at pressure.

APRICOT CHUTNEY

Cooking time: 50 minutes • Makes 1.7 kg/good 3¾ lb chutney

It is better to use dried, rather than fresh, apricots in this chutney for their flavour is more pronounced. The modern tenderised apricots are ideal for they can be cooked without soaking. If using the type that needs soaking, place in the vinegar and leave overnight before cooking. The amount of pickling spices in this recipe is very generous, so use just half the recommended amount if you do not enjoy highly spiced foods.

Metric/Imperial	Ingredients	American
225 g/8 oz	dried apricots	1¼ cups
600 ml/1 pint	white wine vinegar	2½ cups
2	garlic cloves, optional	2
1	lemon	1

2 teaspoons	mixed pickling spices, see page 139	2 teaspoons
450 g/1 lb	cooking apples, weight when peeled and cored	1 lb
450 g/1 lb	light brown sugar	2 cups
75 g/3 oz	raisins	generous ½ cup
150 g/5 oz	sultanas (seedless light raisins)	1 cup
to taste	salt and freshly ground black pepper	to taste

Cut the apricots into small pieces and place in the preserving pan with the vinegar. Peel the garlic cloves (but do not chop them) and pare the top zest from the lemon. Put the garlic, lemon zest and pickling spices into muslin and tie securely. Place in the pan with the apricots and vinegar. Simmer steadily for 30 minutes. Peel the apples and either grate or chop them very finely. Add to the apricots with 2 tablespoons (2½ tablespoons) lemon juice and the sugar. Stir over a low heat until the sugar has dissolved. Add the dried fruit and a little seasoning. Simmer steadily until the consistency of a thick jam. Remove the bag of pickling spices. Spoon the chutney into hot jars and seal down.

Variations

Apricot and Lemon Chutney: omit the pickling spices and garlic cloves in the recipe above but use 2 large lemons. Halve these and squeeze out 4 tablespoons (5 tablespoons) juice. Discard the pips then shred or chop the peel and pulp of the lemons, as though making marmalade. Soak in the vinegar overnight then continue as Apricot Chutney.

Fig Chutney: use dried figs instead of apricots in the first recipe with the same amount of pickling spices and garlic. Brown malt vinegar gives a richer colour to the preserve.

Peach Chutney: use dried peaches instead of apricots in the main recipe or the Apricot and Lemon Chutney above.

Prune Chutney: substitute the same weight of prunes for apricots in the main recipe (weigh the prunes when stoned). The garlic cloves are particularly suitable for Prune Chutney. The flavour of tea is often associated with prunes for it gives them a richer flavour. Tie a tea bag (preferably Earl Grey or China tea) with the pickling spices and garlic and cook with the other ingredients.

AUTUMN CHUTNEY

Cooking time: 1¼ hours • Makes 3.8 kg/8½ lb chutney

This chutney is an excellent way of using the last of the autumn fruits, including marrow. The suggested proportions of fruit in the method can be varied according to personal taste, so long as the total weight of fruit remains the same. This is essential to balance the amount of vinegar and sugar.

Metric/Imperial	Ingredients	American
2 kg/4½ lb	mixed fruits, weight when prepared, see method	4½ lb
675 g/1½ lb	onions	1½ lb
450 g/1 lb	green or red tomatoes	1 lb
750 ml/1¼ pints	vinegar	generous 3 cups
2 teaspoons	mixed pickling spices, see page 139	2 teaspoons
2	garlic cloves	2
450 g/1 lb	sugar, preferably dark brown	2 cups
450 g/1 lb	raisins	generous 3 cups

The best mixture of fruits is 450 g/1 lb each of cooking apples, marrow, pears and plums with 225 g/8 oz (2 cups) blackberries. Peel and core the apples and pears; peel the marrow and remove the seeds; stone the plums. Cut these ingredients into fairly small pieces. Peel and finely chop the onions; skin and chop the tomatoes. You could use half green and half red tomatoes. Pour half the vinegar into the preserving pan, add the onions. Tie the pickling spices in muslin with the peeled garlic cloves and add to the pan. Simmer for 15 minutes. Add the prepared fruits and the rest of the vinegar and cook gently until the fruits are soft. Add the sugar, stir over a low heat until dissolved, then put in the raisins. Stir again and cook steadily until the chutney is like a thick jam. Remove the bag of spices. Spoon the chutney into hot jars and seal down.

Variations

- A little salt and freshly ground black pepper or cayenne pepper can be added to the ingredients above. Taste the chutney when almost ready then add seasoning if desired. A little ground ginger can be added to give a stronger flavour.

Golden Chutney: follow the recipe above but use a mixture of cooking apples, fresh apricots, pears and peaches. Omit the blackberries, marrow and tomatoes but make up the total weight (2.5 kg/5½ lb, i.e. 2 kg/4½ lb mixed fruit plus 450 g/1 lb tomatoes) with the fruits listed. Use white malt vinegar or white wine vinegar and white sugar together with sultanas (seedless light raisins) instead of raisins.

Pear and Apple Chutney: follow the recipe for Autumn Chutney on page 164 but use only cooking apples and pears, instead of the mixture of fruits, to make 2.5 kg/5½ lb. This chutney is excellent when flavoured with 3 teaspoons of ground ginger. About 5 tablespoons (6¼ tablespoons) diced preserved ginger can also be added with the raisins.

BLACKBERRY (BRAMBLE) CHUTNEY (1)

Cooking time: 1 hour • Makes good 2.25 kg/5 lb chutney

Blackberries make an interesting chutney which is particularly good served with a strongly flavoured liver pâté. It is necessary to sieve the fruit to get rid of the very hard pips.

Metric/Imperial	Ingredients	American
450 g/1 lb	onions	1 lb
1 or 2	garlic cloves	1 or 2
600 ml/1 pint	white malt vinegar	2½ cups
1 teaspoon	mustard powder	1 teaspoon
1 teaspoon	ground ginger	1 teaspoon
½ teaspoon	grated or ground nutmeg	½ teaspoon
450 g/1 lb	cooking apples, weight when peeled and cored	1 lb
1.35 kg/3 lb	blackberries	3 lb
450 g/1 lb	sugar	2 cups
to taste	salt and freshly ground black pepper	to taste

Peel and chop the onions and garlic very finely. Put into the preserving pan with about half the vinegar and the spices. Simmer gently for 15 minutes. Dice the apples and add to the pan with the blackberries and the remaining vinegar. Simmer for 30 minutes or until the fruit is very soft. Rub through a nylon sieve and return to the pan. Heat to boiling point, add the sugar and stir over a low heat until this has dissolved. Season to taste. Raise the heat slightly and simmer until the consistency of a thick jam. Spoon into hot jars and seal down.

Variations

Blackberry and Apple Chutney: use the recipe above with only 900 g/2 lb blackberries and 900 g/2 lb apples (weight when peeled and cored). The amount of ground ginger could be increased to 2 teaspoons.

Damson Chutney: follow the recipe for Blackberry Chutney but use a good 1.5 kg/3½ lb damsons. Simmer these with the other ingredients until soft. Either remove all the stones or rub the fruit through a nylon sieve as for blackberries then return to the pan. Continue as Blackberry Chutney.

Damson and Apple Chutney: follow the variation for Blackberry and Apple Chutney but use 900 g/2 lb apples (weight when peeled and cored) and nearly 1.125 kg/nearly 2½ lb damsons. Simmer these with the other ingredients until soft then either remove the stones or rub through a sieve. Return to the pan and continue as the recipe.

BLACKBERRY (BRAMBLE) CHUTNEY (2)

Cooking time: 1 to 1¼ hours • Makes approximately 2.5kg/5½ lb chutney

This recipe gives an interesting but mild-flavoured chutney. To increase the flavour see Variations below.

Metric/Imperial	Ingredients	American
1 teaspoon	mixed pickling spices, see page 139	1 teaspoon
450 g/1 lb	onions	1 lb
900 g/2 lb	cooking apples, weight when peeled and cored	2 lb
900 g/2 lb	blackberries	2 lb
2 teaspoons	grated lemon rind	2 teaspoons
450 ml/¾ pint	white malt vinegar	scant 2 cups
350 g/12 oz	sugar	1½ cups
3 tablespoons	lemon juice	3¾ tablespoons
1 teaspoon	ground ginger	1 teaspoon

Tie the pickling spices in a muslin bag, or see the information on pages 139 to 140. Peel and finely chop the onions; cut the apples into small dice. Rinse the blackberries well, especially if wild fruit, and drain thoroughly before using. Put the onions, apples and blackberries into the preserving pan with the lemon rind and half the vinegar. Add the bag of pickling spices. Simmer gently until the apples and onions are tender then remove the bag of spices. Pour the rest of the vinegar into the pan, add the sugar, lemon juice and ginger. Stir over a low heat until the sugar has dissolved then boil steadily, stirring from time to time, until the consistency of a thick jam. Spoon into hot jars and seal down.

Variations

- To give more flavour add 2 to 3 peeled and crushed garlic cloves to the onions.
- Increase the amount of ginger, either by using 2 teaspoons ground ginger or omitting this and using 1 tablespoon (1¼ tablespoons) grated fresh ginger.
- Give a different texture to the chutney by adding 4 tablespoons (5 tablespoons) coarsely chopped nuts when the chutney is almost cooked. Walnuts or pecans are a good choice.
- There is no seasoning in this particular chutney, but salt and freshly ground black pepper can be added towards the end of the cooking period.

CRANBERRY CHUTNEY

Cooking time: 45 minutes • Makes 1.35 kg/3 lb chutney

This is one of the best of the sweet chutneys. It makes a good alternative to the Cranberry Ketchup below or the cranberry sauce made at Christmas time. This recipe uses a fairly high percentage of pickling spice, but it can be adjusted to personal taste.

Metric/Imperial	Ingredients	American
450 g/1 lb	cooking apples, weight when peeled and cored	1 lb
450 g/1 lb	cranberries	1 lb
2 teaspoons	mixed pickling spices, see page 139	2 teaspoons
300 ml/1/2 pint	cider or white malt vinegar	1 1/4 cups
1/2 to 1 teaspoon	ground mixed spice	1/2 to 1 teaspoon
350 g/12 oz	sugar	1 1/2 cups
175g/6 oz	raisins	generous 1 cup
to taste	salt and freshly ground black pepper	to taste

Put the apples and cranberries into the pan. Tie the spices in muslin and add to the fruit with the vinegar and ground mixed spice. Cover the pan tightly, for the cranberries jump in the air until they are softened. Cook gently for 15 minutes then stir briskly and simmer with the lid off until the fruit is soft. Add the sugar and stir over a low heat until dissolved then put in the raisins and boil steadily until the consistency of a thick jam. Season lightly to taste. Remove the bag of pickling spices. Spoon into hot jars and seal down.

Variations

•   For a more savoury chutney simmer 225 g/8 oz (2 cups) finely chopped onion with the apples and cranberries.

Cranberry Ketchup: follow the recipe above for making chutney. Rub the cooked mixture through a hair or nylon sieve then return to the pan. Add an extra 150 ml/1/4 pint (2/3 cup) vinegar and bring the smooth mixture to boiling point. It should be the consistency of a ketchup but remember it will stiffen as it cools, so add more vinegar if necessary. Taste the preserve and add extra seasoning if required.

Pour the boiling ketchup into heated containers; loosen the caps as described on page 125, then place in a sterilizer or deep pan filled with boiling water (see page 125). Sterilize for 10 minutes and then tighten the caps.

DATE CHUTNEY

Cooking time: 10 minutes • Makes nearly 675 g/1 1/2 lb chutney

This is a very easy-to-make and pleasant chutney. No extra sugar is required for the dates provide the sweetness. Store in the refrigerator for 2 to 3 days before using but do not keep for more than 2 to 3 weeks. The amount of pickling spices suggested is generous for the quality of vinegar used so adjust this to personal taste.

Metric/Imperial	Ingredients	American
2 teaspoons	mixed pickling spices, see page 139	2 teaspoons
300 ml/½ pint	brown malt vinegar	1¼ cups
¼ teaspoon	ground ginger, optional	¼ teaspoon
1 medium	mild flavoured onion, see page 161	1 medium
450 g/1 lb	dried dates, weight when stoned (pitted) and chopped	1 lb

Put the pickling spices into the vinegar and boil for 10 minutes. Add the ginger at the end of the 10 minutes if you feel the flavour would be improved. Meanwhile peel and finely chop the onion. Mix with the dates and put into heated jars. Strain the boiling vinegar over the dates and seal down.

HOT PEPPER JELLY

Cooking time: 20 minutes • Makes approximately 2 kg/4 lb jelly

This jelly is one of the most popular preserves in western America. I have been given a variety of recipes from friends, who told me I must include the jelly in this book. It is splendid with cream cheese as an appetiser or with cold dishes. I have experimented with a variety of recipes and this is the one I prefer. It is based on the kind of peppers readily available in Britain. The jelly is full of pepper pieces, and in the variation some of the peppers are sieved to give a smooth texture.

Metric/Imperial	Ingredients	American
3 medium	red chilli peppers	3 medium
4 medium	sweet red peppers	4 medium
3 medium	green peppers	3 medium
450 g/1 lb	cooking apples, weight when peeled and cored	1 lb
450 ml/¾ pint	cider or white wine vinegar	scant 2 cups
900 g/2 lb	sugar	4 cups
175 ml/6 fl oz	Certo	¾ cup

Neatly chop the chilli peppers; if you require a less hot flavour split these first and remove the seeds before chopping. Be extremely careful to wash your hands afterwards, for if you touch your eyes or the skin around them it could be extremely painful. Halve and deseed the other peppers and cut them into 1.5 to 2 cm/½ to ¾ inch dice. Cut the apples into similar sized dice. Put all the peppers and apples into the vinegar and cook for 8 to 10 minutes, or until nearly tender but unbroken. Add the sugar and stir over a low heat until this has dissolved then boil for 5 minutes. Remove from the heat and add the Certo. Stir well to blend. Spoon into hot jars and seal down. It is advisable to store this jelly in the refrigerator, where it will keep for some weeks. Within a few days the mixture forms a jelly. For long-term storage spoon the boiling mixture into bottling jars, and sterilize as fruit purées on page 126. Do not freeze the mixture if you want to maintain the firm texture of the peppers.

Variations

- Put the chopped chilli peppers with half the red and half the green peppers and all the apples into the vinegar and cook steadily for a good 10 minutes. Rub the mixture through a nylon sieve and return to the pan. Add the rest of the diced peppers and cook for 6 to 8 minutes, then add the amount of sugar given above. Stir until the sugar dissolves. Boil for 5 minutes. Remove from the heat and stir in the Certo. Store as recommended above.
- In some recipes the apples are omitted, in which case reduce the amount of vinegar to 300 ml/½ pint (1¼ cups) and the sugar by 100 g/4 oz (½ cup), or 225 g/8 oz (1 cup) for a less sweet jelly.

INDIAN FRUIT CHUTNEY

Cooking time: 2 hours • Makes approximately 3.6 kg/8 lb

The Indian chutneys that follow should all be cooked for a fairly long period, so the dried fruits become very soft. The main recipe includes some of the more exotic fruits that would have been used in the chutney in India, whilst the variations give more familiar alternatives. This first recipe is for a very hot chutney, but the amount of spices can be reduced to suit personal tastes.

Metric/Imperial	Ingredients	American
2	red chilli peppers	2
2	garlic cloves	2
5 cm/2 inches	root ginger	2 inches
1 tablespoon	mustard seeds	1¼ tablespoons
900 ml/1½ pints	brown malt vinegar	3¾ cups
300 g/10 oz	raisins	2 cups
225 g/8 oz	dates, weight when stoned (pitted) and chopped	1½ cups
450 g/1 lb	onions	1 lb
450 g/1 lb	mangoes, weight when skinned and stoned	1 lb
225 g/8 oz	tamarillos or tomatoes	½ lb
225 g/8 oz	apricots	½ lb
450 g/1 lb	cooking apples, weight when peeled and cored	1 lb
1.35 kg/3 lb	sugar	6 cups

Slice the chilli peppers; the pods can be split and the seeds removed to give a less hot flavour. Wash your hands carefully after handling these, see page 161. Peel and slice the garlic and chop the ginger. Put the chilli peppers, garlic, ginger and mustard seeds into the vinegar and simmer for 5 to 10 minutes, depending on how strongly flavoured you would like the pickle to be. Strain and return the vinegar to the pan. Add the dried fruits and the onions and simmer for 20 minutes. Dice the various fruits, add to the pan and simmer for about 45 minutes, stirring from time to time.

Put in the sugar, stir over a low heat until this has dissolved then boil steadily until the consistency of a thick jam. Spoon into hot jars and seal down.

Variations

- For a hotter flavour tie the mustard seeds in muslin and cook with the pickle. The chilli peppers, garlic and root ginger should be cooked with the rest of the ingredients.
- For a less expensive pickle use 1.35 kg/3 lb of cooking apples (weight when peeled and cored) instead of the mixture of fruits.

Curried Fruit Chutney: omit the chilli peppers, ginger and mustard seeds. Heat 1 tablespoon (1¼ tablespoons) sunflower or olive oil in a pan, add 1 to 2 tablespoons curry powder (the amount depends upon personal taste), cook gently in the oil, then add the vinegar, onions and dried fruits, etc. Continue as the main recipe.

MANGO CHUTNEY (1)

Cooking time: 35 to 40 minutes • Makes nearly 1.8 kg/4 lb chutney

As mangoes are expensive fruits in Britain, the main recipe uses them sparingly; the second recipe is more generous. The inclusion of apples below gives a very pleasant preserve. Mango chutney is one of the favourite accompaniments for curry so it is well worth making this. Do not use really ripe mangoes.

Metric/Imperial	Ingredients	American
350 g/12 oz	onions, weight when finely chopped	3 cups
675 g/1½ lb	mangoes, weight when skinned and stoned (pitted)	1½ lb
450 g/1 lb	cooking apples, weight when peeled and cored	1 lb
2 teaspoons	mixed pickling spices, see page 139	2 teaspoons
300 ml/½ pint	white wine vinegar	1¼ cups
1 medium	orange	1 medium
550 g/1¼ lb	sugar	2½ cups
to taste	salt and freshly ground black pepper, optional	to taste

Put the onions into the preserving pan. Cut just over half the mango pulp and all the apples into 2 cm/¾ inch dice and add to the onions. Cut the remainder of the mango pulp into neat slices and put on one side. Tie the pickling spices in muslin and add to the pan with the vinegar. Simmer gently for about 20 minutes until the onions and fruit are getting soft. Grate the zest of the orange very finely, halve the fruit and squeeze out the juice. Add the zest and juice to the pan with the mango and cook for 5 minutes only. Put in the sugar and stir over a low heat until dissolved then boil steadily until the consistency of a soft, rather than stiff, jam. Season lightly to taste, although many mango chutneys are not seasoned.

Remove the bag of pickling spices. Allow the chutney to cool for about 8 minutes in the pan, stir to distribute the pieces of mango then spoon into hot jars and seal down.

<hr>

Variations

- For a milder flavoured pickle boil the pickling spices for 4 to 5 minutes only in the vinegar, strain this and use as the vinegar (without extra spices) in the recipe above.
- For a more piquant flavour add 1 to 2 teaspoons ground ginger with the vinegar.
- For a less sweet chutney reduce the amount of sugar to 400 g/14 oz (1¾ cups).

Mango Chutney (2): omit the apples in the recipe. Use 1.35 kg/3 lb mangoes (weight when skinned and stoned). In countries where mangoes are grown, somewhat under-ripe fruit are chosen; this means the pieces of fruit stay firmer during cooking. Use the same amounts of onions, vinegar, orange and sugar as in the recipe but add 2 peeled and chopped garlic cloves to the onions and 2 hot red chillies to the pickling spices. Boil these in the vinegar for 5 to 10 minutes, depending on how highly spiced you like the chutney, then strain the vinegar and follow the recipe.

Other recipes give the chutney a strong flavour by adding up to 3 tablespoons (3¾ tablespoons) finely chopped or grated root ginger with the onions.

If you like dried fruit in a chutney add 150 g/5 oz (1 cup) raisins to either of the Mango Chutney recipes. The raisins can be covered with a little rum and soaked for 30 minutes before adding to the chutney when the sugar has dissolved.

MUSTARD FRUIT CHUTNEY

Cooking time: 30 to 35 minutes • Makes 2.25 kg/5 lb chutney

Although called a chutney, this preserve has the clarity of a vinegar pickle but mixed fruits are used instead of the usual vegetables. The mustard flavouring is first boiled with the vinegar, and the sugar is added to this so the fruits are tenderized in a vinegar syrup.

Metric/Imperial	Ingredients	American
450 ml/¾ pint	white wine vinegar	scant 2 cups
1½ tablespoons	mustard seeds	1¾ tablespoons
1.35 kg/3 lb	mixed fruits, see method	3 lb
675g/1½ lb	sugar	3 cups

Put the vinegar and mustard seeds into a pan and bring to the boil. Lower the heat and simmer for 5 minutes. For a stronger flavour you could lightly crush the seeds before using them and/or allow the seeds to stand in the hot vinegar until it has become quite cold. Strain the vinegar. Prepare the fruits – they should all be cut into very small pieces, except the cherries which should be stoned and left whole. Try to have a good variation in the fruits used. They could include 2 or 3 clementines and

1 orange – cut away the peel and discard the pith. Cut the peel into very small pieces and leave to soak for several hours in the cold mustard-flavoured vinegar. Remove the pulp from the clementines and oranges and cut the segments into small pieces; add peeled, diced ripe pears, skinned, diced peaches, diced fresh apricots, a small amount of finely diced ripe, but not over-ripe melon, and a little diced pineapple. Weigh the fruits when prepared so you have the right amount. Strain the diced fruits so excess juice is not mixed with the vinegar syrup. This juice could be used in a fruit salad. Heat the vinegar with the fruit peel and simmer for 10 minutes. Add the sugar and stir until dissolved then boil steadily until a light syrup. Add the fruits, simmer gently for about 10 minutes then allow to cool in the pan until the chutney begins to stiffen. Stir to distribute the fruits then spoon into hot bottling jars and seal down.

ORANGE AND LEMON CHUTNEY

Cooking time: 1³/₄ to 2 hours • Makes 1.35 kg/3 lb chutney

This recipe and the variations that follow make very refreshing chutneys. They are excellent accompaniments to many fish dishes, including fish curries, and are also good partners to cheese.

Metric/Imperial	Ingredients	American
3 large	lemons	3 large
3 medium	oranges	3 medium
600 ml/1 pint	white malt vinegar	2¹/₂ cups
1 teaspoon	mixed pickling spices, see page 139	1 teaspoon
2.5 cm/1 inch	cinnamon stick	1 inch
1 tablespoon	chopped root ginger	1¹/₄ tablespoons
225 g/8 oz	onions, weight when peeled and finely chopped	2 cups
450 g/1 lb	caster or granulated sugar	2 cups
175 g/6 oz	sultanas (seedless light raisins)	generous 1 cup
to taste	salt and freshly ground black pepper	to taste

Wash the fruit to remove the wax coating then halve and squeeze out the juice. Discard the pips but shred or finely chop the peel and pulp as though making marmalade. Simmer the vinegar with the pickling spices, cinnamon and ginger for 5 minutes or to personal taste, then strain. Put the orange and lemon peel and pulp into the vinegar and leave to soak overnight or for several hours. Add the fruit juice and the onions and simmer gently until the peel and onions are tender. Put in the sugar and stir until dissolved then add the sultanas and seasoning. Simmer steadily until the consistency of thick jam, then spoon into hot jars and seal down.

Variations

Lemon Chutney: use 6 lemons and omit the oranges in the recipe. This particular chutney is better if the pickling spice and cinnamon are omitted. Use 1 teaspoon white mustard seeds and the grated ginger and heat these in the vinegar then follow the method as above.

Lemon and Cucumber Chutney: use 4 large lemons and 1 peeled and diced cucumber and omit the oranges in the recipe. Peel and finely chop the cucumber and add to the chutney with the chopped onions. Use the mustard seeds and ginger as in Lemon Chutney.

RATATOUILLE CHUTNEY

Cooking time: 45 minutes • Makes 1.8 kg/4 lb chutney

Lovers of the French ratatouille (vegetable ragôut) will enjoy this chutney in which the same vegetables are used. No sugar is used in the main recipe, so this chutney should be kept in the refrigerator or bottled like a vegetable purée, see page 126.

Metric/Imperial	Ingredients	American
450 g/1 lb	aubergines (egg plant)	1 lb
450 g/1 lb	courgettes (zucchini)	1 lb
450 g/1 lb	onions	1 lb
2 to 4	garlic cloves, depending upon personal taste	2 to 4
450 g/1 lb	ripe tomatoes	1 lb
1 teaspoon	mixed pickling spices (see page 139)	1 teaspoon
600 ml/1 pint	white or brown malt vinegar	2½ cups
2 tablespoons	tomato purée (paste)	2½ tablespoons
to taste	salt and freshly ground black pepper	to taste
pinch	cayenne pepper	pinch

Wipe the aubergines and courgettes but do not peel them. Cut into 2 cm/³/₄ inch dice. Peel and finely chop the onions and garlic. Skin and chop the tomatoes. Put all these ingredients into the preserving pan. Tie the pickling spices in muslin, and add to the pan with the vinegar, tomato purée and seasonings – use these sparingly at first. Simmer in an open pan, stirring from time to time, until the vegetables are tender and the chutney is like a thick jam. Remove the bag of spices. Spoon into hot jars and seal down.

Variations

Ratatouille with Peppers: 2 or 3 deseeded and diced red or green peppers can be added to the chutney above or the variation below.

Sweet Ratatouille Chutney: use the ingredients above plus 450 g/1 lb cooking apples (weight when peeled and cored), 150 g/5 oz (1 cup) raisins (these are optional) and 450 g/1 lb (2 cups) brown sugar. Dice the apples

and cook with the other ingredients together with the raisins. When soft add the sugar, stir until dissolved then boil until the consistency of a thick jam. Remove the bag of spices, spoon into hot jars and seal down.
The inclusion of sugar means this chutney keeps well.

You could add 1 or 2 teaspoons ground ginger or 1 to 2 tablespoons finely chopped root ginger to the Ratatouille Chutney or this sweet version.

RED PEPPER RELISH

Cooking time: 30 minutes • Makes 1.35 kg/3 lb relish

This preserve has a slightly less smooth consistency than the Red Pepper Chutney given under Variations below. It makes an excellent accompaniment to curries and hot and cold meat and fish dishes. Red onions tend to have a pleasantly mild flavour.

Metric/Imperial	Ingredients	American
900 g/2 lb*	sweet red peppers weight when deseeded	2 lb*
450 g/1 lb	red onions	1 lb
450 ml/³/₄ pint	white wine or malt vinegar	scant 2 cups
2 teaspoons	salt	2 teaspoons
1 teaspoon	white peppercorns	1 teaspoon
1 teaspoon	celery seeds	1 teaspoon
225 g/8 oz	sugar, see method	1 cup

*approximately 10 large peppers

Halve the peppers, remove the cores and seeds and cut the flesh into 2.5 cm/1 inch pieces. Peel and finely chop the onions. Put into the pan with the vinegar and the salt. Tie the peppercorns and celery seeds in a piece of muslin and add to the pan. Simmer the ingredients gently, stirring from time to time, until both the onions and the peppers are tender (the peppers should still retain their shape). Remove the bag of seeds.
Add the sugar (this can be white sugar or dark brown, which makes a very richly coloured and flavoured relish) and stir over a low heat until dissolved then cook steadily, stirring from time to time, until the consistency of a thick jam. Remove the bag of spices. Spoon the relish into hot jars and seal down.

Variations

Red Pepper Chutney: use the ingredients as above but add 450 g/1 lb diced cooking apples (weight when peeled). Cook these with the peppers and onions. Add 350 g/12 oz (1½ cups) white sugar and 150 g/5 oz (1 cup) sultanas (seedless light raisins) and complete cooking as the recipe above. This variation makes a good 1.8 kg/4 lb chutney.

RED TOMATO CHUTNEY

Cooking time: 40 minutes • Makes good 2.25 kg/5 lb chutney

The first recipe is for a pleasantly lightly spiced chutney but the variation produces a much more highly spiced preserve. The tomatoes should be ripe but firm.

Metric/Imperial	Ingredients	American
900 g/2 lb	tomatoes	2 lb
450 g/1 lb	onions	1 lb
450 g/1 lb	cooking apples, weight when peeled and cored	1 lb
450 ml/³/₄ pint	malt or wine vinegar	scant 2 cups
¹/₂ to 1 teaspoon	ground ginger	¹/₂ to 1 teaspoon
¹/₂ to 1 teaspoon	ground mixed spice	¹/₂ to 1 teaspoon
350 g/12 oz	sugar	1¹/₂ cups
300 g/10 oz	sultanas (seedless light raisins)	2 cups
to taste	salt and freshly ground black pepper	to taste

Skin and chop the tomatoes; peel and finely chop the onions, and dice or grate the apples. Put all the ingredients except the sugar, sultanas and seasoning into the preserving pan and simmer gently until tender.
Add the sugar and stir over a low heat until dissolved then put in the sultanas and seasoning. Simmer steadily until the consistency of a thick jam. Spoon into hot jars and seal down.

Variations

Spanish Tomato Chutney: omit the ground ginger and mixed spice in the Red Tomato Chutney but use the same proportions of the other ingredients with 2 to 3 peeled and crushed garlic cloves – these should be added with the onions. Tie 2 hot red chilli peppers, 2 teaspoons mixed pickling spices and 1 to 2 teaspoons mustard seeds in a muslin bag and simmer with the other ingredients. Remove before putting the chutney into the hot jars. You can accentuate the hot flavour by increasing the number of red chilli peppers or by adding a good pinch of chilli powder towards the end of the cooking period.

Green Tomato Chutney (2): use the recipe on page 162, or the one above, but substitute green tomatoes for red ones. These are not easy to skin – leave the tomatoes in boiling water for at least 1 minute before trying to remove the skins.

RHUBARB CHUTNEY (2)

Cooking time: 30 to 35 minutes • Makes 1.5 kg/3¹/₂ lb chutney

In this particular recipe for chutney the pieces of rhubarb are kept in a good shape by first making a spiced syrup with the vinegar, onions, sugar and dried fruit.

Metric/Imperial	Ingredients	American
225 g/8 oz	onions, weight when peeled and finely chopped	2 cups
300 ml/½ pint	white malt vinegar	1¼ cups
1 teaspoon, or to taste	ground ginger	1 teaspoon, or to taste
1 teaspoon, or to taste	ground mixed spice	1 teaspoon, or to taste
pinch, or to taste	ground cloves	pinch, or to taste
pinch, or to taste	ground cinnamon	pinch, or to taste
450 g/1 lb	sugar	2 cups
150 g/5 oz	raisins	1 cup
115 g*/4 oz	dried dates, weight when stoned (pitted) and chopped	generous ¼ cup
900 g/2 lb	rhubarb	2 lb

*use this metrication

Put the onions into the pan with the vinegar and all the spices. Simmer for 10 minutes, or until the onions are just tender. Add the sugar and stir over a low heat until dissolved then put in the dried fruits and simmer for 5 minutes. Cut the rhubarb into 2.5 cm/1 inch lengths, add to the very hot mixture and continue cooking gently, stirring from time to time, until the rhubarb is just tender but completely unbroken. Allow to cool for a time in the pan, until the mixture thickens slightly. Stir to distribute the rhubarb and dried fruit then spoon into hot jars and seal down.

Is it possible to use honey, syrup or treacle when making chutney or sweet pickles?
Yes, these can add an interesting taste but they should not overwhelm the flavour of the other ingredients.

You could use up to 50% honey and 50% sugar in the recipes instead of all sugar. If using golden (corn) syrup or maple syrup use up to 25% with 75% sugar instead of all sugar.

Black treacle or molasses have such a strong taste that you should only use 1 to 2 tablespoons (1¼ to 2½ tablespoons) with the recommended amount of sugar in the recipe.

SPEEDY BEETROOT CHUTNEY

Cooking time: 10 minutes • Makes 550 g/1¼ lb chutney

This recipe is excellent when you want chutney without the bother of a long cooking time. It should be kept for about 2 days before using so the flavours blend together. Store in the refrigerator and use within 2 weeks.

Metric/Imperial	Ingredients	American
1 teaspoon	mixed pickling spices, see page 139	1 teaspoon

225 ml/7½ fl oz	brown malt vinegar	scant 1 cup
2	garlic cloves	2
1 medium	onion	1 medium
2 teaspoons	brown sugar	2 teaspoons
450 g/1 lb	cooked beetroot (beets), weight when peeled	1 lb
2 tablespoons	raisins	2½ tablespoons
to taste	salt and freshly ground black pepper	to taste

Put the pickling spices into the vinegar and boil for 5 minutes. Peel and roughly chop the garlic and onion, add to the vinegar with the sugar and continue boiling for a further 5 minutes. Allow to become cold then strain. Peel and grate, or finely chop, the beetroot and put into a basin with the raisins. Add the cold vinegar and seasoning to taste. Stir briskly to combine, then spoon into jars and seal down.

Variation

Quick Banana Chutney: follow the recipe but use 450 g/1 lb bananas (weight when peeled) instead of the beetroot (beets). Mash the bananas, add the raisins and gradually blend in the cold spiced and flavoured vinegar. Taste and add a little more sugar if desired. Seasoning should not be necessary for this chutney. Use within 1 day of preparing and do not store for more than 1 week in the refrigerator.

SPEEDY MUSHROOM CHUTNEY

Cooking time: 20 minutes • Makes good 550 g/1¼ lb chutney

This chutney is quickly made and it can be served within 1 or 2 days. Do not keep for more than 2 weeks. It should be stored in the refrigerator. A mixture of mushrooms gives a particularly good flavour.

Metric/Imperial	Ingredients	American
450 g/1 lb	mushrooms	1 lb
2 small	onions	2 small
1 or 2	garlic cloves	1 or 2
150 ml/¼ pint	brown malt vinegar	⅔ cup
1 teaspoon	mixed pickling spices, see page 139	1 teaspoon
3 tablespoons	raisins	3¾ tablespoons
2 tablespoons	brown sugar	2½ tablespoons
to taste	salt and freshly ground black pepper	to taste

Wipe the mushrooms, trim the ends of the stalks and discard these, but the rest of the stalks can be finely chopped and added to the chopped caps. Peel and finely chop the onions and garlic. Put into a pan with the vinegar and the pickling spices tied in muslin. Simmer gently for 10 minutes, then add the raisins, sugar and a little seasoning. Stir over a low heat until the sugar has dissolved then cook for a further 5 minutes. Remove the bag of spices. Spoon into hot jars and seal down.

SPICED PLUM CHUTNEY

Cooking time: 1 to 1¼ hours • Makes nearly 2.7 kg/6 lb chutney

Use cooking plums for this particular chutney, as they have a more definite taste than dessert plums when cooked. Use only half the amount of spices given, then taste the chutney as it reaches the end of the cooking time and add additional spices to personal taste.

Metric/Imperial	Ingredients	American
900 g/2 lb	plums, weight when stoned (pitted)	2 lb
450 g/1 lb	cooking apples, weight when peeled and cored	1 lb
450 g/1 lb	onions	1 lb
2	garlic cloves	2
600 ml/1 pint	white malt vinegar	2½ cups
½ teaspoon	ground mixed spice	½ teaspoon
½ to 1 teaspoon	curry powder	½ to 1 teaspoon
½ to 1 teaspoon	ground ginger	½ to 1 teaspoon
½ to 1 teaspoon	ground cinnamon	½ to 1 teaspoon
350 g/12 oz	sultanas (seedless light raisins)	2¼ cups
450 g/1 lb	light brown sugar	2½ cups
to taste	salt and freshly ground black pepper	to taste
pinch	cayenne pepper	pinch

Halve the plums and remove the stones if possible – if the plums are very firm then leave the stones in to prevent wasting any flesh. In this case allow about 1 kg/2¼ lb in weight. Cut the peeled and cored apples into small dice. Peel and finely chop the onions and garlic. Put the fruits, onions and garlic into the pan with half the vinegar and the spices. Simmer gently until the fruits are soft. If the plum stones were not removed before, take them out at this stage, then add the sultanas, sugar and remaining vinegar. Stir over a low heat until the sugar has dissolved then boil steadily until the consistency of a thick jam. Add seasoning to taste then spoon into the hot jars and seal down.

Variations

Spiced Damson Chutney: use damsons instead of plums.

KETCHUPS AND VINEGARS

Ketchups, or catsups as they are called in old cookery books, are savoury sauces which, because of their vinegar content, keep well if carefully sealed down and sterilized for a short time. (See details on sterilization on page 125.)

Choose fruits that are really ripe for then they provide more juice. Fruits with a really strong flavour, like blackberries and damsons, make excellent fruit ketchups.

It is generally more convenient to store the ketchups in bottles, rather than jars, so they are easier to pour out when required. If using bottles for storage always pad the inside of metal caps with cardboard or thick paper, as for the lids of pickling jars (see page 139), for these caps would rust when used with a ketchup containing vinegar.

Ketchups use much the same ingredients as pickles and it is advisable to read the comments about pans on page 139.

If your family are particularly fond of savoury sauces (ketchups) you can make varieties other than those on pages 180 to 183. Most chutneys can be turned into ketchups. Choose the chutney that includes your favourite ingredients and follow the recipe (see pages 161 to 179).

You could use slightly less sugar for a tarter flavour. When the chutney is cooked, sieve the ingredients and reheat with extra vinegar and seasoning, for a ketchup should be a pouring consistency and have a sharper flavour than a chutney.

The mixture should then be poured into heated containers and sterilized as the directions for Cranberry Ketchup on page 168 or Tomato Ketchup on page 182.

BLACKBERRY KETCHUP

Cooking time: 45 minutes • For yield see end of recipe

Blackberries make a very rich ketchup. A little can be added to sauces to serve with game or other foods.

Metric/Imperial	Ingredients	American
1.35 kg/3 lb	blackberries	3 lb
150 ml/¹/₄ pint	water	²/₃ cup
	spiced vinegar, see page 140	
	sugar, see method	
to taste	salt and freshly ground black pepper	to taste

Wash the blackberries, put into a pan with the water and simmer until a purée. rub through a fine hair or nylon sieve, leaving just the pips behind. Prepare the spiced vinegar as directed on page 140. Use 1 teaspoon mixed pickling spices to each 300 ml/¹/₂ pint (1¹/₄ cups) vinegar and simmer for

5 minutes then strain. Measure the blackberry purée and to each 600 ml/
1 pint (2½ cups) add 50 g/2 oz (¼ cup) white or brown sugar and 300 ml/
½ pint (1¼ cups) of the spiced vinegar plus a little seasoning if required.
Pour into the preserving pan. Simmer steadily until a fairly thick consistency
then pour into hot bottling jars or bottles and seal down. Loosen the screw
bands or clips on bottling jars or the caps on bottles to allow for the
expansion of the glass. Place in a sterilizer or deep pan of boiling water (see
page 125 for details about sterilizing) and boil for 10 minutes. Remove from
the sterilizer or pan. Tighten screw bands, clips or caps.

Variations

Damson Ketchup: use ripe damsons instead of blackberries in the recipe
with 300 ml/½ pint (1¼ cups) water to cook the fruit. When sieved,
measure the pulp and to each 600 ml/1 pint (2½ cups) add 100 g/4 oz
(½ cup) sugar and 300 ml/½ pint (1¼ cups) spiced vinegar together with
seasoning to taste. Continue as the Blackberry Ketchup above.

Gooseberry Ketchup: use ripe gooseberries instead of blackberries in the
recipe but follow the same proportions of water for cooking the fruit as
in Damson Ketchup and the same amount of sugar. This ketchup is
excellent if a little ground cloves is stirred in just before it is bottled.
Add the ground cloves gradually, tasting as you do so.

Grape Ketchup: use ripe grapes instead of blackberries in the recipe –
follow the proportions of water used for blackberries. You could
substitute white wine for the water if desired. If the grapes are very sweet
use the same amount of sugar as for Blackberry Ketchup. If rather sour
then use the amount of sugar given in Damson Ketchup.

Yield

It is difficult to gauge the exact yield but each 600 ml/1 pint (2½ cups)
fruit purée plus the sugar and vinegar should produce about 750 ml/
1¼ pints (generous 3 cups) ketchup. Where the larger amount of sugar is
used the yield should be slightly more.

MUSHROOM KETCHUP

Cooking time: just over 2 hours • For yield see end of recipe

*This is an excellent ketchup for it can be used to add flavour to many
savoury dishes and sauces, including gravies. Good-sized field mushrooms
have greater flavour than the more delicate cultivated button mushrooms,
so use these if possible.*

Metric/Imperial	Ingredients	American
3 tablespoons	*kitchen or sea salt*	3¾ tablespoons
1.35 kg/3 lb	*mushrooms*	3 lb
300 ml/½ pint	*brown malt vinegar*	1¼ cups
1 teaspoon	*mixed pickling spices, see page 139*	1 teaspoon
2 medium	*onions*	2 medium

Sprinkle the salt over the mushrooms, which should be well wiped but not washed. Leave for 24 hours. Boil the vinegar with the pickling spices for 5 minutes then strain. Peel and finely chop the onions, put into the spiced vinegar with the mushrooms and any liquid that has flowed from brining them. Simmer gently in a covered pan for 2 hours. Strain through a very fine-meshed nylon sieve or muslin then pour into hot bottles or bottling jars and seal down. There are sufficiently high amounts of salt and vinegar in this ketchup to act as preservatives, provided the bottle caps or lids fit tightly. As a precaution, though, it can be sterilized as Tomato Ketchup (see below).

Variations

- For a thicker ketchup, rub the cooked mushrooms and onions through the sieve to give a purée and pour this into the containers.
- Eighteenth-century recipes added a few cloves, a pinch of mace and grated nutmeg and pepper to the ingredients in a similar recipe.
- A little brandy can be added to the ketchup: allow 2 tablespoons (2½ tablespoons) to each 600 ml/1 pint (2½ cups) sieved liquid or purée.

Yield

It is difficult to assess the yield of this ketchup for the juiciness of mushrooms varies so much. The final quantity ranges from 600 to 750 ml/1 to 1¼ pints (2½ cups to a generous 3 cups) ketchup.

TOMATO KETCHUP

Cooking time: 35 to 40 minutes • Makes approximately 2.5 kg/5½ lb ketchup

Tomato ketchup is one of the favourite sauces of both children and adults. The home-made variety has an excellent flavour. Choose really good-sized tomatoes that will yield a generous amount of juice and pulp. Do not skin the tomatoes, and be sure to rub the fruit through a hair or nylon sieve, not a metal one, which can spoil both the colour and the flavour. Cooked tomatoes are an excellent source of lycopene, an antioxidant, which is believed to be of value in combating heart disease and certain cancers

Metric/Imperial	Ingredients	American
1 to 2 teaspoons	*mixed pickling spices, see page 139 and method*	1 to 2 teaspoons
450 ml/¾ pint	*white malt vinegar*	scant 2 cups
1.8 kg/4lb	*ripe tomatoes*	4 lb
225 g/8 oz	*onions*	½ lb
350 g/12oz	*cooking apples, weight when peeled and coored*	¾ lb
450 mml/¾ pint	*caster (superfine) sugar*	¾ lb
to taste	*salt and freshly ground black pepper or cayenne pepper*	to taste

If making the ketchup specifically for children it may be wise to use only the 1 teaspoon of pickling spices. For adults, who like more definite flavours, use the larger amount. If undecided, boil the vinegar and half the spices for 5 minutes, taste and judge whether you want to add the rest of the spices. Strain the vinegar. Chop the tomatoes; peel and finely chop the onions and the apples. Put the tomatoes, onions and apples without any liquid into a saucepan and simmer gently, stirring from time to time, until a thick purée. Rub through the sieve. Make sure all the pulp is used, leave only the tomato skins behind. Return the purée to the saucepan with the vinegar and sugar. Stir until the sugar has dissolved then boil steadily until thickened. Season to taste. Place a funnel into the neck of the first hot sterilized bottle and carefully fill with the ketchup. Seal down but loosen the caps slightly to allow for expansion of the glass. Have ready a sterilizer or deep pan with boiling water, for details see page 125. Sterilize the bottles for 10 minutes then tighten the caps.

Variations

- Use a liquidizer instead of a sieve. In this case skin the tomatoes before cooking.
- Use bottling jars instead of bottles. Loosen the screw bands or move the clips slightly from the centre, as described on page 125, before sterilizing the jars and tighten these when the jars are removed from the pan.

Hot Tomato Ketchup: a more piquant tomato ketchup is made by adding several extra dried chillies or chopped fresh hot red chilli peppers to the ingredients above. If the seeds are removed from fresh chilli peppers the flavour is less strong. Always wash your hands well after handling these (see page 169).

FLAVOURING VINEGARS

There is a wonderful assortment of vinegars on the market today, ranging from the familiar and economical malt vinegar to more unusual vinegars, many of which have been given special flavours. These add subtle tastes to salad dressings and various dishes

It is very simple to produce your own flavoured vinegars at home but important to appreciate the natural taste of the various basic products, for the taste of different vinegars comes from their source. Malt vinegars are full flavoured because they are distilled from malt liquor. It is their strong taste that makes them a good choice for pickles and similar preserves. Wine vinegars are produced, as the name indicates, from the acid fermentation of wine. The finest quality wine vinegars have a wonderful flavour. Cider vinegar is somewhat sharp in taste, like the cider from which it originates. Spirit vinegar is another strong-tasting vinegar, while sherry vinegar is slightly sweet. Distilled vinegar is always white and therefore an excellent choice when making pickles or other preserves that need to look pale in colour.

When deciding to flavour vinegar, choose the additional ingredients that blend well with that particular type of vinegar.

HERB VINEGARS

While most vinegars blend with herbs, the best choice would be a white or red wine vinegar or a distilled vinegar. The best herbs to use are lemon balm, chervil, chives, mint, marjoram, rosemary, sage and tarragon. Basil is another herb that can be used but check the flavour of the vinegar after a week since this herb has such a definite taste.

To each 600 ml/1 pint (2½ cups) vinegar allow about 3 tablespoons (3¾ tablespoons) coarsely chopped leaves (only 1 tablespoon [1¼ tablespoons] for sage). For a more delicate flavour do not chop the leaves but gently crush them with soft pressure from a rolling pin. This allows flavour to be extracted. Put the chopped or crushed herbs into the bottles as soon as they are chopped, so no juice is lost. Add the cold vinegar. Store for 2 to 3 weeks, gently shaking the bottles from time to time. Check the flavour and if satisfied that the vinegar is sufficiently impregnated by the herbs, strain through fine muslin or a fine-meshed hair or nylon sieve. Discard the herbs and return the vinegar to the bottles, labelling each bottle with the particular herb used or adding a small sprig of it.

CHILLI VINEGAR

Most vinegars can be flavoured with chillies, including malt vinegar. Fresh chillies have such a definite taste that they blend with even strongly flavoured malt vinegar. Choose red hot chilli peppers for a really strong flavour but green ones for a less hot taste. Allow 4 large or 5 small pods for each 600 ml/1 pint (2½ cups) vinegar. Add to the vinegar and leave for 5 to 6 weeks. To hasten the flavouring of the vinegar, heat it with the pods and leave for 2 to 3 weeks only before checking on the flavour. If satisfied, strain the vinegar. A small dried pod could be left in the vinegar to indicate the flavour.

GARLIC VINEGAR

Any vinegar can be flavoured with garlic. For a strong taste use a small head of garlic to each 600 ml/1 pint (2½ cups) vinegar. Separate the cloves and peel them. For the strongest taste crush or chop the cloves; for a milder flavour leave them whole. Check after 1 week to see if the vinegar is sufficiently strong, then strain.

HORSERADISH VINEGAR

Malt or white wine or distilled vinegars can be used. Scrape the outside of the horseradish root then shred the flesh. Allow 2 tablespoons (2½ tablespoons) to each 600 ml/ 1 pint (2½ cups) vinegar for a fairly mild flavour but at least twice this for a strong taste. Check the flavour after 4 weeks then strain.

FRUIT VINEGARS

These are very much in vogue at the moment, just as they were in Victorian times when housewives took great pride in their stocks of fruit-flavoured vinegars. There are two ways of preserving the delicious flavour of fruit in vinegar. The first is a very simple one, for no sugar or boiling is required. In the second method the fruit and vinegar are heated together and sugar is added, so you have an interesting sweet and sour taste and a vinegar that keeps well.

Raspberries are undoubtedly the favourite fruit to use. When fresh fruit is not available frozen could be used instead. Fruit vinegars add subtle touches to sauces, salad dressings and other dishes. They make a good basis for sweet and savoury dishes, in which the flavour of fruit is an advantage, and a very small amount of fruit-flavoured vinegar gives a new taste to a fruit salad. An old use for these vinegars was to make a refreshing and somewhat unusual drink. They were diluted with a generous amount of crushed ice or ice-cold water.

RASPBERRY VINEGAR (1)
Use a really good quality white wine vinegar for this preserve. Red wine vinegar can be used but the colour may not be quite as appealing for it will be rather dark. A little sherry vinegar or a very small amount of top-of-the-range balsamic vinegar (which is made from pressed grapes and matured for 10 years and, in consequence, is unbelievably expensive), could be added to wine vinegar to give an interesting taste.

While you can put the crushed fruit straight into the bottles then add the vinegar and shake the two ingredients together, more flavour is extracted if the fruit and vinegar are blended together in a mixing bowl. Allow 225 to 450 g/8 oz to 1 lb (generous 1½ to 3 cups) raspberries to each 600 ml/1 pint (2½ cups) of vinegar, depending upon how strongly flavoured you want the vinegar to be. Crush the fruit and pour on the cold vinegar. Leave for a minimum of 3 days, stirring several times each day to extract the maximum juice from the fruit. Strain through a very fine hair or nylon sieve or through muslin and pour into sterilized bottles and seal down.

Because no sugar is used in this form of flavoured vinegar, and there will be quite a lot of liquid from the raspberries, the vinegar must be used within 3 to 4 weeks and stored in the refrigerator. For long-term storage, sterilize. Pour the liquid into cold sterilized bottling jars, put on the lids and caps or clips but loosen these slightly to allow for the expansion of the glass. Stand the bottles in the sterilizer or a deep pan filled with cold water (see page 125 for details of sterilizing). Take 1½ hours to bring the water up to boiling point. Maintain at boiling for 10 minutes. Remove the jars and tighten the screw bands or clips.

RASPBERRY VINEGAR (2)
Use white wine vinegar or sherry vinegar or cider vinegar. In this recipe you have a more concentrated raspberry flavour. Allow 450 g/1 lb (generous 3 cups) raspberries to each 600 ml/1 pint (2½ cups) of vinegar. Crush the fruit in a mixing bowl, add the vinegar and leave for 3 days, stirring several times a day. Strain as directed above, then measure the liquid. To each 600 ml/1 pint (2½ cups) add 225 g/8 oz (1 cup) sugar for a lightly sweetened vinegar or up to 450 g/1 lb (2 cups) for a really sweet liquid. Put into a saucepan and boil briskly for 10 minutes, then pour into hot sterilized bottles or bottling jars and seal down.

OTHER FRUIT VINEGARS
In each case follow the directions for Raspberry Vinegar (1) and (2).

Blackcurrant Vinegar: a wonderfully rich flavour that gives a splendid taste when added to sauces and gravies served with meats like pork, duck, goose or venison. Use red wine vinegar or red wine plus a little sherry or balsamic vinegar. When diluted with hot water the sweetened blackcurrant vinegar makes a soothing drink for a sore throat or a cold.

Blackberry Vinegar: this also has a very rich flavour. Use white or red wine vinegar or cider vinegar, or a mixture of these. It makes an interesting addition to various savoury sauces.

Elderberry Vinegar: the second recipe for Raspberry Vinegar is better when using these berries, for they have a strong taste which the sugar balances. Use red wine or spirit vinegar or sherry vinegar. A little gives a good flavour to sauces to serve with venison, or a stew using venison or beef.

Strawberry Vinegar: since the flavour of strawberries is more delicate than that of raspberries use 450 g/1 lb (generous 3 cups) of fruit in the first recipe. This vinegar can be used in any way suggested for the others. It makes a particularly good cold drink.

DRYING HERBS

A popular way of preserving herbs for winter use is to dry them. This is a very simple process. The herbs take up relatively little space and have a good flavour, especially if used when freshly dried. Do not keep them for more than a year. When following recipes that give an amount of fresh herbs, use only half the amount of dried herbs, or even slightly under half for their flavour is more concentrated.

Pick the herbs on a dry day and use only those that are in good condition, not those that are becoming old and rather tough. Wash the herbs in cold water, pat dry in kitchen paper or a cloth. Lay them on baking trays padded with plain paper. Cover with muslin or gauze (you can buy this from a chemist) to hold the herbs in position and prevent them becoming dusty if you dry them out of doors. Herbs can be dried in an airing cupboard or at a very low heat in the oven. Preheat the oven to 100°C/approximately 200°F, Gas Mark O or S (or whatever is the lowest setting in your gas cooker). Place the trays of herbs in the oven but leave the oven door ajar. In very hot weather dry the herbs out of doors in the sun. When the sprigs or leaves are brittle it is very easy to chop or crumble them. Store in airtight jars or tins so none of the fragrance or flavour is lost.

DRYING HERBS IN A MICROWAVE OVEN
The times given for drying herbs is based on a microwave oven with a 650 watt output. If your oven has a lower output then the herbs will need approximately 10 to 20 seconds *longer* at each stage of the drying process. If your oven has a higher output then *shorten* the drying time by 10 to 20 seconds at each stage. Individual microwave ovens vary a great deal, so the first time you dry herbs open the door (which automatically switches off the power) halfway through the first stage of the drying time and inspect the herbs. Continue like this to ascertain the right timing for your oven.
   Pick and prepare the herbs as directed above. Place a sheet of absorbent paper on the turntable or the base of the oven, then arrange the herbs in a single layer on the paper. Switch on to FULL POWER (High) and leave for 30 seconds. Move the herbs around and turn them over, as this helps them to dry evenly. Continue the process on FULL POWER for another 30 seconds. Turn the herbs over and move them around once more. Repeat the process until the herbs feel dry and crumble readily when handled. Leave the herbs in the microwave oven with the power switched off for 5 minutes; they continue drying slightly during this time. Allow the herbs to stand until cold then crush or chop them. Keep in airtight containers.

STORING DRIED HERBS
Whichever method of heat is used to dry herbs, they retain more colour and flavour if kept in a dark cupboard. This is particularly important if they are placed in glass jars.

INDEX